Also by Chris Horrie

*Sick as a Parrot*
*Fuzzy Monsters*
*Stick it Up Your Punter!*
*Live TV!*
*Citizen Greg*
*Premiership*
*Tabloid Nation*

Also by David Matthews

*Looking for a Fight*

# CHRIS HORRIE AND DAVID MATTHEWS

# *True Blue*

Strange Tales from a Tory Nation

FOURTH ESTATE · *London*

First published in Great Britain in 2009 by
Fourth Estate
An imprint of HarperCollins*Publishers*
77–85 Fulham Palace Road
London W6 8JB
www.4thestate.co.uk

Visit our authors' blog: www.fifthestate.co.uk
LOVE THIS BOOK ? WWW.BOOKARMY.COM

1 3 5 7 9 10 8 6 4 2

A catalogue record for this book is available from the British Library

ISBN  978-0-00-729370-4

Typeset in Minion by Palimpsest Book Production Limited,
Grangemouth, Stirlingshire

Printed in Great Britain by
Clays Ltd, St Ives plc

**Mixed Sources**
Product group from well-managed
forests and other controlled sources
www.fsc.org  Cert no. SW-COC-1806
© 1996 Forest Stewardship Council

FSC is a non-profit international organisation established
to promote the responsible management of the world's forests.
Products carrying the FSC label are independently certified
to assure consumers that they come from forests that are managed
to meet the social, economic and ecological needs
of present and future generations.

Find out more about HarperCollins and the environment at
**www.harpercollins.co.uk/green**

*Chris dedicates his work on this book
to Clare, Lotte and Tom.*

*David dedicates his work on this book
to his mother.*

# Contents

# PREFACE

## *'No, Janet, It's One of My Writing Thingies'*

'What the hell do you think you're doing!!' hissed Janet, her eyes flaming with anger and her voice almost incoherent with rage. Voting was drawing to a close in the 2005 general election and Janet, a family friend and longtime Labour voter, had spotted me outside the polling station in East Sheen, in the wealthy borough of Richmond in south-west London. I was wearing a bright blue Conservative Party rosette with the words 'Vote Conservative' emblazoned on it. I was also acting as a teller for the Tories, gently hassling voters for their polling card numbers as they went into the polling station, set up for the occasion in a local primary school.

At many a left-wing dinner party poor Janet had listened to me jawing on into the night about some socialist theme or other; I had even droned on to her about left-wing politics during chance encounters on the local streets. To Janet, I was a fellow member of the red team. 'How can you be wearing that . . . that . . . thing?' she gasped in horror, jabbing at the blue rosette, 'and after that revolting election campaign!' Physically cowed by Janet's onslaught, I tried simultaneously to hide the blue rosette under my anorak – I thought she was going to rip it off – and hunched up in anticipation of a blow.

'This is not what you think it is, Janet. I can't really talk about it now,' I gabbled. To my horror I saw another official Tory teller – an elderly woman with Margaret Thatcher hair and a piercing gaze – was bustling towards us with her blue ribbons waving in the breeze. Again I pleaded with Janet – through clenched teeth and a fixed smile – and gave what I hoped was a begging, puppy dog-like look. 'Pleeeeze Janet . . . it's one of my writing thingies! . . . we can talk about this later . . .'

Janet shot back: 'Oh no we can't! In fact, make bloody sure you never talk to me again! Have you got that?' I acknowledged her with a sad and shame-filled nod and must have looked, I realized, like a naughty schoolboy. And with that Janet harrumphed off into the polling booth to cast her vote.

On Monday 11 April 2005 my friend the writer David Matthews officially took up residence at my house in Richmond in what the local tourist board still liked to call Surrey but which was, in reality, part of the sprawling but very prosperous south-western suburbs of London. And with that one of the most extraordinary episodes in my life began. The two of us had decided to join the already faltering Conservative general election campaign taking place that year and write about it from the inside. It was to be a literary and investigative project, and we would be working largely undercover.

David and I were interested in finding out what sort of person might, these days, become a Conservative activist and what made them tick. That was the official Mission Statement. But we had another, even more powerful, motive. We just thought that 'joining' the Conservative Party would grant us access to all sorts of situations which would ordinarily pass us by, and we would get to meet people we would never ordinarily meet. The project, as things turned out, was to last well beyond that election – on and off, in fact, for the next three years.

Supposedly, we reasoned, 'Conservatives' should be very ordinary people. That was what the name almost literally meant – sort of 'ultra-normal'. But just looking at the statistics for membership it became clear that this was no longer true – if it ever had been. Joining a political party of any sort was, by 2005, pretty deviant behaviour. (Admittedly, by the time our journey into Blue Britain was over, the image of the Conservative Party had improved considerably, and we were there to see, from the inside, how that transformation took place.)

But in 2005 the Tories were extraordinarily unpopular, especially with just about anyone under fifty. They struck David and me as more like a weird and unfathomable cult than a once unstoppable election-winning force. This was the Conservative leadership era, remember, of Michael Howard and a pre-makeover Ann Widdecombe, when the party's claim to represent modern Britain seemed more than a little tenuous. So we saw voluntary activism in the Conservative cause as so unusual that it represented a sub-culture potentially more interesting than the groups and scenes we had reported on in the past – such as football hooligans, Muslim fundamentalists, professional boxers, tabloid journalists, gun-wielding inner-city criminals and the yacht-dwelling super-rich. All of those groups were, to a degree, tricky to understand, but their world-views were, we reckoned, a lot easier to figure out than the mentality of local Conservative activists in 2005.

I was living in a Conservative ward, consisting of lots of multi-million-pound residences stretching up to the walls and iron gates of Richmond Park, a royal deer park with actual herds of deer in it. The parliamentary seat was held for the Liberal Democrats at the time by Jenny Tonge, a medical doctor who seemed to have pretty extreme views about most things, especially the Iraq war. Jenny had endured a tabloid lynching after she advocated bombing the Taliban in Afghanistan with money and loaves of bread instead of cruise missiles. And yet the Richmond Tories could make no headway against somebody as plainly cranky and annoyingly worthy as her. Why was this happening? Had the population of Richmond, consisting as it did of one of the largest concentrations of rich, elderly white people in the country, suddenly decided that even it didn't like the Tories?

Our plan was to treat the Conservatives and a broader swathe of 'small c' conservatives (such as country sports enthusiasts, village cricketers and the Women's Institute) as a broad tribe or clan whose social anthropology we wished to study. We would work our way through their habitats in the manner of Colonel John Blashford-Snell (the pith-helmeted jungle explorer who turned up at one of the Conservative drinks parties we attended) and note their rituals. As we discovered, some of the people we met really were, in the nicest possible way, from another planet – not necessarily a worse planet than the one David and I live on, but certainly a very strange one.

David and I worried – briefly – about the ethics of 'joining' a party which we did not approve of, and aiding a cause that we felt was neither in the interests of ourselves nor the people we cared about and loved. Would we be able to live with ourselves if we accidentally helped to get a Tory elected to Parliament? Wouldn't we be helping to propagate a world-view with which we fundamentally disagreed? What if the Tories liked us and started trying to make proper friends with us? We decided, though, that getting the inside track on the Conservatives and conservatism was a Legitimate Journalistic Exercise in the Public Interest: and that, together with it being fun and broadening our horizons a bit, trumped all our other concerns.

In the appropriately anonymous surroundings of a Battersea pub we decided that we would only be evasive if we needed to be. (If we said we were journalists we would get the usual flim-flam). We felt perfectly justified in taking this approach, because working as reporters we knew that Conservatives, like almost all politicians, aren't above being evasive themselves.

And while working on this book, we saw Conservatives giving enormously misleading accounts of things to journalists who approached them overtly with, as it were, their press cards poking out of their hat rims. We felt we needed to get beyond that.

So I admit that some mild subterfuge was involved in the process of researching the book. But there was never any malice. Most of the people we met were, we felt, essentially harmless and, if anything, just a bit lost or stuck in a rut. The Conservative Party, and other Conservative institutions, offered these people a much-needed anchor in their lives. We felt sorry for some of those we met, liked one or two and were repelled by a few.

At the outset we also resolved, as far as possible, not to do any harm to the Conservative cause in the process of writing the book, or to impose any additional costs or avoidable difficulties on Conservative supporters. For example, if we were given party leaflets to deliver we always delivered them. We had no contact whatsoever with the direct political rivals of the Conservative Party during the writing of the book. Nor did we divulge any Conservative secrets or engage in any sabotage. There was often the chance to provoke or entrap a Tory into a newsworthy 'gaffe' – especially on the issue of race – but we resisted that temptation.

In our dealings with the public we were determined not to damage the Conservatives, but we also decided not to give them undue assistance if we could avoid it. When party officials eventually trusted us to knock on people's doors and try to persuade them to vote Conservative, we were not the party's greatest salesmen. We restricted ourselves to neutral and truthful remarks delivered in a polite but flat tone of voice, such as 'Hello, we are canvassing for the Conservative Party' or questions like 'Are you planning to vote for the Conservative Party?' If people on the doorstep asked us about policy matters we would answer as accurately as we could, saying, for instance, 'Well, the

Conservatives believe that more money should be put into having cleaner hospitals.'

The plan was to join up and – while scanning discreetly for useful information – fade into the background. But that was not going to be easy. Neither of us looked or sounded anything like typical Conservatives. We were both relatively young by the standards of Conservative Party members (David is in his early forties and I'm in my early fifties). I am a scruffy ex-northerner, former squatter and one-time political activist for the likes of CND. David is a cooler, much more elegantly dressed and less politically obsessed character, and he is black. On top of this, we were also living at the same address, generally hanging out together as a closely bonded pair of males and casting a lot of meaningful glances at each other. We honestly did not think it through – we should have – but this led some Tories to jump to the conclusion that we were a non-camp mixed-race homosexual couple.

When any Conservative Party members grilled us about politics, it was very simple to repeat whatever right-wing tirade we'd heard about the matter at a previous drinks party or canvassing session. In fact, though, most of the Tories we met didn't seem to be particularly interested in talking about politics, re-inforcing our belief that being a Conservative was as much about belonging to a tribe with comfortingly familiar rituals as it was about having a firm grasp of a set of political principles.

We felt that most of the Tories we met made instant decisions about whether or not we were worth talking to. All of them seemed to think that there was something fishy about us, especially when meeting us for the first time. In any Tory situation I felt that roughly two-thirds of those present would give me the cold shoulder, and only a few would want to welcome me. In David's case the proportion of people who gave him a wide berth rose to around three-quarters – especially outside London – and it was hard to escape the conclusion that this was because he was black. Oddly, though, whereas I was exposed to outright hostility once or twice this never seemed to happen to David.

In the main, the Tories we met seemed fantastically uncomfortable around David, and it seemed to be because of the colour of his skin. I felt that none of them believed David's story that he was a disenchanted Labour voter who wanted to cross the line (we could not, of course, establish this beyond doubt; perhaps once those involved have read this book they will let us know). The feeling we had was that virtually everyone we met thought that David was either on the make – offering to add a spot of much sought-after 'blackwash' to the Conservative Party's predominantly white profile – or some sort of spy, perhaps for a newspaper or for another political party. On one occasion he was mistaken for a Premier League footballer by an Italian sex kitten of mature years dressed in gold lamé, whom we met at a Conservative cocktail party in Richmond. She chatted David up while at the same time promising meetings with people back in Italy in the 'construction industry' who could guarantee massive returns on any investments he might like to make using the gigantic wages she assumed he got in return for playing for the Fulham Hotspurs or whoever it was.

What they made of me I was never able to work out. Long after I left the Richmond Conservative Party behind, in order to progress around the rest of the Home Counties on my Tory journey with David, they would telephone from time to time asking if I wanted to become a local councillor in Richmond which, they said, they could 'fix'. That was the first step towards a full-time professional political career. All that suddenly stopped when I politely asked the local organizer, Mr Leach, to stop calling me. (I told him that, although I had been perfectly happy to join in the 2005 election campaign in Richmond, 'that phase of my life was now over'.)

Leachy seemed hurt and bewildered by my departure and, on a personal rather than a political level, I had some sympathy for him. His social life seemed, to a large extent, to revolve around the local Conservative Association, whose membership included many very, very old people. I think he saw me, despite my greying hair, as vigorous new blood, and perhaps the first swallow of a new spring of enthusiastic support for the Conservative movement, someone who might help to revitalize the thing he loved.

'Why have you gone off us?' he asked plaintively. 'You know you could have a really great future with the Conservative Party ... You did such marvellous work for us during the election campaign ... We really need energetic young people like you, you know ...'

# ONE

# The Sound of the Suburbs –
# Richmond, Surrey

Joining the Conservative election campaign was very simple. We just walked off the street into the party's Richmond constituency office, which was on East Sheen high street, near to where we were living. The Conservative Party's premises were next to a butcher's shop and a takeaway pizza place. We had prepared the ground by calling the office the previous day when, to our surprise, the phone had been answered by Marco Forgione – the Conservative parliamentary candidate for Richmond – in person. We recognized the name from the blue election hoardings which were starting to appear in some of Richmond's more ample front gardens.

When we sauntered into his office – pausing only to wipe our feet noisily on the welcome mat – Marco looked astonished. He rose from behind his desk in that very slow way you see in gangster films, when the bank clerk stands up gingerly while at the same reaching for the alarm button hidden under the desk. Looking well into his forties, Marco had a manic smile, dark hair and devilishly sparkling eyes. His smile revealed a slight gap in his teeth, which gave him his distinctively boyish look. With his mouth open and his eyes as wide as saucers, he struggled to speak before greeting us in a stilted voice.

With the awkwardness beginning to build nicely, a high-spirited OAP named Robert bowled into the room, emitting a stream of completely unfathomable banter and ignoring us completely. We looked pretty out of place, so we later thought that he might have taken us for photocopier technicians or something similar. When Marco cut into Robert's bonhomie to introduce us, the old gent almost jumped out of his skin. 'Good grief!' he said, recoiling as though he'd just stumbled across a nest of rats.

Robert was charm itself and instantly likeable – much more so than Marco, who was pleasant enough, but, like many professional politicians, came over as a bit oily. And Robert had what seemed to us a really killer look – he sported a luxurious Second World War Spitfire-ace-meets-Rajput moustache, slicked-back hair, multi-coloured cravat and a vast blue silk hanky tucked into the top pocket of his brass-buttoned blue blazer.

When Marco introduced us as 'new members of the team' Robert twitched with apparent bafflement. Then, composing himself, he launched into a long-winded speech designed to clinch the vote of what the Richmond Tories liked to call 'a wavering Liberal Democrat' (we were to hear a lot about these creatures, who seemed to be largely mythical). As Robert waffled off into a shaggy-dog story about the local Liberals, Marco nodded at him with a mixture of patient tolerance, punctuated by a slightly panicked air when Robert began to veer into politically incorrect territory, as he often did.

Robert said that when the Liberals had been in charge of the local council, they had set up a rehab clinic for drug users and alcoholics. But then, he said, the council 'just had to go one step further – and set up a second clinic just for ethnic minorities'. He paused, as though expecting laughter or possibly applause. 'Now,' Robert continued, deciding he had paused long enough, 'I can see why some Asian women, for example, might need to be treated on their own, because they have their own customs and so on . . .'

Marco seemed very uneasy with this racially-based talk. But it was something I noticed throughout our Tory journey.

Whenever David was present, older Tories would often spontaneously start talking about racial matters. It was like an itch they had to scratch. And it struck both of us as incredibly gauche. Maybe it was just their way of trying to be friendly, or even welcoming.

Perhaps sensing the bad vibes from Marco, Robert suddenly changed the subject. 'Do you know, in the end it's all about pavements,' he said, puffing out his chest, 'pavements and dog messes.' Marco relaxed, but started to look bored. At length, Robert explained that since the Conservatives had got back in control of Richmond council they had, cunningly, copied Liberal Democrat tactics and repaired 'hundreds and hundreds of pavements, all over the place'.

We got the formalities out of the way and it wasn't long before we were junior players in the campaign to elect Marco Forgione. That meant delivering campaign leaflets or, as Marco liked to put it, 'blitzing the streets'. We'd seen plenty of politicians using a battle bus for touring from one triumphant PR stunt to another – occasionally they would splash out on a helicopter or even a private jet. But for Marco, transport consisted of the much more modest Battle Banger, which was usually parked outside the constituency office, next to a karaoke noodle bar.

The Battle Banger – an ancient, dented, off-white Rover with a cracked windscreen, barely legal tyres and a peeling tax disc – was a complete heap, and had, we guessed, a resale value of about £150. In the back window was a yellowing Countryside Alliance sticker, which was probably a relic of Marco's previous incarnation as the unsuccessful Conservative parliamentary candidate for Yeovil in Somerset. The Battle Banger looked as if it had been welded together from two stolen cars and driven down from Glasgow.

The Battle Banger's interior complemented the exterior: it was a tip. There was litter everywhere – scrunched-up newspapers, sweet wrappers and mud-covered leaflets, along with Marco's collection of music cassettes. The cassettes included *Ibiza Uncovered (The Return)*; *Frank Sinatra's Greatest Hits*; *Classics For a Summer Day*; *American Pie* by Don McLean and, most bizarrely for a Conservative candidate, *The Best of Two Tone*, by a clutch of late seventies Midlands ska bands. We also noticed a page printed from the internet giving directions to a model railway club in New Malden and, in addition, technical information about the equipment club members owned – types of trains, track gauge and so forth.

Our first day of campaigning for the Richmond Tories consisted largely of giving out leaflets up and down the streets around the Vineyard ward, an enclave of slightly bohemian Georgian streets just to the north of Richmond town centre. The Vineyard ward covered the area of Richmond Hill, which includes some of the most expensive residential property in the country. One particularly upmarket group of Georgian mansions in Richmond Hill sits high up on a terrace overlooking the Thames, from which there is a beautiful view of bucolic woods and flooded meadows in the foreground and the entire county of Surrey in the distance.

We parked up near the Georgian mansions and Robert, with child-like delight, set about getting the Battle Banger ready for a spot of what he called 'loudspeaker work'. Chuckling softly to himself as his cravat flapped gaily in the breeze, he began to lash the loudspeaker system onto the roof with bits of string. Then he linked it to a valve amplifier which looked so old and battered it might once have belonged to the Troggs. The amp was plonked on the back seat of the Battle Banger and was powered by an oil-streaked car battery which smelled strongly of acid.

As he was going about all this, Robert dropped the ball of string onto the street and it rolled under the car – just the first of a series of minor operational disasters that seemed to bedevil the Richmond Tories whenever they ventured forth into action. Instinctively, Robert tried to retrieve the ball by pulling on the strand already tied to the roof rack of the Battle Banger. It took him a while, and several good hard jerks, before he realized that the more he pulled on the string, the more the ball would unravel. Marco decided he would leave the string problem to Robert, who scratched his head thoughtfully.

Instead, Marco turned to us and, with what looked like a wicked glint in his eye, produced a pair of large bright blue satin 'Vote Conservative' rosettes. 'Do you guys want to wear one of these?' he asked. We hesitated and exchanged glances. 'You don't have to if you don't want to,' he added, a touch teasingly, perhaps thinking this might weed out anyone who wasn't a true Tory. We had to agree – or risk blowing our cover – so Marco went into overdrive, fussily helping to fasten the rosettes onto our chests. When he'd finished he stood back to admire his handiwork and said with exaggerated pride, 'There you are . . . FAN-TASTIC. You are proper Tories now . . . FAN-TASTIC!'

Later, David and I talked about the moment the blue rosettes were pinned onto us: it was a far more traumatic experience for me than it was for David. As I wandered around the quiet residential streets of Richmond Hill I felt incredibly self-conscious, a bit like a half-hearted novice streaker. I genuinely thought that I would encounter a lot of hostility from people – and get lots and lots of dirty looks and perhaps even worse than that. But I was wrong. I scrutinized the faces of the few passers-by I saw and, as they clocked me, to my surprise there was no reaction at all. It was an important moment of revelation for me. I had enormously overestimated people's interest in politics and the significance they attached to political symbols. People just didn't seem to care.

David thought the pinning on of the rosettes was probably an attempt by Marco to play some basic mind games – it was either a wind-up or a loyalty test of some sort. And, being

David, he wasn't going to let Marco psych him out quite so easily, so he had taken the rosette with a beaming smile on his face. The chances of David having an embarrassing encounter with anyone he knew were practically zero, since he was only living in Richmond temporarily. An East Ender by birth, he had recently lived in Willesden, in suburban north-west London before moving to Battersea, south of the Thames. Knowing pretty much only me in this part of London, David would be more likely to bump into somebody he knew in Romania than in Richmond.

But David was uncomfortable, nonetheless, while wearing a blue rosette. On this and other occasions he got stares from other black people that he found a bit unnerving. He said that black passers-by would see him, then the rosette, then do a double-take straight at him as if to say, 'Fool!' Richmond's white majority, David felt, either ignored him or regarded him with the usual air of, variously, fear, resentment or wonderment. His biggest fear was that he would be mistaken for Ainsley Harriott.

A couple of days later I met up with Marco in a down-at-heel pub that nestled among the opulent Georgian homes of the Vineyard ward. There I found him holding court with the day's campaign team, which now consisted of not just Robert and myself but also half a dozen local stalwarts, mostly elderly yet formidable Tory women. They were part of a larger group of Conservative women who were clearly the engine room of the local Conservative operation. For Robert, the sex ratio was great news as he revelled in the company of all these women and flirted with them constantly, if harmlessly – to the amusement of all concerned.

Marco addressed these iron ladies in staccato phrases, stringing his favourite expressions together in an accent that uneasily mixed received pronunciation with Estuary English. 'Well,' Marco said, 'we are doing very well, vrrrrr well in this ward.

Vital ward. Vital! Important. What's really encouraging? Labour people are coming straight over to us. Not stopping at the Lib Dems. Our vote? Solid. FAN-TASTIC. Lib Dems? Soft! Vrrrr vrrrrr soft!'

As far as we could tell, the only evidence that Labour people were coming straight over to the Conservatives was the arrival on the scene of David and me. Marco was, in fact, basically showing us off as evidence of his dynamic and effective leadership. If people like us – so far beyond the Conservatives' usual pool of voters – were coming over to the Tories, Marco probably reasoned that his party was heading not only for victory, but for the biggest landslide in electoral history.

But despite Marco's enthusiasm, the iron ladies listened to him with what struck us as thinly disguised contempt. Their leader was an elderly woman called Pam who looked fragile and fearsome in equal measure – terribly thin despite efforts to bulk herself out with a pea-green padded Barbour-style body warmer. With her weathered features and rural outfit she looked as if she might live on a farm. In fact, she made lampshades and sold them on the internet.

Pam spent a lot of time chatting to her friend Jane, a short, plump woman of about seventy who wore her white hair swept back under a 1950s-style Alice band. Jane seemed to have more intellectual gravitas than anyone else in Team Marco – including Marco himself. Unusually, she talked about politics from time to time, often referring to what she had read in the *Daily Telegraph*. (It was odd to meet someone who referred to the *Telegraph* with such reverence and such confidence – doubtless justified – that everyone else in her circle would also have read it that morning.)

Eventually Jane decided to call my bluff. 'Why have you joined us?' she said. 'You don't look like a Conservative to me. You seem quite nice. Don't you know we are the nasty party?' There were cackles all round at this. I repeated my cover story that I was a Labour voter, but I didn't like Tony Blair because of the war, and that there was no point in voting Liberal because that would only help Labour. Jane listened to this sophistry, blinked, and looked bemused. It struck me that she did not believe a single word.

A few moments afterwards, as if to bring me up to date on the politics of the election campaign, Jane said in a stage whisper of foghorn volume: 'You know, the Lib Dems are very, very strong here – verrr strong – because they have got a FANTASTIC candidate, a really, really capable candidate – and that makes SUCH a difference . . . yessss – a really EXCELLENT candidate . . . such a difference . . .' If this was bait, Marco decided not to rise to it. His mobile phone rang and he excused himself before rushing off on some vital mission or other.

Later, following an afternoon of door-to-door canvassing that merely revealed the rock-solid nature of Liberal support in that part of Richmond, Jane complained bitterly about Marco. She said he had been parachuted into Richmond, had no roots in the area and was, generally speaking, a bit of a lightweight. 'The Liberals know how to do it,' Jane grumbled. 'They are like we were years ago. They are at it all the time. Coffee mornings, jumble sales, petitions. We don't do anything. You can't just bring the party to life at election time. It won't work.'

As we canvassed another leafy avenue flanked by expensive houses – territory in which you might reasonably expect the householders to vote Conservative – Jane began to despair. Exasperated, she threw her arms in the air and cried out, 'There's nothing here!' She meant there were scant promises of Tory votes, and added, mystified and almost tearful, 'All of this was ours when Maggie was in! Don't they realize that their taxes will go up! What are they thinking?'

My time with the Richmond Conservatives passed quickly and soon I had become a key player in their election campaign – and so, to a lesser extent, had David. With so few keen activists there was a vacuum at the heart of the organization, and we had been sucked into it. What made us even more valuable was that hale, hearty and physically fit party workers were especially thin on the ground. These problems seemed to be nationwide but in Richmond the rot was so bad, we discovered, that the party was paying a firm that used Eastern European immigrants to deliver campaign literature door to door. The story appeared in the Liberal-leaning *Independent* and made out that the Richmond Tories were a bunch of utter hypocrites, employing the very immigrants on whom many right-wingers wanted more stringent controls.

A few days into the campaign I found myself in Robert's car, with him at the wheel, driving towards yet another canvassing rendezvous point to deliver yet more leaflets (I had put aside my concerns that this was taking bread from the mouths of asylum seekers). During the journey Robert happily recounted stories about his escapades as a Tory campaigner, such as the time he had stood as a candidate in an unwinnable seat in the North East in the 1980s. As Robert told it, one day Cecil Parkinson arrived at a railway station to support his campaign and to speak at a public meeting. According to Robert, 'Cecil' had turned up at the station and, instead of saying hello, had pointed at a 'lady station guard' and said, 'Look at the enormous knockers on that!'

As we trundled slowly along Hugo, the other passenger, was not the least bit interested in Robert's stories. Instead, he was sitting in the back seat, wriggling like an excited puppy and pointing at all the VOTE MARCO signs he had put up in people's front gardens. Hugo was staggeringly enthusiastic about political signage. As Robert rambled on, Hugo would butt in excitedly with 'Oooh – look at that one up there! That's a bloody great position! Everyone will see that! Hey! Three signs in a row! I hope Marco drives this way and sees that! Over the back there, there's a street you can't see from here, but there's loads and loads of signs! Yep, loads of them! Loads of them.'

As we arrived at a busy road junction Hugo pointed out a large but dilapidated house with a big garden, and Hugo shared his plans to persuade the householder to let him plant an enormous VOTE MARCO sign in the front garden. 'She's barking mad,' Hugo confided, 'and her house is a complete wreck. I think there's something seriously wrong with her. But I think she might let me put a sign up – she's mad enough.' Sure enough, a few days later a gigantic blue sign was securely and proudly standing in the garden, plonked down like the Stars and Stripes on the surface of the moon.

As we drove past a thicket of orange diamond-shaped Liberal Democrat signs along the main road, Hugo filled up with respectful admiration. 'You know, those Lib Dem signs are much better than ours, the colour is much better and it stands out more. You've got to hand it to them.' After that Hugo decided he wanted to cheer everyone up and badgered Robert – who was telling a very long story about some sort of mishap with John Major's portable soapbox during the 1992 election campaign – into taking a considerable detour around Barnes Common. This was so that we could see the sign Hugo had erected in the garden of the multimillion-pound mansion that belonged to Chris Patten – the wealthy former Tory minister and last governor of Hong Kong.

'He agreed to have the sign up straight away,' Hugo yapped. 'I met him and he was really nice about it.' Hugo then insisted we take another detour so that we could see the signs he had erected along the edge of Barnes Common itself. A neat row of blue signs planted amid some brambles came into view. 'Yes! Reeee-sult!' Hugo cried, punching the air. He had been worried, he explained, that because they were on common land 'vandals' might have pulled them down.

Later that afternoon Robert dropped me off at Tory HQ and

I walked the short distance back to my house where I was due to meet David for a spot of evening canvassing. It was five o'clock on a bright spring evening. I turned the corner and was confronted by the sight of an eight-foot wooden pole with a VOTE MARCO FORGIONE – CONSERVATIVE poster stuck to a large piece of hardboard in the style of an estate agent's For Sale sign. As chance would have it David turned up at exactly the same time and, pointing at the sign, began laughing like a drain.

He watched me look at the sign and then go into a state of shock: 'Oh f***! Look at that,' I said. And I kept repeating this two-word mantra, involuntarily burying my head in my hands. Being a coward, I peeped in through the window to see if my wife was in. She was. 'Oh f***, oh f***!' My wife is a dedicated Labour supporter (and feminist!) and, even more than this, very committed to gardening and the overall look of the front of the house. She had reservations about the project in the first place. This was not going to play well with her.

I hit upon the brilliant plan of blaming David. It was in fact true that David had agreed to 'display a poster' during his original, fateful phone call to Marco. What he had in mind was maybe an A4 poster that could be put in the window and then obscured by shrubbery in some way. Instead, we had ended up with this carbuncle, this Day-Glo Nelson's column of political shame. In the event my wife, who had grown wearily used to my escapades over the years, displayed a boundless degree of tolerance. She restricted her retaliation to a series of withering looks, adding the observation that the very sight of the sign made her flesh creep.

I mulled over the sign question with David as we drove through Richmond Park to the rendezvous point in Tudor ward where we were scheduled to start canvassing with Marco and his 'boys and girls' (our experience to date led us to expect they would actually be mature women). I was feeling very paranoid about it. And I was very paranoid about the sign. I was in a dark place at the time, partly because of the powerful kidney drugs I was on, which had mood-altering and anxiety-heightening properties.[1]

The Tories were devious, I reasoned. They had obviously arranged for the sign to be stuck up as a way of smoking us out. It was a test. David, who was not on drugs and who had a healthier and less Machiavellian outlook anyway, was more inclined to think that it was just routine idiocy and, perhaps, wishful thinking. 'These people just go round putting up these signs,' he explained, adding: 'It's a waste of f***ing time and effort. But it is what they do.' And he shrugged and told me to calm down a bit.

It seemed likely that the Tories thought there was something suspicious about David and me. But we were doing no harm. And what were they going to do if they felt they needed to act? March up to David and say, 'You cannot possibly be a Conservative – we can tell because you are black'? Some of them might think that, but they were not going to come out and say it.

Notwithstanding the powerful side effects of my kidney drugs, it didn't always feel great to be deceiving Marco, Robert, Pam and the rest of the Richmond Tories. But, then again, a bit of research on Marco revealed that the image he liked to present wasn't, as we saw it, always completely in tune with the reality. A quick look on the internet had turned up the fact that when he had joined the Tories in the mid-1990s the party's national machine had trumpeted him as a prized Labour 'defector'. But while he had said he had been a Labour sympathizer shortly after studying at university, it soon emerged that he had never in fact been a Labour Party member. There were

[1] I am much better now.

other inconsistencies and exaggerations in his background, so the last thing he could complain about was people not presenting a full and accurate picture of themselves, politically speaking.

David and I mulled it all over as we drove through Richmond Park to the evening rendezvous in the car park of a sports centre. Marco was waiting for us with a small knot of two or three blokes. A tall man called Frank loomed physically over the proceedings, but the brightest spark was Sean, a forty-something who was introduced as an official of some sort for the party. Sean had all the lists and papers we needed sorted out in advance, and introduced the concept of 'running the board' – whereby one member of the canvassing team didn't actually knock on doors at all but, instead, kept the running total of promised votes up to date.

We were to canvass the Tudor ward, a relentlessly suburban patch with an entirely different feel from the more fashionable Vineyard ward. Housing in the Tudor ward was much more modern, with a good sprinkling of boxy sixties- and seventies-style semis with built-in garages. Parts of the ward looked like the remnants of a privatized council estate, with boring looking but good quality cottage-style red-brick semis.

The key thing about door-to-door canvassing, the Richmond Tories emphasized to us, was not to waste time trying to change anyone's opinion. That would be done by the TV appearances of the party leader Michael Howard ('God help us!' I said to David), by the negative smear stuff on the front pages of the tabloids, by the leaflets and by the national billboard advertising campaign (featuring, on this occasion, the vague and frankly useless 'dog-whistle' slogan 'Are you thinking what we're thinking?').

Big Frank drove us to the canvassing starting point, a few streets away. I was still feeling a bit sick because of the arrival of the sign at home, and I was at the worst point of my kidney drug therapy, so I was slightly out of it and everything seemed a bit weird and threatening. Big Frank was openly hostile and unfriendly – narrowing his eyes for one heart-stopping moment and saying with real menace: 'Haven't I seen you somewhere before?' Frank's car didn't help either. It was a monstrous Mercedes-like affair which seemed hermetically sealed. The mood was tense and there was no conversation. Instead the car was filled with the booming sound of Barry White which happened to be playing on Frank's choice of easy-listening radio station. For a little while it was like being in a David Lynch movie – sailing through the suburbs in Frank's hermetically sealed bubble with a bunch of odd characters and this insane sex music blasting over the stereo.

Robert had previously told me all about Tudor ward. It was pretty solid Conservative territory, a 'Thatcherite' place where the house prices were steep but not ridiculously so. That was because the transport links to London were no good, interrupted by the Thames on one side and Richmond Park on the other. In a borough which had one of the oldest populations in the country, this was where younger couples could just about get on the housing ladder.

Tudor ward was where the 'hard-working families' lived, the typical potential swing voters to whom politicians of all parties like to pay homage. From what we could tell, Tudor people were moderately well off and had white-collar jobs; they were the kind of people who were probably juggling their mortgages and credit card debts while trying to work out whether they could really afford private education for their kids.

Voters around here, Marco said, were sensitive to taxation and changes in interest rates. Once we were on the doorstep it quickly became clear that, although there were plenty of Tories in the Tudor ward, there were also plenty of non-voting former Tories who were still angry with the Conservatives for overseeing interest rate hikes more than a decade earlier. When you met such people they were pretty hostile, in the main, to politics of any kind. We received comments such as: 'You only come round here when you want our vote' – as though that was somehow a bad or irrational or hypocritical thing to do rather than an obvious and perfectly reasonable one. It seemed to me and David that these people wanted a straight cash bribe in return for their vote. None of them seemed to exude much ideological zeal or public spiritedness. I had the feeling that with most of them you needed to repeal the law on the secret ballot, so that they could then simply sell their vote to the highest cash bidder.

The official Conservative campaigning materials didn't really help us deal with these characters. What they were really after was the abolition of all taxes and all laws that adversely affected them, combined with draconian measures against everyone else in the country. The leaflets were vague, and talked about side issues such as hospital cleanliness. What you needed here was something more along the lines of VOTE TORY AND WIN A MINI METRO. To get through the psychodrama of canvassing we developed a technique we came to call 'Zen' canvassing, based on the main official slogan of the Conservative campaign which was 'Are YOU thinking what we're thinking?'

David and I would repeat this meaningless sentence and then wiggle our eyebrows inscrutably, while noting the perplexed reactions of the householder. One middle-aged woman – who looked a bit Lib Dem – asked, 'Is this a joke?' to which I replied, 'No, no!' before showing her the slogan on an official leaflet. I coughed and announced, 'I am canvassing for Marco Forgione and I was just wondering "Are yoooooo thinking what we're thinking ... erm ... hmmmm ... are you?"' The woman warmed up and seemed amused: 'Well, what is that ... what are you thinking?' I said I didn't know and, anyway, that was not the question. She took a leaflet and said that in fact she always voted Conservative and would probably do so again.

With the first phase of the evening's canvassing over, Marco and his team gathered on a street corner to tot up the number of likely Conservative votes. There were a lot of shrugs and pulling of faces, and a feeling that they had really just been going through the motions. There was a Tory vote here but there were few signs of enthusiasm. Big Frank enlivened proceedings by telling the story of how a house he was canvassing had been stormed by armed police. Frank said he told the cops, 'Don't arrest me, I am only canvassing' and this witticism was treated by Marco and company as though it were a fresh from the lips of Oscar Wilde. 'What were they, Frank? Irish? Or Muslims?' Marco asked.

After this Team Marco fanned out across the ward for a little more light canvassing until it got dark. At one house a woman detained me on the doorstop while she fetched her grumpy teenage son, and then used me as the exhibit in a show-and-tell lesson about how local politics, councils and the entire constitutional system worked. The kid looked at me blankly, then began to smirk in a hostile manner.

By the time I arrived at the pub, everyone had disappeared except David, Marco and a clean-cut Canadian volunteer in his twenties. The section of the pub we were sitting in and the downbeat feel of the bar matched Marco's conversation. He laid out all the reasons that the Tudor ward householders had given for not voting Conservative. I said I'd found people receptive, but Marco said: 'The thing is, you can't believe a word most of them say to you. They will say they are going to vote for you, and then not do it. Others will say they are against you, then they change their minds.'

Then Marco started grilling me about the giant blue Conservative election poster that had appeared in my front garden. Was I happy with it? he asked. I nervously dodged the question – fearing Marco was trying to gauge my true loyalties – and replied that my wife was 'hopping mad' because 'it doesn't go with the curtains' and 'she's essentially non-political'. That last bit about my wife being non-political was, I think, the only out and out lie I told throughout the entire project. The real reason my wife was hopping mad was not down to mismatched interior décor or political apathy, but because she hated the Conservatives with a passion and now had a huge VOTE MARCO FORGIONE – CONSERVATIVE placard positioned on her lawn.

Apparently satisfied, Marco headed to the bar for a second time. I wondered if he was trying to pump as much lager as possible into us in order to discover the reality behind the shifty demeanours of his latest recruits. He came back with more beer, tossing a packet of crisps onto the table.

'I knocked on one door,' said Marco brightly, 'and this old Glaswegian guy came out. Verrrr much the dyed-in-the-wool Old Labour supporter, and he said: "I don't like Blair. Not at all. But if you think I am going to vote for a f***ing Welsh Jewboy like Michael Howard you must be f***joking!"' There was silence, and an agonized pause. David came to the rescue and – as the on-hand race-relations expert – defused an awkward moment. 'Better put him down as a "don't know", then,' he quipped.

Later I asked David whether he had encountered any racism on the doorstep in Richmond, not just in Tudor ward, but everywhere we had canvassed in the borough. Or indeed, whether people had been at all surprised to find a black man wearing a blue rosette and asking them whether they would be voting Tory. David said there had been hardly any noticeable reaction to his skin colour on the doorstep, or any suggestion that a black Tory might be an oddity.

A few days later I took my first turn at shouting Conservative slogans into the Battle Banger's microphone, my words being completely mangled as the ancient amplifier and speaker broadcast them around Richmond's quiet streets.

This, like wearing a Conservative rosette for the first time, had been – despite my commitment to the writing project – a troubling experience. There I was being driven around my borough bothering people with Conservative propaganda, and I expected them really to hate me for it.

But, as with the rosette, I had been genuinely surprised to find that people either ignored us or had only given mildly annoyed looks – because of the noise, I suspected. There had been some vaguely approving but amused smiles, of the sort given to morris dancers or people rattling tins for Cats Protection, but no one had thrown a brick at us or even flicked a V-sign.

Robert had been at the wheel and, with a wry smile, had written out a script for me on the back of an envelope from the water company. The script read: 'For Cleaner Hospitals, Vote Conservative'. If I got bored with that, Robert said, I could change the line to 'For More Police, Vote Conservative'. When I shouted, maybe a little bit sarcastically, 'Vote for Marco Forgione – your LOCAL Conservative candidate', Robert said, with an enthusiastic cackle, 'That's a good one!' Marco, as part of his election strategy, was indeed claiming that he was a local man, although this struck us as a somewhat unusual claim to be making, given his strong family and business links to the West Country.

Nobody would have been able to make out a word I was saying, however, since the distortion and feedback from the clapped-out battery-powered valve amplifier was so extreme. At one point I wound down the window of the car – it was a warm day – and that produced a persistent, whistling feedback so sweet and sustained that it could have formed part of a Jimi Hendrix guitar solo.

As Robert drove and I shouted – sometimes relieving the boredom with 'For Cleaner Police and More Hospitals, Vote Marco Forgione' – I thought how pointless it was to shout at people in this way. It seemed to be nothing more than a habit among local political campaigners which dated back to a time before television, when a megaphone was the only way to communicate with people in large numbers or over a distance. Now it was just a noisy but empty ritual, one of the things you did at election time.

Eventually I was invited into the belly of the beast – the back room of the Richmond Conservative Association office itself. I was given a desk and a telephone and a telephone canvassing job. I had to convince Richmond's Tory supporters to show up at a public meeting with Michael Howard and also confirm that they would turn up to vote on election day.

The inner sanctum – the size of a decent sized sitting room – was windowless and dominated by a long boardroom table in the middle of the floor. Around the table sat six elderly women stuffing leaflets into envelopes. From one wall a chocolate-box portrait of the Queen looked on, and on another hung an oil painting of the Houses of Parliament. The place was dingy and threadbare, yet this was the nerve centre of the Conservative operation in Richmond.

'Chris is just going to make a few phone calls for me,' said Marco, grinning in a sickly way. 'Is that OK, ladies?' There was no reply. I sat down facing the wall and picked up an ancient telephone with a curly wire, keying in the numbers and working my way down a list of Tory sympathizers. Another element of this ring round was to ask if they would help with electioneering. The majority of those who answered the phone sounded very old – many with ailments which they used, quite reasonably, to excuse themselves from helping out with political activity.

The routine went something like this. I would say: 'Hello, is that Mrs Smith?' Then one of the six ladies – they were watching my every move – would interject with something like 'Oh, I know her, she can't help – she's terribly crippled.' The ladies would talk about me as if I wasn't there: 'Why have they asked him to phone all these people,' they would say. 'I know all of them, they are all my friends.'

Sometimes, I got through to a younger, and presumably able-bodied, Tory supporter, who would make excuses to get out of helping with the campaign. The ladies would then cheer themselves up by making vitriolic personal comments about the person on the other end of the phone, along the lines that he or she was a traitor, hypocrite and fair-weather supporter who had been only too keen to help when the Tories were riding high.

As I worked down the list, I began flipping through a script left by the phone. It was obviously to be used when cold-calling people. Among the various instructions was a crib sheet to be used if the person on the other end of the line was a Lib Dem who might just be persuaded to vote Tory. There was some very negative, personalized stuff there about Jenny Tonge, the retiring Liberal MP, claiming that she had stepped down as MP 'probably because of her stance on hard drugs'.

As for Susan Kramer, the new Lib Dem election candidate, the script made it clear I should emphasize that she was an 'outsider' and a 'foreigner' who had 'few links with Richmond' and had 'lost in other constituencies'. The script also said Kramer was Hungarian, although why all this should matter, particularly given that Marco's links with Richmond didn't seem particularly strong either and he was of Italian extraction, was anybody's guess.

Taking a momentary break from phoning the existing supporters, I turned to face the ladies and said: 'It says here that Kramer is Hungarian. I didn't know she was Hungarian.'

'She's a Jewess,' one of the ladies replied, 'but we aren't allowed to say that. We get told off if we say that. So all we can say is that she got off the train from Hungary.'

\* \* \*

The next day I was out of the office and back on the road. A Tory convoy had been organized, with the aim of 'blitzing' Barnes, the well-heeled, faintly bohemian area which much of the BBC's top talent calls home. By mid-morning a cluster of four or five cars – expensive but boring mid-range saloons – had parked up at the rendezvous point. Some of the cars had blue balloons attached to them and a couple had 'Vote Conservative' posters in the side windows.

As the housing density in the area was so low – the ultimate luxury in London – there was no need for parking restrictions, and consequently no danger of getting a parking ticket. The line of parked cars was soon noticed by two local Anglo-Indian boys, about eight and nine years old.

'Who are these people?' asked the younger one, possibly attracted by the balloons.

'The police,' the older one asserted.

'What are they doing?'

'They are doing a survey of people,' he stated categorically. Bored, they returned to slurping ice cream and dropping litter on the street.

Eventually, the Battle Banger hoved into view, with the amplified voice of Lampshade Pam broadcasting noisily through a loudspeaker tied to the roof rack. She sounded like Björk with a mouth full of marbles talking through a fuzzbox. Her message was simple, if not very easy on the ear: 'VRNNRTT KORNSVVVKKNNNITIVE VRRRNNNTTT MMMMNNNAEEKKKOW FOOORRRRGEE OWWWWN-EEEEE.'

The Battle Banger trundled up the street and abruptly came to a halt. Pam, sitting in the passenger seat, was thrown forward. The car was decked out in an array of 'Vote Forgione' posters with blue helium balloons trailing behind, some of which had already started to deflate. Marco jumped out of the car to meet the team.

The man behind the wheel of the Battle Banger – an aggressive-looking middle-aged activist – leaned across Pam, wound down the window and growled a garbled message to the effect that we were to follow him down to 'The Glebelands' in central Barnes. There was great excitement among the Tories. This was the patch of Susan Kramer, the Liberal Democrat candidate for Richmond.

Kramer lived in a mansion – the £5-million type – close to the centre of Barnes village, the expensive heart of the area. 'It's time to really put the boot in,' said one canvasser with enthusiasm. 'Yeahhhh,' agreed the driver of the Battle Banger, with grim determination: 'let's DO it!' There were now about ten of us in total, and we all climbed into the cars and sped off.

When we arrived in Glebelands, everyone parked in front of the Kramer residence, which stood in a wide, tree-lined street completely devoid of people. The Battle Banger hovered for a while, with Pam on the loudspeaker, chanting with added gusto, 'FER KLINNER HAIR-SPIT-YULES! MHER PLISS ONDER STRIT! VERT KIN-SEVE-VEET-TEETH' over and over again.

As Pam's racket continued, we hung about on the pavement. Ostensibly – with sheaves of leaflets at hand – we were just hoping to talk passers-by into voting Conservative. But as there were no passers-by, it was pretty clear the Richmond Conservatives were simply having fun by trying to annoy Susan Kramer.

After a few minutes, to our complete amazement Kramer's husband actually arrived on the scene and began talking to the Tories. Instead of starting a slanging match, however, he exuded goodwill and bonhomie. It was a master class in the art of passive aggression. 'Good morning,' said Mr Kramer, 'how is it all going . . . it's great to see you all here. This is really fantastic for democracy. Well done, well done.'

This genteel stand-off concluded after a few minutes, following which the driver of the Battle Banger revved up and zoomed into the distance. Fun over, the Tory mob then began to disperse, pounding the surrounding streets and pushing their leaflets – the implied message of which was 'Vote Liberal and get a gypsy encampment at the bottom of your garden' – through as many letter boxes as possible on Kramer's patch.

As we were bumbling around near Kramer's house a TV crew – meaning one microphone-wielding reporter and one cameraman – turned up. They were from a Dutch news channel and were profiling Richmond as one of the key seats in election 2005. From the standpoint of a Dutch television reporter Richmond, I learned, is an interesting place, as there are lots of opportunities for references to cricket on the green, tea shops, boating on the Thames and so on.

The reporter then asked me off camera why I thought such a prosperous place was held by the Liberals and not by 'your party, the Conservatives'. I told them the truth as I understood it – Barnes was a fairly trendy area. Lots of rich folk working in television lived there and they tended to be opposed to the Conservatives on moral and philosophical grounds. The Dutch reporter was starting to look bored so in a moment of inspiration I added: 'Also – gay people.

'There's loads and loads and loads of gay people here in Barnes, just like in Amsterdam,' I added. 'They're stinking rich, but they don't vote Conservative because they're gay, and I for one very much welcome that.' The Dutch reporter was momentarily thrown, so, in character, I stumbled and corrected myself: 'Sorry – I don't mean that I welcome the fact that gay people don't vote for us – that is something I regret. What I welcome is that there are such a lot of gay people around here and in the world generally.'

The Dutch reporter was now completely thrown. 'You do not seem to me to be very much like a Tory Man,' he said, evidently wondering what to make of all this gibberish about gay people.

'That's right,' I said, brightly. 'I am normally a very strong Labour supporter, but I don't like some of the things Tony Blair has been doing, like the war in Iraq. Same as you in Holland. So I have decided to give out some leaflets for the Conservatives to see what will happen. And also I am partly doing this as an experiment. To see how they will react to me.'

The Dutch reporter was, again, lost for a moment. Finally he said: 'Noooohhh – I'm not believing this, that a left-wing man can be voting for such a very right-wing organization as the Conservatives Party, I have never heard of this. This is not possible.' But then a light bulb seemed to go on above the reporter's head, and he added with some incredulity: 'Can I film you saying all of these things? About you being a Labour man who does not like Mr Blair any more?'

'Sure,' I said. I delivered the lines to camera, while wearing my blue rosette. I added the news that Greg Dyke, the socialist former Director General of the BBC, had earlier that day told Old Labour people such as himself to vote Lib Dem in order to give Tony Blair a good kicking. I went on to explain, for the benefit of Dutch television viewers, that Dyke's advice was a waste of time because, without a proper proportional representation system, the election was a two-horse race.

'In this election when the votes are counted it either means Tony Blair is going to be Prime Minister or Michael Howard is gonna be Prime Minister,' I summed up. 'So if you don't want Howard you are stuck with Blair. And vice versa. And that's the fact of it and all the rest is just hot air.'

The reporter didn't seem entirely convinced that this could motivate my apparent overnight journey from left-winger to right-winger, but he had a new angle on the election and was grinning from ear to ear. He gave a thoughtful and appreciative 'Hmmmmmm' which seemed to say, 'I know you are up to something, but I am not quite sure what it is.'

*　*　*

Michael Howard didn't seem to be a particularly popular character with the local Richmond Tories, and the name of the then Tory leader was hardly mentioned during the campaign in Richmond. For a party which often created a cult of personality around its leaders – from Churchill to Thatcher – this was odd. Howard was, however, due to arrive in Richmond to give a boost to local campaigners, and that gave me and David the chance to see at close quarters how the Tory leader's spin machine operated. The morning rendezvous point was Richmond Green, an open space in the middle of the town. When Team Marco – including us – arrived, a flunky from Conservative Central Office confronted our group.

The flunky was much younger than anyone else among the gathering Tory campaigners – maybe twenty-five. He was unsmiling and yakked on a mobile, which he had clamped to his ear, continuously. His telephone conversations employed modern lingo and jargon, spattered with the f-word, just like a normal person of his generation.

Howard's motorcade drew up and parked in a side street without much fuss. There were three or four vehicles led by a black shiny car containing what looked like security men and more officials from Central Office. Howard's own car came next, unmarked but bearing the unmistakable sign of power and money – darkened glass windows. Inside was his fragrant blonde wife, Sandra, along with some more helpers. Bringing up the rear was a navy blue minibus full of the journalists and TV cameras, and behind that another unmarked car, presumably full of yet more secret police.

A whole gang of Tory heavies emerged from the cars, including a squad of pushy media minders from Central Office. Like the flunky we had seen earlier, these apparatchiks were much, much younger and more dynamic than the Dad's Army of local Tories we'd so far been involved with. They had about them the look, manners and vocabulary of tabloid journalists – as though they had been seconded from the *Sun* for the duration.

Two or three bored-looking camera crews emerged from the minibus. The BBC's man, the vulpine James Landale, strode about looking imperious and tremendously unimpressed with everything. But the star – far more luminous than Michael Howard – was Trevor McDonald, who, as well as being a top newsreader, was also a resident of the East Sheen ward. Trevor began walking about in stately fashion, waving regally to those passers-by who recognized him. Last out of the minibus were the lower-status non-TV hacks, including a young male newspaper reporter with a punk hairdo from the Press Association, and a plump and jolly female reporter for a local radio station.

Howard emerged from his car wearing a mirthless smile and shook Marco's hand. There was no small talk – no 'How's it all going, Marco?' – just straight on to 'Right! Where am I supposed to be walking? Let's get started!' The walkabout kicked off, with Howard first pressing the flesh with the local Tories, shaking hands and pepping them up. 'Thank you verrr much for coming here today,' he said in his curious sing-song voice.

The Tory leader looked frightful – caked in so much make-up to the point of appearing like a waxwork dummy, with strange jerky, wooden movements to match, and a faraway look in his eyes, as though he was running on autopilot. His wife Sandra was beaming at everyone all the time in a way that seemed to suggest she was about to say something, but she never did. Not once. Not even a 'Hello'. She was completely mute, yet remained in a state of apparently continuous imminent pronouncement.

The hacks understood that they had to wait for the brief ritual of party leader patting local party workers on the back to take place before the real business of the walkabout began; it was all part of a game they had played many times before. Howard and Marco then marched off around Richmond Green and towards the high street at a cracking pace – almost a jog. The Sky TV News cameraman filmed every moment, jogging backwards as he shot them from the front, shuffling sideways like a crab. The Central Office people seemed very annoyed that there was such a tiny turnout of local supporters and began bossing me and the others about. 'No, no, no!' they would bark. 'You need to get in much closer behind Michael . . . Much, much closer.'

People twenty yards away would clock the blue rosettes and TV cameras and cross the street to get away. There was only one way, the Central Office officials seemed to have decided, to make sure Howard could be filmed interacting with passersby. And that was to pounce on the more unwary as they emerged from shop doorways.

It worked like this. Howard would stop chatting to Marco – mid-sentence – and then swoop on an unsuspecting punter coming out of a shop and, to the bewilderment of the punter, initiate a conversation. The press pack, Central Office minders and Marco's local Tories would then bunch up, with the hacks pressing forward, trying to earwig the conversation, and hoping for a gaffe of some sort to come tumbling out of someone's mouth.

When Howard swooped – and it was a bit Dracula-like, as he tended to be taller than the older shoppers he encountered, the younger ones having already scuttled off – the victim would quickly spot the cameras and the hacks with notebooks, and then try to get out of the way. If escape was impossible, the victim tended to adopt a bemused, 'game for a laugh' expression, perhaps realizing that they were going to be on TV and wanting to look amenable and as normal as possible. A few seemed to recognize Howard, but none seemed to recognize Marco.

At one point Howard descended on a scruffy man who was probably in his seventies. The man was wearing cheap clothes – a baseball cap, soup-streaked tracksuit top with out-of-date

Arsenal insignia, badly fitting jeans and scuffed trainers – and carrying his shopping in two grubby plastic bags. The old boy started talking about how he lived on the nearby Ham estate, claiming there was a lot of trouble there, with lots of youths hanging around and swearing, 'throwing bottles about' and generally making his life a misery.

Howard listened for a bit and then butted in, outlining a plan to cut the welfare benefits of parents of kids that had been reprimanded for anti-social behaviour. 'We have some very tough measures for dealing with the yobs you are talking about,' he said, edging away. But the man came back, a quizzical look on his face. 'What about putting them all in the army?' he growled. 'What do you think about that?' The media scrum tightened, sensing that Howard was now in potential gaffe territory.

But Howard smoothly ignored the question. 'Well,' he said, 'we do have some very tough measures, some very tough measures indeed, for dealing with yobs who do make life impossible for good, hard-working peepil . . .' Before the old boy could push his plan for dragooning hoodied ASBO yobs into a conscript army any further, Howard beamed at him with a smile both brilliant and seemingly devoid of any sincerity whatsoever. 'Thank you, thank you,' he said, 'must press on, thank you so much . . .' Patronizing smiles broke out among the Tory officials.

As the Howard mob shuffled off along the street, the punky Press Association hack broke off to interview a man who had just come out of a betting shop, claiming to have put £100 on Michael Howard to win the election at 30-1. The story of the bet was the only part of the Press Association story that made the local paper and it was very much the comedy highlight of an otherwise completely gaffe-free – and therefore, as far as the journos were concerned, unproductive – walkabout.

Finally, Howard disappeared into a Chinese restaurant for an hour to be interviewed by Trevor McDonald. Everyone else – the less starry television journalists, the newspaper hacks and the plump female radio reporter – was left on the street in front of the restaurant to fend for themselves. It was now pouring with rain. One minder from Conservative Central Office sheltered in the restaurant's entrance, barring the way like a bouncer. Another started sparring with Radio Woman, saying it had all gone very well and that 'MH' had received a 'really great, warm reception'.

'Well, come on now, this is not exactly hostile territory for you,' said Radio Woman.

The Tory press minder replied, in a wounded voice, 'It was totally solid Lib Dem last time, totally solid, but this time it is really moving.'

'In your dreams,' snorted Radio Woman, before announcing that, since Howard would be in the restaurant for a long time, she was going off to get coffee in Starbucks. 'In your dreams,' she repeated as she departed.

Later, Howard was due to give a formal speech to supporters at a local community centre. He appeared through a side door and made magisterial gestures to calm the crowd, arms outstretched, smiling and soaking it all up, as his head bobbed up and down like a nodding dog toy. Once or twice, he seemed to point to somebody in the middle distance, as though he was on stage at a vast arena.

In reality, he was only in a tiny hall with no more than a hundred people present, all crammed tightly together by party officials so as to create some atmosphere. However, the deception worked to great effect. When we later saw the two-second sound bite that appeared on television, it really did look as though Howard was addressing a mass rally.

The Conservative supporters lapped up all this nonsense in a manner that was polite rather than ecstatic. Like fans of the Rolling Stones, the greying crowd was holding back until a favourite song was rolled out – then they would really let rip.

When, I reckoned they were wondering, was Howard going to get to the signature tune of the campaign – that is, the harsh measures the Tories would take against criminals once they were in power?

'We are going to put the criminals behind bars – and the do-gooders back in their box' was the furthest Howard would go on that issue. Box? What box? As far as I could tell, the crowd was confused by this odd remark. It seemed to be one of the 'dog whistle' signals that newspapers' political writers had told everyone to expect; but what the crowd wanted, it appeared, was proper whistles that they could actually pick up without having super-sensitive dog hearing. Such as, maybe, 'Lock 'em up and throw away the key.'

At the end of his speech, Howard received a standing ovation – no real surprise at a stage-managed event such as this – but it was a pretty sad scene. At least half the audience did not even try to stand up, and this seemed to be because they were either very old or disabled. Many of those who did stand up struggled to their feet slowly and with evident discomfort. In some cases, by the time they had made it the ovation had finished, leaving them looking stranded and bewildered. Howard did his nodding and waving rock star thing again and the audience sat down, some of them very slowly. And then he was gone.

Polling day dawned and David and I were roped in for 'one last push' as part of the plainly doomed national and local campaign. We were given the task of standing outside the East Sheen polling station – actually the local primary school – and asking voters for their names as they arrived to vote. We had to look up the name on a list of voters and tick them off. The idea was, by process of elimination, to identify known Conservative supporters who hadn't voted, so that other workers could call them up and persuade them to get to the polling station.

This process, known as tellering, had been organized by John Leach, a stalwart of the Richmond Tories, who had phoned us a few days earlier. (Marco had told him we were 'living together' and 'very keen to help'.) We found Leach's name surreal, and yet another reminder of how, during our time with the Richmond Tories, truth was often stranger than fiction. Could a Tory organizer have a more comedy name than Mr Leach? To us, it was like a version of Happy Families drawn up by Dave Spart of *Private Eye* fame – Mr Parasite the stockbroker, Mr Leach the Tory party organizer.

Leachy was another long-in-the-tooth Tory – he was the retired founder and former chief of the Londis supermarket chain. When he called, he said he was planning to drive down to the polling station himself on election day, but in the background his wife could be heard reminding him that he had to go to a funeral. Leachy's manner brightened, as though he was looking forward to the funeral as a treat, or a really nice day out.

Leachy had delivered to our home, by hand, the complete tellering kit consisting of a notepad, a novelty official Conservative Party biro (made in China), a spare blank blue rosette (without the Vote Conservative sticker) and written instructions. These warned that there would probably be an enemy Liberal Democrat teller present at the polling station, but this should not be a cause for worry because 'some of them are quite human'.

Tellering was extremely boring. There was a rush in the morning, as people voted on their way to work, and another rush around teatime. In between there were long spells when there were no voters at all. From time to time Leachy or one of his elderly pals would arrive at the polling station and take away the lists of voters I had compiled, tut-tutting about the low turnout in general – which, in an overwhelmingly Tory ward like East Sheen, was a worrying sign. He would sigh, ask, generously I thought, if I wanted him to bring me a cup of tea in a thermos flask and then he would hobble off again.

I got chatting to the Lib Dem teller, who seemed friendly enough but a bit wary of me. He was a retired business studies lecturer at what had been South Bank Polytechnic. He seemed to have an encyclopaedic knowledge of the local Tory Party, and kept asking if I knew this or that councillor. Later he was relieved by another Lib Dem teller, an eccentric, elderly bohemian looking woman who was wearing a long hippy-style skirt, a sort of suede jacket, beads and sandals – very much a faded Joan Bakewell look. She had previously made educational TV programmes for the BBC, featuring glove puppets. The Lib Dems, in other words, were living up to their stereotypes just as much as the Tories.

Meanwhile, David was helping to identify promised Conservative voters who had not been ticked off by me and other tellers across the constituency, and then rushing off to knock on their doors and badger them into voting. After the polls closed we met up in the house of a Conservative councillor for East Sheen. The councillor's front room (standard Georgian furniture, blue silk upholstery, gilt-framed oil paintings, cabbage rose floral explosion elderly female Conservative chintz look) had served as a key command centre in the ward.

There were half a dozen people at the house and we were offered a glass of sherry and a piece of sponge cake. The BBC exit poll was already predicting a national victory for the Labour Party, but the TV wasn't on. An elderly gent, close to tears, said, 'We have just not got our vote out. They have stayed at home.' The others shrugged and agreed. It was hopeless – far worse than the exit polls had suggested. Then, at about 10.30, the councillor suddenly announced that it was getting late and turfed everyone out.

By election day the Vote Marco sign in my garden had drooped alarmingly, and in fact was leaning at an almost 45-degree angle into the garden. Much of it was covered up by an out-of-control clematis, growing profusely in the unusually wet, warm spring. Nobody in my household had vandalized the sign, but if nature wanted to knock it over nobody was going to stand in the way. And, as Hugo the sign guy had bitterly regretted, Tory poster printing was done on the cheap and so the colours were starting to fade, heading towards a sort of Ecology Party turquoise green.

For good measure my son, then at primary school and something of a wag, had drawn a primitive skull and crossbones on the poster with a marker pen, and I had frustrated a further plan of his to add a black plastic skull and crossbones pirate flag. Various spiders and other insects had taken up residence in the soggy hardboard and my teenage daughter had added a Labour Party leaflet, secured with Blu-Tack. Mould was beginning to invade the edge of the placard and it was, all in all, starting to turn into a sort of voodoo totem poll with all sorts of political bunting and tat flapping from it. If it had stayed up long enough maybe somebody would place a human skull on top, like one of those props from *Apocalypse Now*.

At one point during the campaign there was a gathering of my wife's family at a house a little further down the street. I had been amused to see various non-political in-laws, cousins and nephews walking past the sign and looking at it in vaguely anxious perplexity. When I arrived at the party they seemed frosty at first, but said nothing about the blue carbuncle. I then explained The Project, swearing them to 'semi-secrecy' (whatever that meant), and they warmed up considerably.

One brother-in-law, who used to work for a giant pharmaceuticals company, said he knew that a form of temporary insanity was a common side effect of the medicine I was taking for my kidneys, which could also bring on a sort of instant physiological and neurological old age. He had, before I explained The Project to him, genuinely thought that the drug therapy might be the reason for the appearance of the sign.

When I got back to the house, I told David that we had

chalked up the first truly scientific conclusion of the project. The conclusion? That normal, middle-class professional people – who had normal, responsible jobs with big firms – now honestly thought the most obvious explanation as to why somebody might switch their vote from Labour to Conservative was acute drug-induced insanity.

Michael Howard lost the 2005 general election and handed Tony Blair a third term in office. It was an open secret that Blair would in due course hand over to Gordon Brown. It did seem in a way that the Conservative Party of old had passed away and would require a complete relaunch. Marco increased the Conservative vote in Richmond slightly, achieving a swing of 1.9 per cent to the Tories from the Liberal Democrats.

A couple of days after election night we attended an excruciating thank-you party for the Conservative campaigners in Richmond. We met up again with all the characters we'd come across during our time inside Marco's campaign – Robert, Lampshade Pam, some of the 'iron ladies' I had worked the phone with, Hugo the sign guy, Marco himself and a group of very old Tories whom I had not seen during the campaign. Most people seemed either very depressed, or they were so old they were past caring.

In defeat Marco made pretty much exactly the same speech as he had made four years earlier when he stood in Yeovil during the 2001 election (we looked it up on the internet). His spiel made it sound as if he was planning to stay and fight another day. In fact, Marco left both the area and politics itself soon afterwards, taking up a job as the marketing man for a technical college in Kent.

As the party was winding down an elderly and slightly deaf Tory – who looked well into his eighties, if not older – invited us to the Richmond Conservative Association's annual dinner. It was easy to remember when the event took place, the old guy said, because it was always held on the Queen Mother's birthday. One of the younger Tories (in his fifties) explained, shouting the information into the old man's hearing aid, that the Queen Mother was dead. The old man replied with a fearful and utterly lost look: 'Oh! Are you sure? How terrible. Are you sure? How did that happen?'

Coincidentally, the Richmond Conservative Association's annual dinner was due to take place in an Italian restaurant called San Marco. It was an appropriately named venue as Richmond was soon to be sans Marco, since he was about to depart to pastures new. To paraphrase Shakespeare, the Richmond Tories were pretty much sans eyes, sans ears, sans teeth, sans taste, sans Marco – sans everything.

# TWO

# Village Cricket People – Rodmell, Sussex

'Rural England is the real England, unspoilt by factories, financiers, tourists and hustle,' wrote A. G. Macdonell in *England, Their England*, his classic 1933 novel. The book concerns the exploits of a young Scotsman, Donald Cameron, as he tours southern England and some of its more conservative byways. The most famous episode in the book is a blow-by-blow account of a cricket match between a gang of First World War invalids from London and a team from the village of Fordenden, still hailed by many critics as one of the greatest pieces of sports writing. The episode was, though, anything but fictional. Literary historians have established beyond doubt that the match Macdonell describes actually took place in the village of Rodmell, in Sussex, not far from Brighton.

'The entire scene was perfect to the last detail,' Macdonell wrote of his visit to Rodmell. 'There stood the Vicar, beaming absent-mindedly at everyone. There was the forge, with the blacksmith, his hammer discarded, tightening his snake-buckled belt ready for the fray.' According to Macdonell, the locals in this idyllic hamlet sat around the cricket pitch with tankards of ale while 'blue and green dragonflies played at hide and seek among the thistledown and a pair of swans flew overhead. An ancient man leaned upon a scythe, his sharpening-stone sticking out of his velveteen waistcoat. A magpie flapped lazily across the meadows. The parson shook hands with the squire. Doves cooed. The haze flickered. The world stood still.'

After my experiences in Richmond the world of Conservatism just appeared a bit sad to me. The party and its followers hardly seemed worth writing about, except, perhaps, as an exercise in gloating. A year passed, during which I saw off a near fatal illness, which got worse before it got better, and which had made my life such a misery during the 2005 election campaign.

Meanwhile, David had been off on another project, investigating the world of Sierra Leonean war criminals and, on the side, writing about the lifestyles of gangsters and the super-rich for glossy magazines. After the 2005 election Tony Blair's government had become so unpopular that the Conservatives, still unpopular themselves, started to creep up on the inside of Labour in the polls, giving them an outside chance of once again forming the government of the country. Michael Howard stepped down from the Conservative leadership and handed over to the much younger, more media-friendly figure of David Cameron. Cameron began to work his magic, at least at the level of national politics and television, and the Conservatives looked like coming to life once again as a force in their own right. What interested us was whether things were changing at the grass roots of the party and, more broadly, in the attitudes of 'small c' conservatives who might support the party.

A second stage of our Tory journey thus began, and it was to take place against the backdrop of the growing unpopularity of the Labour government and incessant talk in the national media of a rightward shift of the political tectonic plates of the country. We had entered what was for us the alien world of Conservatism through the front door of my local Conservative Association office. We now planned to re-enter by the back door of day-to-day life among conservative people. Our itinerary was to include gatherings of the Women's Institute, bank holiday pilgrimages to Winston Churchill's house, agricultural shows and village fetes, polo matches and summer garden parties, rubber chicken circuit fund-raising dinners, and immersion in a 'Nimby' campaign in Oxfordshire. This, we felt, was the 'real' or 'small c' conservative England on which the fortunes of the Conservative Party ultimately rested. Rodmell, the focus of Macdonell's journey seventy-five years ago, seemed the best place to start – especially as we'd learned that the village still had a cricket team. So we went to the village to watch Rodmell play a one-off invitation match against a local Sussex league side called, of all things, Blackboys.

In 1933, Macdonell described Rodmell as a village of red-roofed cottages gathered around the flint tower of the church, set in meadows bursting with wild flowers and buzzing with bees. It was still a lot like that, at least along the tree-lined lane leading away from the main road and down towards the church, school, graveyard and cricket pavilion. Here, cottages were of the picture postcard variety with clouds of roses around the door and riots of wisteria and other climbing plants. One cottage had a perfect thatched roof, set off by crisply painted white wooden clapperboard exterior walls. Others were of ancient red brick set in wooden frames.

The 1939 census, taken on the eve of war, six years after Macdonell's novel was published, put the population of Rodmell at 359 people living in 101 occupied properties. At that time the village had two farms, a shop, a post office, a petrol forecourt, a blacksmith's forge and a school as well as the pub. 'Today,' said a booklet produced recently by a local historian, Rodmell was a 'commuter/retirement village with a similar population but with little employment in agriculture'. The independent farms had hit financial ruin and had been merged. The resulting larger farm had, in 1999, moved to a complex of industrial-looking modern 'crinkly tin' sheds outside the village. The shop and post office had closed long ago. The blacksmith's forge was still there, but now, from what we could see, it was essentially a car body repair shop.

The village primary school had almost closed at one point, but was now thriving and was highly rated in the school performance league tables. This, we gathered, was because kids were bussed in by thrusting middle-class parents from urban areas a few miles away in Brighton. Few of the children in the school were connected with Rodmell, the chairman of the parish council told us, since so many of today's inhabitants of the village were well beyond the age where they were bringing up young children. The younger executive-commuter types living in the village tended to send their children to one of the many private schools to be found in the area.

The village notice board was festooned with leaflets giving out information of use mainly to older people with a lot of time on their hands: watercolour painting exhibitions and classes; classical music recitals in churches in surrounding villages; a forthcoming midweek evening concert in the pub to be given by a folk combo called the Wayfarers – who were apparently an ancient Peter, Paul and Mary tribute band.

Inside the renovated cottages, instead of going to church and getting ready to play cricket, people were watching Sky Sports or playing computer games on giant plasma TV screens. Some of the cottages had garages built on the side, tastefully done to match the original brick, timber and tile work, their weathered oak-style doors left open – ostentatiously, we thought – to display a variety of gleaming Porsches, BMWs and top-of-the-range Audis. It was unlikely that the owners of these luxurious cottages would be seen dead consuming scampi in a basket in the village pub, or in the church, which looked underused and served, mainly, it seemed, as a tourist attraction and a local monument.

Many of the first wave of incomers to the village had been hippies fleeing urban areas, and semi-bohemian and intellectual people connected with the University of Sussex, which had expanded in the 1970s. In Rodmell a process had occurred similar to the 'gentrification' of the inner cities – squatters and bohemians had made once-dilapidated areas like Islington and Spitalfields trendy and well-off professionals had followed later.

One of the cottages we visited was home to an arty type who had opened it to the public, advertising the fact with a newsagent-type A-frame sign erected next to a single brightly coloured floral deckchair. The deckchair constituted an al fresco café at which 'Sussex cream teas' were available for £3.50. The deckchair was not provided for people to sit in – it was being used as a sign in the lane, advertising the cream tea deal, a neat combination of surrealism and hard-nosed commercial nous. This open-door policy meant that we were able to get inside one of the Rodmell cottages and thus reveal the truth about what goes on behind the figurative net curtains of rural Sussex.

We entered, stooping to get through a doorframe originally designed for medieval peasants bent double by a lifetime of toil in the fields. The building was a low-ceilinged former hovel, now gentrified, consisting of a small front room, a small back room, an upstairs and an outside toilet. Discreet handwritten signs on lilac notelets with tiny drawings of flowers said PLEASE DO NOT TOUCH, forbidding the unknowing punter from laying a finger on the sort of items that were standard fare at any car boot sale. As soon as we crossed the threshold there was, I felt, a wrinkling of the nose, a sign of distaste at our presence. 'Can I help you?' said the owner of the nose, a self-styled water-colour-artist-cum-instructor, willow-thin and probably about fifty, as she emerged from the back room with a look of alarm in her eyes.

An unconvincing dialogue ensued about a furry portrait of Virginia Woolf, made from bits of old carpet sewn together and stuck in a wooden frame (£350). We could feel the owner's eyes drilling into us as we surveyed the artfully arranged wares, principally examples of pink-tinged wholesome chintzy niceness. On offer were handmade silk pincushions, homemade paintings of flowers, gingham tablecloths, an Isle of Wight tea towel and scented candles set in tiny flowery china teacups.

Our hostess was suspicious of us and understandably so. David, tricked out in combat pants, dark glasses and a baseball cap, was the walking, attention-grabbing essence of the inner-city criminal (as the Richmond Tories used to put it). In the rural world-view there was just no credible explanation as to why a black man would travel to a village in Sussex to inspect a £70 pokerwork representation of a windmill, or peer through wraparound shades at a purple silk tasselled macramé plant potholder on sale at the bargain price of £22.50. David later said that the cottage owner might well have taken us for a gay couple up from Brighton for the day.

It was just a short walk from the artist's cottage to the field where the village cricket pitch lay. Set into the hedge surrounding the field was a concrete machine-gun bunker dating from the Second World War. Puzzlingly, the field was relatively flat. The pitch described by Macdonell had a slope on one side with such an incline that, as he described it, when the bowler started his run-up he could not be seen by the batsman at the crease. In Macdonell's day the bowler would only come into vision, like a distant ship appearing above the horizon, as he puffed up the incline ready to deliver the ball. The pitch also seemed far smaller than that described in 1933, and further away from the pub, which, in the twenty-first century, was not adjacent to the pitch but on the other side of the village.

Rodmell Cricket Club had erected a brick-built pavilion – complete with flagpole – in the 1980s. There was an arrangement with the local council whereby the council mowed the field and local schoolchildren could use it for sports days and the like. On the day we visited, the wives and children of the Rodmell cricket team had gathered in the pavilion to make cucumber sandwiches.

The consensus among them was that the *England, Their England* cricket match had taken place in a field now known as Cricketing Bottom on the other side of the village. The likely site of Macdonell's cricket match now had the 'crinkly tin' farm buildings on top of it, erected to replace the old ones in the centre of the village, which had been bought by developers and turned into luxury homes.

The irony hardly needed to be pointed out. The Rodmell of *England, Their England* had been 'unspoilt by factories, financiers, tourists and hustle'. Now a charmless, factory-like farm building covered the cricket pitch where dragonflies had once buzzed about the players. The village was now a popular place for financiers to live. Indeed, the farmer's house and barn was now occupied, we discovered, by the finance director of a very large energy company. In summer, the village was flooded with tourists, many of them visiting Virginia Woolf's house (she lived in Rodmell from 1919 until her death in 1941). And there was plenty of hustle, too – from the hippy capitalism of the cottage artists to the ersatz country fayre of the village pub and the rampant hype of local estate agents.

The new cricket pitch was in a more exposed position than the old one, but it did have a view across the valley. That was, however, spoilt by the sight of a gigantic white chalk scar on the other side of the valley at Beddingham. This marked the location of an enormous landfill site used to dispose of rubbish from Lewes and most of Eastbourne. Initially, and unbeknown to the people of Rodmell and the surrounding villages, the site had also been used to store radioactive waste from Cumbria, a profitable business and, at least according to a spokesman for the company which operates the site, a safe one. 'The waste is so low-level we can transfer it on the back of an ordinary lorry. It is handled in the same way as asbestos sheets. It's put in a pre-excavated pit.' Safe or not, it still sounded a bit unnerving and not very A. G. Macdonell.

When we visited, the Rodmell village cricket team was, not surprisingly, a reflection of the village's new population of commuters and people who worked in finance. They were not very serious about cricket, and did not seem to know each other particularly well. The team included several accountants, an 'estimator' (whatever that meant), the aforementioned finance director of the multinational energy company and the director of a primary healthcare trust. They tended to commute to big city offices during the week, and play out the role of stout yeoman or country squire at the weekend. One of the team told us, 'I never played cricket until I moved here – it is just that this field is here so we think "why not use it"?'

The locals were kitted out in pristine old-fashioned cricket whites, caps and cable-knit jumpers of the sort that had not been worn by anyone serious about cricket for decades. In contrast Blackboys, who were regular players, wore modern Nike-style gear, with their names emblazoned on their backs, like today's professional cricketers. It had taken the Rodmell team a long, long time to find a date in their diaries when they were able to put a team together, perming a squad of a dozen or so from the male population of approximately two hundred.

Rodmell versus Blackboys turned out to be a ridiculously one-sided match. Blackboys batted first, and within minutes their batsmen were confidently dispatching the ball to the boundary. Rodmell's opening bowlers were not bad, and looked as if they had played plenty of cricket long ago at school. But when the pair had each bowled their maximum number of overs, several unskilled pie-chuckers had to take their turn bowling. Further diminishing Rodmell's chances of winning the match, their fielders were hopeless. Later, the consensus was that they had dropped a total of nine catches, and also received injuries ranging from getting hit in the face by the ball to tripping over.

As Blackboys' innings went on, their batsmen were soon

whacking the ball clear out of the ground at will. They played their shots with increasing power and verve and eventually the ball rocketed straight at the spectators in the pavilion, missing David and me – and also the skull of a six-year-old child – by millimetres before smashing a neat cricket-ball-sized hole in the glass of the pavilion door. After a couple of hours, Blackboys were 196-1. Had this been a five-day test match they would have been on track to declare at 3,000-odd runs for, say, eight wickets.

It was a big target, and when Rodmell came out to bat they didn't look as if they would meet it. In fact, they were bowled out for forty-three. Reactions to the drubbing seemed to vary. Some of the very worst performers were self-effacing and tried to turn it into a joke, but others were clearly irked and there was a very uncricket-like snippy feeling in the air, with the slightly better players exuding resentment towards the passengers and no-hopers. It was not as though Blackboys were up to much either. The Rodmell game was to be their first win of the season and, two months and nine games later, it remained Blackboys' only win of the season.

The last Conservative Prime Minister John Major is famous for a speech in which he quoted George Orwell on the English love of village life. 'Fifty years on from now,' Major had said, the country would still be a place of 'long shadows on village cricket grounds, warm beer, invincible green suburbs and old maids bicycling to Holy Communion through the morning mist'. By the time we arrived in Rodmell ten of those fifty years had elapsed since Major left the scene. And in Rodmell at least we discovered that his vision had already vanished almost entirely.

According to a plaque on the wall of the twelfth-century church, the last burial in the graveyard at Rodmell had taken place in 1992, the year John Major was elected Prime Minister.

It seemed to us that, however you wanted to define it, there was very little in the way of Conservatism in Rodmell. Farming had been replaced by agribusiness and the village had become part reluctant tourist attraction and part estate agent's dream – thatched-cottage living on the edge of a city and only half an hour's drive from Gatwick – a picture, we reckoned, repeated all across the rural (or once rural) south of England. The rosy image people liked to have of the countryside was of a timeless, gentle place of seasonal rituals, home to farmers, craftsmen, vicars and parochial, patriotic yokels. The reality, as it appeared to us, is that it was populated by number crunchers and workers in the 'knowledge industry', most of whom had not a local outlook but an international and strongly pan-European one.

# THREE

# Dam Busters and Morris Dancers – Woodbridge, Suffolk

After the 2005 general election defeat, and the arrival of David Cameron as leader, the Conservative Party quickly reduced the amount of energy it spent talking about criminals and the need to be tough on them. The thinking was that banging on about crime linked the Tories, in the public mind, to a past generation of boggle-eyed authoritarians who wanted to bring back hanging and corporal punishment, and who were unhealthily obsessed with all that sort of thing. In the hope, presumably, of making the Conservatives sound more approachable and less nasty and weird on the subject, one of Cameron's first significant acts as party leader was to give a speech saying the public needed to try to understand criminals. This scored headlines saying Cameron wanted everyone to 'hug a hoodie'.

But how would all this go down with the grass roots, many of whom, I reckoned, believed that cracking down on criminals was one of the main things that being a Conservative was all about? Some of the right-wing law and order fundamentalists had, in fact, already deserted the Conservatives and joined the United Kingdom Independence Party – UKIP for short – originally formed in a wave of disgust over the pro-European stance of the Conservative Party and the political classes generally. So when I read that UKIP was to hold a conference devoted solely to the subject of law and order, it seemed like the chance to get a good insight into a type of red-blooded law and order enthusiast who thought it was no longer right or proper to support the Conservative Party.

The conference was held in the Suffolk town of Woodbridge at the end of May 2008. It wasn't hard, as we parked up outside a supermarket, to find the conference venue. All we had to do was follow the strains of 'Rule, Britannia!' and the theme from *The Dam Busters*, which formed part of a medley of patriotic tunes being blasted out from a public address system inside a community centre, and flooding out into the supermarket car park through open emergency exit doors.

There were about sixty people inside the hall – all of them white and mostly elderly – sitting in rows of cheap plastic and tubular steel seats, facing a stage. Looking down from the stage was a row of six grim-faced UKIP leaders and luminaries who resembled a latter-day politburo reviewing a Red Square parade from the top of Lenin's tomb. They sat behind a trestle table decorated with the red and white Cross of St George flag and a Union Jack. My arrival with David seemed to cause a stutter in the proceedings. We looked so out of place that it seemed the folks on the stage were, we thought, wondering whether they ought to confront us in some way, or perhaps stop proceedings to ask us who we were and what we thought we were doing.

But they said nothing and just sat staring at us as the patriotic music faded and things began to get going. The introductory speech of welcome was given by John West, a very thin man wearing a shapeless suit, on the lapel of which glinted an enamel Union Jack badge. John spoke with a harsh, nasal cockney accent and his eyes had a slightly faraway look. His delivery was the percussive jabbing of a megaphone-wielding street politician or market trader. 'Now then – why're we holdin' a confrunce on loranorder?' John asked. 'It's cos we're losin' the war on crime . . . a hundred and thirty million crimes are committed in Britain, every sinkle year.' John ploughed on, throwing out the welter of similarly alarming statistics and doom-laden killer factoids which, we were to discover, were very much the hallmark of UKIP speech-making. John spoke quietly, but his message boomed and echoed around the mostly empty hall thanks to overamplification. 'Do ya remember David Camrun's advice to hug a hoodie?' he sneered. 'Huh! So much for the Conservatives bein' the loranorder party. WE are the new loreanorder party now!' John paused, seemingly expecting applause, which did not come. He deflated a little.

John had brought his wife Alison along and she was sitting beside him on the platform. Husband and wife teams seemed to be more common on the political right, where there is capital to be gained from being seen to embody traditionalist family values – the examples include former MP Neil Hamilton and his wife Christine, and the current MPs Nicholas and Ann Winterton. Alison had shoulder-length black hair, cut severely, and wore a lilac skirt suit and high heels. She had a Lancashire accent which was as strong and irritating on the ear as her husband's cockney.

Alison based her speech largely on crime stories she had read in the *Daily Telegraph* and on the internet. The UKIP speakers seemed to like the information superhighway a great deal – it provided them with endless new snippets about crime – and they were evidently a lot more familiar with the new age of email and online politics than most of the Richmond Tories I had met. Criminals, thought Alison, were simply refusing to take personal responsibility for themselves – 'criminals don't have to choose to re-offend,' she told the audience.

But Alison's main beef was with 'sur-called experts' who lacked common sense and didn't seem to have 'a grip on reality'. These so-called experts, said Alison, came up with trendy ideas like ASBOs. These initiatives were meant to deter crime but then, she said, ASBOs had come to be worn as badges of pride by 'gangs who wander the streets'. So-called experts sent offenders on luxury adventure holidays, which were just a 'slap on the wrist'. Under a UKIP government, she said, schools would have the freedom to use corporal punishment if they wanted to: 'Kids are out of control and we need to take back control of our streets.' It struck us that everyone in the room looked as if they had heard this speech or some version of it many, many times before.

Later a younger man called Rob Burberry was called to speak. He was introduced as a former special constable and an ex-policeman, and a member of UKIP's youth wing. Rob told a favourite tabloid news story about an alleged criminal who was chased onto a roof by policemen in the Midlands. The police could not follow the man onto the roof because of health and safety considerations. There was a bit of guffawing and jeering at the mention of the much-derided politically correct concept of 'health and safety'.

Rob laboured through the story, which everyone already seemed to know, to the extent that some were actually mutely mouthing the words. But the audience seemed to be enjoying it, as if a much-loved song were being sung by an interesting young performer. Rob reached the climax of his account by saying that the police had supplied the suspected criminal with a bucket of KFC. To illustrate the point, Rob had brought an empty red and white striped KFC 'bargain bucket' with him. He waved it in the air and said, 'We need less of these . . .' – he picked up a policeman's helmet which he had brought with him and said – '. . . and we need more of these.'

After the speeches there were questions from the floor. 'Should we bring back borstal?' asked a member of the audience. 'Yes – very much so,' Alison responded. An elderly guy in a blazer and slicked-back hair didn't ask a question, but instead made a speech of his own. He wanted to abolish the Race Relations Act; abolish the Howard League for Penal Reform and abolish the Commission for Racial Equality. 'And while we are at it,' he continued, in the midst of an apparent brainstorm, 'we should abolish those foreigners who are always interfering and always sticking up for prisoners, erm, what are they called now? They begin with an "A". Erm . . .' Someone shouted out, 'Do you mean Amnesty International?' The old guy's face lit up with recognition. 'Yes! That's them! Amnesty International – they are a bloody nuisance, too.'

Another interjection from the floor put the focus back onto the borstal question: 'Y'know, I think the Americans have got the right idea; they have places called boot camps, and they work,' said a voice from the audience. Alison replied, 'I totally agree wi' that.'

Another question came from an elderly Mary Whitehouse lookalike. What about the 'scourge of sex and violence on television', she wanted to know. Rob, the ex-police officer and Kentucky Fried Chicken expert, spoke up: 'I would like to say something about that as a qualified journalist. I am not for state regulation of the media. It sounds communist to me.' An old woman in the audience shouted out: 'They can download it anytime on the internet anyway.'

Yet another woman stood up and said UKIP needed to 'get tough on drugs – and we need to do something about these ghastly hand-held video games. I saw one of these things – it was the property of an Arab boy – and on this . . . this . . . this "thing" – there was a cartoon of a man being chased by a man with a knife and he caught him and stabbed him and the whole screen went red.' She added: 'I sent a letter to John Selwyn Gummer about it.' Another audience member demanded that 'bad language on TV should be criminalized'.

As the questions continued, we looked at the women in the UKIP audience. They were thinner on the ground than the men, but style-wise they were more diverse – largely eschewing the dark trouser suit and limited make-up look beloved of female politicos in favour of far less anonymous styles.

Favourites were the Essexy one of worn-out gold lamé accessories, luridly coloured hair and orange make-up; and the more
upmarket country dowager look with lots of polka dots and
navy blue, usually set off by clouds of naturally snow-white
hair, chalk-white face make-up, bright red lipstick and randomly
applied blusher.

During the lunch break David and I were followed out of
the building by Chris Hudson, the UKIP official in charge of
proceedings. 'Do you mind if I join you,' he said, pulling up a
chair as we sat outside a pavement café, just off the main street
near the railway station, checking our notes and trying to enjoy
the early summer sunshine. Chris wasn't letting on, but he obviously wanted to know who we were and what we were doing.
We explained that we were writing a book about politics and
he immediately seemed nervous. He was anxious to admit, in
what we thought was a very disloyal way, that some of what
we had just heard in the conference was 'very silly' and 'crap',
but that there was 'a lot of sense talked in there as well, mixed
in with the nonsense'.

Chris was an affable looking chap straight out of gin and
tonic belt, golf club central casting. He had grey hair, a purple
tie and a pocket hanky, beige trousers and a stripy shirt, dark
jacket, glasses, pot belly and a florid complexion. He also had
a mellifluous voice, and a whispery way of speaking with just
a touch of Captain Mainwaring about it, punctuated by sudden,
unexpected and surprisingly choleric bouts of expostulation.
Together with John West, the cockney who had been sitting
next to him on the stage, the two of them resembled a right-
wing version of Laurel and Hardy.

'I'm a libertarian,' Hudson said out of the blue but not without
some passion. 'Not a liberal – a libertarian.' He then suddenly
expanded the conversation to the subject of Freemasonry, and
the vast power, and entirely underestimated influence over
events, he seemed to believe the Masons exerted. His basic view,

it occurred to us, was that the EU itself – opposition to which was UKIP's very *raison d'être* – was a giant Masonic conspiracy.

Still, Chris had been pleasant enough and even quite amusing. The Freemasons didn't, in fact, need to murder him – or whatever it was Chris reckoned they might do to their opponents – because he was doing a good job of that himself. For lunch he had an artery-clogging fried egg and bacon sandwich which was so greasy it looked as if it had been cooked in diesel oil. A scalding hot jet of fat and egg yolk shot out and hit his shirt as he bit into it.

As Chris wiped the egg yolk from his shirt, a group of morris dancers with blacked-up faces and green costumes wandered past our table: 'Look at those nutters – that's the green party,' quipped Chris. In fact, as if our day in Woodbridge wasn't already strange enough, a national morris dancing festival was also taking place. When we had arrived in town the first thing we had seen was an ensemble dressed in sixteenth-century clothes and playing ancient drums, pipes and violin-like instruments. Little gangs of morris dancers and other people in strange, ragged scarecrow-style costumes – looking like the Joker's henchmen – had been drifting around Woodbridge all morning.

After lunch the first event was a raffle draw. I had taken a shine to the framed painting of Winston Churchill – the artist had managed to make him look more like Phil Collins – which was the first prize, and so I bought a lot of tickets. The second prize was a tin of Danish biscuits. Sadly there was no fruitcake among the prizes on offer. David Cameron had described UKIP as 'fruitcakes, loonies and closet racists', so I would have made a straight cash bid if there'd been some UKIP fruitcake on display. Other lower-ranking prizes included an Airfix kit of an American warplane, possession of which would have been my idea of paradise, aged nine. I won nothing, but of the many raffles we were to enter during the process of writing this book, UKIP's boasted the tackiest and maddest looking prizes of all.

In the notably drowsy afternoon session Chris, our lunch companion, was the first up to speak. When he was eating his grease-bomb sandwich and going on about the Masons and how horrible everyone in UKIP was, he had seemed very chummy and pleasant, with his hearty and jokey 'I don't take this at all seriously' Captain Mainwaring manner. But now that he was doing his act on stage he suddenly seemed much darker.

'Why don't we get it into our heads that there is a criminal class that is criminal – and bad,' he said, warming himself up at the mic. Then he started to crank up the menace of what he had to say, turning on 'lily-livered liberals' who were constantly scheming to destroy the country for reasons unknown and unstated, but probably sexual in some despicable way. 'We can kiss all the girls goodbye and welcome a Dark Age,' said Chris, apropos of nothing. Chris had indeed turned very sinister but he was smooth with it, like a Bond villain. 'The British people are fair-minded. But I believe we've had enough of those bully boys and bad boys . . . Nothing can stop us from putting the "great" back in Britain . . .'

Despite the hair-raising content of the speech the audience seemed slightly bored by Chris's delivery and his strange, almost random juxtapositions. Perhaps it was too sophisticated for them; or perhaps simply too weird. 'As Alan Clark said, anything can happen at bridge,' Chris suddenly said. 'Alan Clark suggested we just round up the IRA men and shoot them,' he added. Chris's strangely disjointed presentational style might have been attributable to the fact that he had not, apparently, bothered to write a speech. Instead he just picked up a copy of that morning's *Daily Mail* and waved it at the audience, as though it was a secret document he had found somewhere in a vault. On the front page there was a story about the Soham murderer

Ian Huntley: PRISON GUARDS TOLD: BE NICE TO HUNTLEY.

'BE NICE TO HUNTLEY?' Chris Hudson now hiss-whispered into the microphone, bringing a touch of *The Silence of the Lambs* to proceedings. 'Oooooooh, yes! I'd like to be nice to Mr Huntley – I can tell you.' Someone from the audience yelped 'Give 'im the rope!' Hudson nodded graciously and imperiously at the suggestion: 'Quite . . . No, I don't want to "be nice to be Mr Huntley".' And then, after the whispering, he suddenly yelled: 'Stop it now! It is nonsense!', causing some people in the audience actually to jump in their seats. After that he rambled on, working up a head of steam from time to time, when he would shout things like 'We must stop this madness now!'

At moments Chris would go quiet. Maybe he was trying to digest the egg sandwich. Or perhaps he was thinking about thumbing through the rest of the *Daily Mail* to try and find fresh material because, frankly, the Huntley riff had run out of juice pretty quickly. He settled instead on a very long rap about the Chinese government, and their bracingly ruthless approach to illegal drug use. As Chris told it, Chinese authorities had recently identified a town where a fair number of drug dealers lived and the Chinese Army had gone in there and killed pretty much everyone – thousands of them. The audience loved this story, and seemed not to have heard it before (rare, and creating the suspicion in my mind – perhaps unfairly – that he was making it up): 'Yes. That's right. That's the way to do it' seemed to be the attitude.

'EU integration? Stop it now! It's nonsense! . . . Nothing on earth can stop us now . . . We must succeed – our survival as a people depends upon it . . . We are all about freedom, freedom until the last of us dies.' Chris rounded off with the old slogan: 'Let's put the Great back into Great Britain' and with that he sat down to deafening silence.

Chris's speech was followed by questions from the floor. The first came from a middle-aged guy with wild, wiry hair and glasses with eighties disco frames. He ignored Chris and addressed his remarks to John West.

'You would have a very hard job to find anyone in the whole country who disagrees with you, John,' said the questioner, adding, 'everyone – without exception – would agree with all of that. But the problem is . . . how are we going to spread the word? How can we get on the media, John? It seems impossible.' The questioner then told the story of how he had personally pirated a few dozen UKIP DVDs, given a supply to his local newsagent and then paid for an ad in the newsagent's window advertising the free DVDs. 'Only three people took one, and one was the newsagent himself . . . I asked him, "What did you think of it" and he said, "I was frightened."'

John did not really seem to know how they could get the press to promote the UKIP message, but he was able to offer reassurance: 'Our vote is increasin' – and we are holdin' conferences like this, and we use videos on YouToob an' finally we've got leaflets.' John added: 'This conference itself is being videoed right now and bein' put onto YouToob.' That was true, but it was also true that a YouTube video of the party's 2006 conference had only clocked up 620 views in two years on a planet of seven billion. This was a far smaller YouTube audience than for the average blurry home video of a pet hamster with a paper hat on posted up by children with too much time on their hands.

The show wound up with a long and routine denunciation of Islam and a good old chew over the issue of Asians living in Britain. There were various predictably draconian proposals aimed at turning British Asians into white people, while simultaneously preventing any more Asians from arriving in the country – particularly Afghans and Pakistanis. Chris described 'fundamentalist' Islam as a form of mental illness. Generally being non-white was seen as an illness or disability and all the debate seemed to be around whether or not it was curable.

As a discussion of Islamic sharia law developed, Chris embarked on a shaggy-dog story. He said the only time he had seen somebody executed was in Saudi Arabia. 'They had executions in public and there was quite a crowd. May I say as a white fellow that they used to push me to the front.' He described how the executioners had taken an adulterous woman and crushed her under a lorry load of bricks. 'On a lighter note,' he added, 'I have to say a man had his hand chopped off for thieving. His second offence was stealing an artificial hand – and they couldn't do anything about that.'

The last act of the conference was the singing of the national anthem. A bizarrely elaborate choral version of 'God Save the Queen' was played over the PA and it went on for ages, right through the rarely heard second verse, which is all about confounding popish plots and other non-PC material. Those who could manage it stood ramrod straight in military formation. As the conference broke up we spoke briefly to one or two people, including John West, the organizer. He told us that he was the press officer for UKIP in Suffolk, and he was the prospective parliamentary candidate for Ipswich North. But he had a day job as well. He was a governor of Suffolk NHS Mental Health Trust.

# FOUR

# *Get Me the Ugandans! –*
# *Wandsworth, London*

By the spring of 2008 the Conservatives had developed a commanding lead in the national opinion polls. It was the first time for more than a decade that they had been ahead and they looked like staying there. This scenario raised an important question, upon which the future of the country possibly depended. Were the Tories in the lead because people had really decided they liked them again? Or were they ahead because people just didn't like Gordon Brown?

Against this backdrop, the London mayoral election, scheduled for May, looked as if it would be the first real test of the Conservative revival. Would people actually tick the box marked 'Conservative'? Or would they veer away at the last moment, their hands stayed by the sheer social embarrassment which, for more than ten years, had stopped many from voting Tory? The mayoral contest was not, however, a simple fight between the Labour Party and the Conservative Party. It had its own peculiarities.

The two most prominent peculiarities were the two leading candidates themselves – Ken Livingstone, a maverick who could present himself as a figure apart from the Labour mainstream, and Boris Johnson, the controversial journalist, TV performer and MP whom the Tories had selected as their candidate. Johnson, well-known for his turns on *Have I Got News For You*, had started as the rank outsider, but his campaign had gone well and his poll ratings had swollen steadily, just as the air had seeped out of the Labour Party bubble.

David and I arranged to join up with a group of pro-Boris campaigners in the Conservative-controlled borough of Wandsworth in south London. Wandsworth was often held up by the Thatcherite free-market Tories as a good example of how the party should run things both in office and when campaigning on the streets. We were interested to see how this much-vaunted operation worked. If the Tory campaigners in Richmond had, in 2005, been like Dad's Army, would the Wandsworth Tories be more like the militant estate agent and City financial workers who had taken up residence in the area, roaring around town in trendy, aggressive motor cars, cutting deals, hanging out in tapas bars and jogging relentlessly?

Another reason for visiting Clapham was that this was where younger Tories might be discovered – we certainly hadn't found many in Richmond. The streets around Clapham Common offer decent housing stock which is often bought by professional twenty- and thirty-somethings who often tend, as they grow older and settled in their ways, to develop Tory views. Parts of Clapham are known as 'Nappy Valley', because it's here, among the parks and boutiquey shops, that wealthy London couples come to raise toddlers, and make a killing by gentrifying their houses, before moving out to the leafier suburbs and inhabiting a proper four-square suburban mini-mansion with golf course nearby. It is thus the self-improvement capital of south London, with health club after health club, yoga centres, the sounds of continual drilling and sanding that mean homes are being improved, and, at least until the credit crunch of 2008/9, continual property speculation.

With our track record of involvement in the 2005 election campaign in Richmond (however less than fully committed) it wasn't hard to make an entrée into the Wandsworth Conservatives. Making things even simpler, David had a flat, and therefore a working postal address, in Battersea, in the middle of the borough of Wandsworth. We arranged to meet up with the Wandsworth Tories at the County Hotel, just off Clapham Common, for a day's 'mass canvass' of the Common area. When we got there, about a dozen people had turned up, including Richard 'Dick' Tracey – the local candidate for the London Assembly, and a former cabinet minister – and a clutch of office workers, some of whom seemed, from their gossip, to work full time as administrators for the Conservative machine.

The Tory mayoral campaign had an ecological slogan: 'Vote blue, go green'. Despite this, and the fact that there was a bus stop near the County Hotel, a huge former roadhouse-type pub which – inevitably since this was Clapham – had been transformed into a combined gastropub and conference venue, all the Tory canvassers had, as far as I could tell, arrived by car. These were typical Tory cars, too – middle-of-the-road, mid-priced saloons, for driving around Middle England. The exception to all this normality was an old-fashioned Citroën 2CV plastered with hundreds of small brightly coloured 'Vote Boris' stickers, all arranged in a surprisingly psychedelic pattern. The proud owner of the 2CV was a red-faced middle-aged man called John who was dressed in a mustard-coloured jacket and bright red corduroy trousers.

All the canvassers seemed to have known each other for a long time, and the event had the air of a jolly social get-together. After some small talk, we were introduced to Melanie and Paul, with whom we would be canvassing. Melanie – vivacious, in her forties or early fifties (it was impossible to say exactly how old) – love-bombed us with expressions of delight: 'Lovely! Sooooper! So maaaaaah-vellous that you are with us!' Apparently she was a divorcee, though we could not be sure about that either. But it did seem that, for the duration of the mayoral contest at least, she was campaigning full time for the Tories in a voluntary capacity. Paul, a quieter and much more dishevelled figure, was more guarded. He had a well-worn face which seemed to say: 'Well, I've seen it all now.'

Paul was a chain-smoking, hard-nosed political hack. His air of frayed cynicism and general shabbiness appealed hugely to us. We might have called him wrong, but he seemed more pragmatic than many of the Conservatives we met. He had once made a living from politics, working as paid, full-time Conservative organizer and electoral agent. But after the 1997 Labour landslide – which had greatly reduced job opportunities within the Conservative Party – his fortunes had seemingly dimmed. Later, when we got talking to him, Paul was at pains to emphasize his working-class roots and lack of expensive education. He was a far cry from the 'toffs', as the *Daily Telegraph* put it – the Old Etonians Boris Johnson and David Cameron – who were now back in charge of the party for the first time since the sixties.

Paul told us that decades ago he had been successful in the catering business, and had found a niche organizing the food for Conservative functions. From feeding Conservatives, by the late seventies when party fortunes were on the up and up, it was a short step for Paul to become a political organizer on their behalf. Paul told us he had been active in Cardiff – helping to slash the constituency majority of Jim Callaghan, Old Labour's last Prime Minister – before landing a plum job as a Tory agent in Cumbria.

In Cumbria, Paul had found himself dealing with what he called 'proper Tories'. He liked these exotic creatures who, from the perspective of a self-made man, he regarded as 'y'know . . . aristocrats with castles'. It had been an easy job because a network of Tory squires and their wives ran political life, such as it was, in the villages. But it seemed that Paul had made the error of assuming the good times would go on forever, and that the Tories would be in power perpetually. Instead of hanging on to what he had, he tried to climb the ladder, taking a job at Conservative Central Office in London, in charge of the whole North East region. After the Tories were annihilated in that part of the country in 1997, Paul found himself on the way out.

Paul said, sadly, that he 'couldn't really complain' about that. But even after all these years, we reckoned, it still hurt. The taint of failure seemed to hang over him, mingling with the clouds of fag smoke. His chances of getting a job like his old one, even if the Tories returned to power, seemed slight. He might have been joking, but he told us that he had to supplement his income by selling his possessions at car boot sales. He didn't much like London, but he was stuck there, freelancing as a political consultant.

Melanie couldn't have been more different – glossy, hyperactive, wealthy and, to use one of her favourite words, 'posh'. She had short blonde hair – cut in a trendy, youthful style – swept back and held in place by a pair of designer sunglasses. She wore plenty of make-up, along with pearl earrings, sparkly bling accessories, a tight navy blue top and black figure-hugging jeans. Style-wise, the whole effect was upmarket Tory crossed with seventies disco diva. Her vertiginous heels clacked out advance warning of her arrival, and, given the number of cracked paving stones she was going to have to negotiate while canvassing, she looked like a Claims Direct compensation case waiting to happen. Melanie was a loud and proud Tory, and instead of the discreetly chic green BORIS lapel badges favoured by most of the campaigners, she wore a gigantic bright blue rosette, ribbons akimbo as she tottered along.

Melanie talked incessantly in a piercing staccato full of sharp vowels, coquettishly saying 'dhhharling' a lot and dispensing air kisses to everyone she knew. When we attempted to engage her in a conversation about the state of Wandsworth borough's schools, she revealed that her own children attended a £20,000 a year boarding school in Oxfordshire. She seemed contemptuous of Paul – with his scruffy look, cheap clothes and nicotine-stained fingers and teeth – chiding him from time to time and generally bossing him about.

Melanie drove us in her car – a shiny Galaxy people carrier, of the sort beloved by Clapham's 'yummy mummies' – to the starting point for the canvass run. The car was full of Boris leaflets tailored not just for Wandsworth but for other parts of London – Melanie was involved in local campaigns all over the capital. She said there had been 'a lot of rubbish in the papers' about Boris, supplemented by the BBC, 'which is just an arm of the socialists, as you know'. Even more bizarrely, she said that *The Times* was against Boris because 'as you know . . . it is a socialist newspaper'.

The short drive turned into an unavoidable lecture from Melanie on how to deal with the various situations which might occur on the doorstep. She briskly told us that discussing Tory policies in detail was a potential minefield, which could be dodged by directing people to a website called 'www dot . . . something'. There the approved versions of the policies were listed – like, we thought to ourselves, the small print on a toxic loan. Beyond this the idea was simply to tell householders anything they wanted to hear and then beat a hasty retreat. As we listened in silent, pretended fascination, there was plenty of eyeball rolling from Paul.

As Melanie parked up in one of the leafy, gentrified streets near Clapham Common, Paul gave us a terse twenty-second briefing on how to record the electorate's voting intentions. A piece of paper listed the names and addresses of local occupants. We were to write 'C' for a promised conservative vote and 'S' for socialist (rather than 'L' for Labour). 'A' stood for 'against' and 'P' for 'possible'. Lib Dems were not an issue in Wandsworth, said Paul, adding that the borough had once been solid Labour but the Tories, to general astonishment, had won control of it in the 1980s. The Tories had 'nursed' each ward they captured and now they were firmly in control and seemed unshakable, even at the height of New Labour's popularity. It seemed to us that the underlying reason for Wandsworth's switch from Labour to the Tories was the gentrification of the area, which had completely changed the composition of the population, especially in the wards we were canvassing. The area was younger, richer, trendier and whiter than it had been in the past.

Paul said our mission was to identify accurately which households were planning to vote Tory so that on polling day they could check that every last promise of a Conservative vote had been delivered. This was the whole point of the operation and it was a waste of time trying to explain any policies to anyone. He then explained what to do about 'foreign sounding names' by using a foreign sounding accent, a sort of mixture of *'Allo 'Allo* and Sacha Baron Cohen's Borat. 'Iffa dey say dey don't wanna vota for di Boris Johnson . . . forget it.' It was just his way of trying to enliven an otherwise potentially dull chore with a bit of ham-fisted humour. Compared to Melanie, Paul was a cynic, but he said he had seen earlier canvass returns and he was 'absolutely certain' that the Tories were going to win in Wandsworth and throughout London. We characterized his approach as 'let's get this over and done with so we can go to the pub'.

The houses we canvassed first were fairly substantial terraced Edwardian properties, a cut above the cramped rows of Victorian terraces which cover much of this part of south London. Their small front gardens provided a comforting buffer between the front door and the street. Edwardian literature is full of references to distressed gentlefolk who, after losing their fortune or inheritance, had to move out of Mayfair or Chelsea to Clapham. The houses still had the aspirational touches of those days, such as front porches decorated with glazed tiles. By the late noughties, almost every house in the area had been improved to death – chunky designer front doors, razor sharp Venetian blinds, white walls, natural wood floors, Habitat furniture, plasma screen televisions – tens of thousands of pounds had been spent on each one in terms of interior decorating alone, and much of the money was borrowed. Most residents had placed a 'no junk mail' sticker on their shiny minimalist letter boxes.

In contrast to Paul, Melanie was going on about how much she liked canvassing. 'It's like being a salesperson,' she said, as though she was spending the day slumming it as a double-glazing huckster. It was 'really great' Melanie said, when you got a big team together and 'stormed' an area like this, mob-handed – it was 'great fun'. Melanie knocked briskly on the doors and launched into her polished spiel. 'Oh, hello. I am canvassing for Boris Johnson for Mayor. May I count on your vote?' The potentially vote-losing c-word – 'conservative' – was not used; the favoured approach was simply to refer to the whacky TV star Boris by name. One person told Melanie that she was going to vote for Boris because she liked him and then added, 'It's not because I don't like Ken – I like him as well.' Melanie was taken aback and blurted, 'Well, I think he [Livingstone] is a poisonous shit.' Some of the householders were a bit wary, but there were few signs of open hostility. Generally, the man on the street ignored us as we marched from house to house, but at one point the driver of a passing car honked his horn supportively. Melanie was visibly thrilled. 'Oooo . . . We got a little toot!' she said excitedly.

After an hour we found ourselves outside a relatively dilapidated, unimproved house – possibly the only one left in the ward. The paint on the door was peeling and the place looked as if it was divided into rented flats. As we crashed through the unhinged front gate Melanie stopped us to deliver a mini-lecture. A lot of people thought that only 'posh' people voted Conservative, she explained. That was wrong, she said forcefully. Poor people 'on the roughest kind of estates', she said, were 'more Conservative than anything'.

When we rang the bell, a scruffy and impoverished looking middle-aged woman in a T-shirt and jeans came to the door. Melanie launched into her patter and the woman said that she was 'sick to death' of Ken Livingstone, whom she had voted for in the last mayoral election. The woman told us she worked at the local DIY superstore and did not earn very much. Because of the recent abolition of the 10p tax band she said she was going to have to get a second job. Melanie came over all concerned and said that Boris was 'absolutely and completely and utterly opposed to the "10 per cent tax thing"'. Then she cut to the chase. 'Can we count on your precious vote?' The woman answered in an infuriatingly indirect way, with more hand gestures. 'Well, me granddad were Conservative mayor of a big town in Surrey, so I suppose I have to, don't I?' she drawled. 'Absolutely!' Melanie chirped. As soon as the door was shut, Melanie turned to us with a look of disapproval and ticked the 'A' (for 'against') box. 'She will never vote for us,' she snapped, adding, 'wrong body language.'

As far as we could see there were virtually no black people, residents or otherwise, in the area we canvassed; but at one house an Asian woman came to the door. She was very polite and said that she was going to vote for Boris. Again, when the door was closed, Melanie paused and, after due consideration, put the Asian woman down as a 'possible'. Without evidently thinking too deeply about what she was saying, Melanie added: 'Muslims are like that. They smile, and they say they are going to vote for you. But they don't.'

We were now approaching a row of bigger houses on a quieter road overlooking Wandsworth Common – an area local estate agents and residents called the Toast Rack. The area consisted of streets of brick-built Edwardian town houses which, when we were there, were selling for as much as £2 million each. Here, the latest home improvement trend was to extend underground, by excavating the basement and turning it into a family room or entertainment space. The cost of having this done was about £200,000 – which, at the time, would pay for itself almost immediately by bumping up the potential sale price of the house. Builders' vans were parked in many of the streets, one of them sporting the livery of The London Basement Company – 'specialists in basement conversions'. Phil Spencer, co-presenter of Channel 4's fashionable 'property finding show' *Location, Location, Location*, lived in the area and, we were told, was having his basement extended. However, the local Nimby movement, the Toast Rack Residents Association, was worried that the new basement extensions could undermine foundations and divert the local water table.

In canvassing terms the Toast Rack was tough going. Very few people were in or answered the door. As in Richmond, those who did come to the door tended to be au pairs or staff, often Eastern European and therefore probably lacking the vote. We then moved on to tackle some cheaper properties including blocks of 'social housing' flats, possibly owned by the local authority or a housing association, which acted as a sound barrier between the noisy main road and the rows of gentrified terraced houses. The problem here for canvassers was getting somebody to open the exterior communal front door, which was usually heavily fortified and operated by means of a very confusing entry phone. After messing about with that, and a lot of trial and error, we eventually got into a block of flats after speaking to an uncomprehending Australian. Melanie rolled her eyes as she waited for him to open the door. 'That's the problem with flats: full of transitory people.'

As the door finally swung open, Melanie clacked her way in, her high heels echoing around the stairwell as she stormed up the stairs at a furious pace. We didn't bother with the Australian because he was not named on the canvassing list and therefore did not have a vote. All we got for our efforts was a brief encounter with a tremendously old woman who had a Zimmer frame on wheels. 'I'm not in the mood for politics this morning,' she said. On the strength of this, Melanie put her down as an 'S' for socialist.

As we left the building Melanie began a lecture about an 'unwinnable ward' in the south of Wandsworth, near the border with Labour-controlled Tooting, where she had stood recently, and unsuccessfully, as a council candidate. A third of the ward was social housing, she explained, and there were 'lots of Labour voters'. Some of the flats in the area were 'really horrible, really filthy some of them'. Exasperated, Melanie removed her cardigan to reveal a tight white vest, and also a fair amount of flesh. In her tight jeans, high heels and skimpy top she looked like a veteran eighties rock chick, à la Pat Benatar. 'It is so hot I've had to strip down,' she trilled. 'Not very appropriate for a Conservative I suppose, but there you are.'

Later, as we drove back to the County Hotel, Melanie told us how that very afternoon she was going to do a second stint of canvassing in Little Venice, a very wealthy area located around a canal junction in west London. Just as the poor were the mostly likely Conservative voters, Melanie now informed us that, just because the rich of Little Venice were 'posh', it didn't mean they would vote Conservative. Some, she said, could be rich 'because they were Jewish'. Unprompted, she said that she had recently canvassed around the multimillion-pound mansions of St John's Wood – close to Little Venice – where 'everyone' was Jewish and not many of them were Tory. She added that she had also been dispatched to canvass around Regent's Park, where, once again, 'everyone' was Jewish, but the canvassing stint had clashed with Passover and had thus been a waste of time.

Melanie said that this showed that the local party organiza-tion in the area was no good and didn't know what it was doing. Paul decided to tell us that he wasn't Jewish himself, but that he knew Jewish people, that some of his best friends were Jewish and that he had recently been to a Jewish community event of some sort in Belsize Park. Once again, when David was around it seemed that matters of race seemed to crowd to the forefront of Tory minds. Melanie and Paul were like the Richmond Tories – trying to show they were hip on matters of race relations, and in doing so making slightly clumsy banter about racial and ethnic differences, while simultaneously trying to tell us how open-minded they really were.

When we got back to the County Hotel there was a small group of black people wearing Tory rosettes milling about. It turned out that they were not, as it first appeared, local supporters of the Conservative Party. In reality, they appeared to be Ugandans who had arrived in London for the duration of the Boris campaign as part of some sort of exchange or educational scheme. The scheme, it seemed, was supposed to be about giving people from newly democratic countries the opportunity to observe, at first hand, how British democracy worked. In fact, with their blue rosettes, the Ugandans were, whether they knew it or not, functioning as an advertisement for the supposed new inclusiveness of the Tory party under the Old Etonian leadership of David Cameron and Boris Johnson. There were some people from Montenegro as well, also wearing blue rosettes and 'Vote Boris' stickers.

Back in the top room of the County Hotel Melanie went around explaining that the day was so warm that she had had to take her top off. 'I look like a bit of a tart, don't I?' she said to an older woman in a sludge-coloured tent dress. Melanie then handed over her canvassing gear and got ready to depart. 'Goodbye, darlings, goodbye,' she said theatrically, and disappeared. Most of the other canvassers headed off into the County Hotel's beer garden for a drink. The mood was excellent because it was sunny and, at the same time, quite clear that the Boris campaign was going well. By this stage the Ugandans seemed to have been shipped off to some other part of London, where, happily for the Conservatives, voters might well mistake them for black Londoners who had signed up with the Tories.

In the beer garden Dick Tracey was chatting away with a gang of people who worked at Conservative Central Office. A Central Office worker showed him one of the Ugandans' business cards, which identified the man as the mayor of a town somewhere in Uganda. The group joked about how to win elections in Uganda and that they probably used elephants to get around. 'Would that be part of expenses?' chuckled one, adding that 'you would have to watch out for lions' while canvassing.

John, the owner of the 2CV Borismobile, then said he had been walking along the road when he saw a group of 'funny looking chaps' with big Tory rosettes. These were the Montenegrins: members of a right-wing party who, like the Ugandans, had in theory come to study the Conservative campaign. John then did a comedy impression of the Montenegrins, in which they were struggling to make themselves understood on the doorstep, and talking about their great leader Boris. The big joke was that Boris is an Eastern European name. All the Tories wanted to know who these mysterious Eastern Europeans were, and what they were doing.

An elderly woman said she knew something about them. 'Oh, it's Operation . . . whatsit . . . Operation Democracy?' she said mournfully.

Tracey thought it was funny that she was so down in the mouth about the project, whatever it was. 'Surely, since you, after all, work for Central Office, shouldn't you be more enthusiastic about this?' he asked her.

She pulled a face: 'All these working parties . . . I dunno . . . they are just hot air . . . They are just a fantastic waste of time and money,' she added with exasperation, 'all these rich people give us all their money in good faith and we waste it on nonsense like that.'

A few days after our outing with Melanie and Paul, the Conservative mayoral candidate himself turned up in Clapham to do a walkabout. Boris Johnson arrived in an unmarked silver Audi, and came marching down the hill with two smartly dressed young security minders at his side. You could spot Boris's trademark blond haystack from a long way off. He also had something of the air of Winston Churchill about him: crouching, grunting, gesticulating, making regal arm gestures and pointing as he moved from place to place. The idea was for Boris to walk up and down the street attracting attention and impressing local voters. Northcote Road is lined with ersatz Latino bistros, coffee shops, baby boutiques selling Fair Trade wooden toys, innumerable seven-days-a-week estate agents, tapas bars, breakfast bistros selling croissants and Portuguese-style pavement cafés. Here, Boris would fly the flag and have pictures taken of himself at ease in this, the land of the Young Urban Professionals.

The first Tory to arrive at the rendezvous point was an old boy, eighty if he was a day, in a floppy panama hat. A small crowd soon developed, about twenty in all, including David and me. There were a few other older men dressed like panama wearer: white trousers, collared shirt, jumper and round spectacles – a cricket-derived look beloved, as far as we could tell, of public school and university educated Tory males. It wasn't an impressive turnout, given that Boris was not only the regional chieftain of the Tory tribe, but also a TV star, professional entertainer and all-round controversialist. Around half of the little group were full-time Central Office staff, who tended to live in this part of London anyway, or just across the river in Fulham or Chelsea.

The Central Office hacks were younger than the others, and

more callow. They looked a bit bored and name-dropped and gossiped about people who were unknown to us but sounded like key players in the Tory campaign. The Central Office people were dressed casually – it being Sunday – which meant that the men wore rugby shirts and ironed jeans, all very clean and neat. The female Central Office workers – the Borisettes – were dressed in white T-shirts with I'M BACKING BORIS on the back and an Andy Warhol-type primary colours portrait of Boris on the front.

Today nobody was wearing traditional blue rosettes, except for two or three Ugandans, who had made a reappearance. They were the only black people except for David in this temporary flying circus. With their blue ribbons, and lacking T-shirts bearing the slogan 'Official Observer' or anything of that sort, they would naturally be taken for Londoners who supported the Tories which, whatever else they were up to, they were not. Their job was to give out stickers saying 'I'm Backing Boris' to anyone who wanted one, which they did mutely.

When Boris arrived, he was steered towards the Ugandans straight away, and chatted for some time to a woman who was wearing a bright purple trouser suit. With his accent and self-effacing mumbling it can be hard, at the best of times, to understand what Boris is saying. The Ugandan discussion – out of our earshot – could, we reckoned, easily have been pure rhubarb-rhubarb, uttered for any passing camera crews to notice. When Boris and the Ugandan woman had finished talking, a Central Office lackey introduced one of the Ugandan men as the mayor of what was probably his country's equivalent of Manchester. Boris seemed genuinely perplexed and taken aback: 'Really? How extraordinary!'

Some of the handful of old ladies – genuine local Tories who looked as if they had years of service behind them – were starting to get a bit restless, and seemed eager to show fealty in person to Boris. However, Boris was instead presented to a group of three or four Montenegrins who, like the Ugandans, appeared to have been furnished for the occasion by his campaign organizers. The Montenegrins were much younger than everyone else – average age twenty years old. They seemed to defer to a hyperactive young woman with a curly reddish-brown henna hairdo straight from the Toni & Guy style book. She wore a leather jacket, a big military-type belt, low-slung jeans and sunglasses and kept running here and there, expostulating in rich and ringing Slavic syllables. Her compatriots were two guys: one a tall, well-built sort, the other a much shorter and scrawnier chap. They hung around in their baggy jeans, hoodies, leather jackets and good quality fake designer shades, smoking cigarettes. With Balkan politics having seen centuries of vendettas and ethnic cleansing, we wondered what these characters made of an election in which the main issues seemed to be bendy buses and the consumption of alcopops on trains.

Nevertheless, the Montenegrins added a much needed element of youth and semi-cool streetsy glamour to the proceedings. Boris moved along the road and they tagged along closely behind, sounding like disputatious bodyguards as they chatted and argued among themselves. When Boris and the Montenegrins arrived at the first of the pavement cafés, they stopped and started shaking hands with each other. Boris then did his rhubarb-rhubarb routine, ostensibly chatting with them as if they had just met. In this way, the Montenegrins, like the Ugandans, played the role of extras for the whole day. Sometimes they would run along the street in front of him, so that he could bump into them and shake their hands over and over again. They accepted stickers from him, or from helpers such as ourselves, as though they had never seen any of us before. Then they would peel off and run up the street a little way, and stand at the ready outside another café or fancy cake shop. They seemed to enjoy this piece of Conservative street theatre – an excellent introduction to the nuts and bolts of political campaigning in a true democracy.

With the Montenegrins disappearing and reappearing, Boris would barge into the conversations of people sitting at the pavement cafés, gurning and cajoling, urging them to vote for him. When he stopped, the rest of the party would bunch up, including the beribboned Ugandans, the pompous Central Office types, the T-shirted Borisettes, Boris's security men, the eccentric ancient retainers, three or four other Tories and a knot of other oddballs and us. Then we would move on again, towards the waiting Montenegrins. Boris moved quickly among the coffee drinkers and shoppers, avoiding controversial topics of conversation, or pretty much any political subjects at all. He was proficient at spotting the target demographic and reading their body language – his canvassing radar was highly tuned. His overarching strategy was to preach only to the converted. He would quickly scan row after row of coffee drinkers, inadvertently making himself look shifty. His aides looked constantly nervous, barely able to disguise the gaffe-angst behind their thin, indulgent smiles.

Whenever his radar picked up an easy target, Boris would growl: 'Hi! I'm Boris Johnson, Conservative mayoral candidate. Can I count on your support?' A scrum of Tories would gather, listening intently to the reply, as though they were expecting a major revelation of some sort. But anyone addressed in this way usually just looked highly embarrassed and said 'yes' or 'probably'. Boris would then do a bit of bumbling: 'Good, excellent, marvellous', and then he would scuttle off. He got a much better reception, I noted, than that given to Michael Howard by the people of Richmond in 2005. On that occasion I saw people in the distance cross the road to avoid contact. This time just about everyone seemed to think the Boris carnival was a great laugh, and one or two actually looked pleased to meet him.

After wheeling through a few cafés, Boris came across John's sticker-covered 2CV Borismobile parked up on the street, the one we had seen on our day with Melanie and Paul. Boris went into a big routine: 'This is an outrage! Who did this!? Where is he!? Where is the culprit!? I want to see the man responsible for this!' cried the candidate, waving his arms about like a blond orang-utan. John arrived on cue, decked out in a blue blazer which emphasized his broad neck and *A Year in Provence* look, and was convulsed with laughter. 'It's like the Popemobile!' Boris brayed. The Tories found this wildly amusing, and Boris, naturally, played to the crowd. 'Tell you what,' he beamed, 'why don't you drive it and I can stand up in it. Is there a sort of roofy thingy where I can stand up like the Pope and wave at the masses as you drive along?' John was laughing so hard that he looked as if he was going to collapse. Meanwhile, several older Tories took snapshots with digital cameras.

The 2CV moment looked, to my perhaps overly cynical mind, as if it had been staged, but immediately afterwards an unscripted drama began to unfold. As if from nowhere, two scruffy student-type dudes appeared from the crowd brandishing homemade signs wrapped up in Clingfilm. The first student's sign read DON'T VOTE FOR A JOKE. He bustled in next to Boris and held the sign like a judge in an ice-skating competition. Edging sideways, the man tried to keep the sign in position above the Johnson thatch as he strained with the already difficult task of introducing himself with a degree of dignity.

The second studenty dude buzzed around a few yards from Boris carrying a sign with the more direct message: VOTE KEN. He was also holding a bundle of anti-racism leaflets produced by Ken Livingstone's supporters. Initially, all that was visible of these leaflets were the letters BNP and a Union Jack flag. This caused a lot of muttering among the Tory ranks. The DON'T VOTE FOR A JOKE dude then made a token attempt to talk to Boris, struggling to keep his adrenalin under control while yelling, 'Come on then, why don't you want to debate your policies? It's because you haven't got any, have you? It's because you're a joke, innit?' From a slight distance this looked exciting – as though there was going to be pushing, and maybe punches thrown. The Tory old ladies in particular seemed ready for aggro, and started gripping their rolled-up umbrellas more tightly.

'Who are these people?' we asked John, who was already stoked up and red at the gills because of his moment of glory with the Popemobile. 'The Fucking Socialists!' he hissed back. Meanwhile, John's partner had waded into the action and was using her official Tory umbrella to obscure the JOKE poster and, entirely accidentally, giving the student holding the sign the occasional stiff poke. Right on cue the smaller Montenegrin youth arrived and began to talk animatedly. Then his taller mate arrived. They looked like they were seriously up for a fight and the tall one started to put a headlock on one of the studenty dudes. But the Central Office people restrained the Montenegrin and he had to make do with various Balkan arm-waving and finger gestures, accompanied by disgusted looks and the shouting of what were presumably severe insults in his native tongue.

When the studenty dudes still refused go away, John the 2CV man suddenly lost his cool and began pushing and shoving, and the melee found itself pressed up against an estate agent's window. Brollies were waved about in more determined fashion. Even the second student type, who had kept his distance and was carrying the VOTE KEN sign, got pinned against the plate glass. The Tories' blood was now up and if the student types had legged it at that point, they might well have been chased down the street. Instead, one of the Central Office rugby shirt guys came over and, adopting a mockney accent to show he meant business, said: 'Look, chum – you are not wanted here.

Now this is a very big street. You don't have to be right here now, do you?' I was impressed. This guy was either a fairly accomplished street brawler or, more likely, a barrister used to dealing with assault cases. Another Central Office flunky warned the studenty dudes along similar lines, that if there was trouble it would be their fault. What they were doing was provocation and the police would understand that. The dudes seemed to get the message and skulked off to make a nuisance of themselves elsewhere. By that time Boris had been herded well away from any potential embarrassment.

Further down the street, Boris was working the pavement cafés again, talking to passers-by – mid-morning dog walkers and baby buggy pushers amid the inevitable joggers. We had reached the end of the parade of cafés, and we gathered in front of an evangelical church. Boris checked the timetable with his minders and then turned to face his gaggle of followers, now forming a semi-circle on the pavement before him. 'Well done, Wandsworth. Well done, team,' he said with a hint of self-deprecating sarcasm. 'All we've got to do now is get all these yuppies round here to get out and vote for me. OK? Great. Marvellous. OK. Good!' And with that he headed off towards his gleaming Audi, parked up in a side street. Most of the minders followed, apart from one of the men from Central Office. He was in charge of the Operation Democracy foreign legion and was furious that some of these walking political props had gone missing. 'I've got the Montenegrins,' he hollered, 'but where are the Ugandans? Get me the Ugandans! They've got to be there for the TV crew in Balham when Boris arrives!' One by one the Ugandans were rounded up, but not before the Central Office man had screamed, 'And where's the other one?' cutting David a look as if to say, 'Are you the other one?' David ignored him and walked off.

The campaign – minus Boris – sprinted through the BMW- and 4x4-choked streets of Wandsworth, up past the Toast Rack and on to the Polish Club in neighbouring Balham. The club was crowded with people browsing the Polish deli produce set out on stalls along one side of the meeting room. Some second-generation Poles had been bussed in from real Polish London – places like Ealing and Ravenscourt Park – where they were on the local council. There were some ancient Polish people present – probably anti-communist refugees – the one ethnic minority that the Tories could rely on. There was also a sinister looking blond skinhead with a Polish slogan on his sweatshirt lurking in the shadows. The club was a dark, run-down hall with a grimy stage, the sort of place where you could hold a low-budget wedding reception.

Boris arrived, and wandered around doing his rhubarb-rhubarb act while being trailed by representatives of obscure media outlets – among them a Polish radio reporter and a Japanese TV news crew. Off to one side we heard Boris's minders, realizing there was not much real media action to be had in the club, yelp frantically, 'Get him out of here.' The reason for their panic was a complete mystery. In the bright TV lights a female Polish councillor from Ealing was relating an anecdote about how the traffic lights in Ealing had completely failed one day but the traffic had been great, flowing freely. Her line of argument appeared to be that, once in power, Boris should remove all the traffic lights in London in order to improve traffic management. Boris nodded and used his fallback phrase for the umpteenth time: 'How extraordinary!'

There was some confusion about whether or not Boris was going to give a speech, but, in the event, he didn't. Instead, a leaflet written in English and Polish, which included a tentative endorsement of Boris by a leader of the Polish equivalent of the Tory Party, was circulated. As Boris left the club, he paused in the entrance to survey the rain lashing down outside. At least a dozen or so people were milling around, including the Japanese news crew, which seemed to be treating the event as though it were the inauguration of the monarch or similar potentate. Someone from Central Office produced a brolly to shield Boris from the elements. As he jockeyed his way out of the building, Boris glanced quizzically at David, who was badged up with his blue rosette, and then froze for a moment. Boris seemed to be thinking: 'Haven't I seen you somewhere before?'

Earlier on, during the 'Nappy Valley' tour of Clapham's cafés and buggy shops, David had indeed stopped Boris to pose with him for a trophy photo. The blond bombshell had looked nonplussed. Here was a politician who had once described black people as 'piccaninnies' with 'watermelon smiles' being accosted by a rather large and very swarthy chap for a fan-style photograph. The Tories had been delighted, however, twittering 'marvellous' at the sight of this touching display of interracial harmony. It was just as likely, though, that they were thrilled (if David was in any way representative) at the thought of the landslide which would result from any switch of political allegiance on the part of black Londoners, most of whom voted Labour. That, David and I judged, was pretty unlikely. The only other black people we had seen taking part in the campaign had been not black Londoners, but black Ugandans.

On the night of what turned out to be Boris Johnson's election as Mayor of London we had decided to head for the 'committee room' of the Conservative Campaign in Battersea, which was located in the basement flat of a male local councillor, who lived with his partner, a female Tory activist. It was dark by the time we got there. The flat was not far from the Thames, located on a traffic-swamped main road, crammed between a viaduct carrying roaring commuter trains and a massive roundabout. The steep concrete steps down from the street to the councillor's front door were grubby and horrible. The front window was set well below street level and protected by heavy iron bars.

We rang the bell on the windowless front door and waited. After a minute or two the door opened slightly and we could hear a dog growling and the sound of hyperactive paws scratching on a hard floor. 'Who is it?' said a suspicious female voice. 'Is this the Battersea Conservatives?' David asked, his gold tooth glinting in the harsh sodium light. 'We were helping out earlier and . . .' Before the sentence was finished, the door opened and the dog thrust its yapping head into David's crotch. A woman emerged from the shadows and restrained the dog. 'Don't worry, he won't hurt you,' she said, 'do come in . . .' We entered the flat, grinning inanely.

The flat was cramped, with a very low ceiling. The female activist wore one dog-eared fluffy pink bedroom slipper, but kept the other foot bare. Adding to this slightly unkempt look, she was wearing an old pair of glasses, a shapeless black top and grey slacks. She said that she and the male councillor had lived in the flat for twenty-five years. She said she managed properties, lots of them, in the area. She complained that she was extremely tired, having been up for a dawn canvassing stint and, in addition, had been woken at 4 a.m. by the sound of 'some bint' being noisily sick outside her bedroom window.

The male councillor had told us there would be other activists coming round but they were nowhere to be seen. He was in the back of the flat, in a small, boxy, bunker-like room beyond the little kitchen. He was on the computer, staring excitedly at the screen, reading canvassing returns generated by a computer program called Blue Chip, which kept track of how the final stages of the campaign were going locally.

The main message from Blue Chip was that things had gone very well. The overall turnout was high; and almost all the promised Conservative voters in the ward had arrived at the various polling stations. The election, the male councillor reckoned, was pretty much in the bag. Earlier that day we had delivered election leaflets but now there was nothing left for David and me to do.

Back in the sitting room, we resisted the female councillor's best efforts to pump us for information about our backgrounds. Right in the middle of the minuscule sitting room was a dog cage and for me – I have had an intense dislike of dogs since childhood – the presence of the hyped-up mutt was unnerving. It said a lot about my prejudices that I could not believe the flat was home to a Conservative couple, as it was entirely unlike the Tory homes we had entered in Richmond, which tended to be extremely chintzy and smelling of lavender. The colour scheme was earthy – brown velvet sofas and green velvet cushions – and two life-size oil paintings of nudes dominated the room. The shelves shook from time to time as trains thundered past the back yard.

The only books I could see in the sitting room were a copy of *Gangs* by Tony Thompson, a sociology textbook and an economics book about the production of T-shirts. Apart from this it looked as though the councillor and the activist got a lot of information from the internet, and the *Ecologist*, the conservationist magazine with a right-wing pedigree currently edited by Zac Goldsmith (the magazine had originally been established by the Goldsmith clan to promote the cause of reducing the world population). Apart from boxes and boxes of 'Vote Boris' leaflets, there was also a well-thumbed copy of a pamphlet called 'The Poverty of Multiculturalism'. The pamphlet had a cartoon of Britannia wearing a burka on the cover.

After a while, a male friend of the couple turned up with his bike. He walked into the sitting room, complaining that it was a chilly evening. 'The worst thing,' the friend mused, 'is that when I get cold I can't warm up again.' The male friend wandered off into the bunker room, where he started looking at Blue Chip with the male councillor. The friend suddenly announced: 'You know what I could murder right now? A big kebab?' 'Ah, yes – the dodgy doner,' said the female activist.

'Yeah, yeah,' said the friend. 'When I was in the navy I used to buy kebabs two at a time – one for dinner and one that I would keep overnight and eat cold for breakfast.' The friend then began telling stories about his life in the navy. 'What we would do is get a bunch of guys together,' he said, 'and we would go to a bar and strip naked and sit there drinking . . . completely naked, sitting there in a line . . . until we got turned out.'

'You don't get that sort of thing any more,' the friend added, 'because we don't send out ships any more to fly the flag.' The male councillor tut-tutted and said, 'That's right.' The friend soon started boasting again, saying if there had been CCTV in the streets in the 1980s and 1990s he would have been arrested many times for being drunk in the streets and causing trouble. 'The charge would have been "drunk in charge of a kebab",' David chipped in, which brought a roar of laughter.

To David and me the strange, stilted conversation was all getting a bit like *Abigail's Party*, the Mike Leigh play. The awkwardness dragged on until a female friend of the couple arrived, minutes before the polls closed, at 10 p.m. The female friend was an elderly woman, seventy or more and very thin. She had a collapsed bouffant hairdo and a sort of urban farmer's wife look – all dark greens and browns with a sleeveless jacket, slacks and brogues. The female friend and the female activist obviously went back a long time, because they began shrieking and making jokes about men they both knew. The male council-lor and the male friend were still in the bunker, Googling something and talking in muted tones, while the two women kept up their continuous high-pitched hilarity.

Perhaps picking up on the upbeat conversation, the dog clamped itself to the female friend's leg. On cue, the friend, in her quavering cut-glass accent, quoted a slogan on a coffee mug she had spotted on a shelf. 'If I can't hump it or eat it, I'm not interested,' she pronounced, adding, 'well, three cheers for that!' Then, suddenly turning grim, she started complaining about a friend who had 'a randy beagle – a ghastly awful little creature'. She added, 'I kicked it somewhere and you couldn't castrate it after that – there was no need to!'

For David and me, still fairly unused to Tory types, it had been a strange evening. Maybe it all seemed very normal to them. But as we sat there, a momentous day in politics was drawing to a close. The next day, as the results of the election came through, three things became abundantly clear. Boris Johnson was now Mayor of London; Labour had been slaughtered throughout the country in the local government elections; and, although little had changed at the grass roots as far as we could see, the Tories, previously assumed to be stone dead, were suddenly, and dramatically, back in business.

# FIVE

# Houses of the Holy –
# Henley, Oxfordshire

When Boris Johnson won the London mayoral election in May 2008, he resigned his job as Conservative Member of Parliament for Henley, triggering a by-election in the Oxfordshire constituency. The by-election had originally been scheduled for the autumn, but the Tories hurriedly brought it forward to late June so that they could capitalize on their recent land-slide victory in the Crewe and Nantwich by-election. Henley is one of the safest Conservative seats in the country and, with a brief exception more than a century ago, the seat has always been held by the Conservatives. David and I reckoned the official Henley by-election hustings, to be held a week before the vote, would be an excellent place to find some prosperous provincial Tories. So off we went.

The venue for the hustings was Dorchester Abbey, a cavernous medieval structure which dwarfs the surrounding village of Dorchester-on-Thames, on the northern extremity of the Henley constituency. By seven o'clock, when we arrived, a crowd had started gathering in the nave of the church, and wine and orange juice were being sold. The hustings goers – most of whom were quite elderly and looked like Tories – had formed themselves into sociable clumps. They were all in a good mood – unsurprising, really, given their party's rising popularity in the polls – and were swapping information about their health concerns and exchanging news of their various relations and mutual friends in the clubby way we had come to expect. The Conservative candidate, John Howell, was a plump and unremarkable middle-aged man in an ill-fitting suit who went from group to group, sometimes slapping his fellow Tories on the back. Whatever you might think about Howell, from the way he was working the room you could tell he was a seasoned professional politician.

The other noticeable figure was the vicar, a bossy, short woman of about thirty. She radiated inner wellbeing and the sort of zealous self-confidence that only comes to a person convinced that eternal life is in the offing if the right moves are made. The vicar rounded up the crowd – probably a couple of hundred – and got them to sit down. Bustling about, she lined up the candidates along a table at the front, just behind the pulpit. The Conservatives, Labour and the Lib Dems were all represented along with UKIP, the Greens and just one of the fringe candidates, a pleasant, slightly careworn-looking chap called Dick Rodgers who represented a Christian outfit called the Common Good Party. Later, Rodgers revealed that he had travelled down from Birmingham on his motorbike in order to take part in the campaign and that he was planning to spend the night in a tent in order to keep his election expenses down. Except for David, everyone we could see was white.

It was a meant to be a hustings – open to all, so that voters could talk to candidates – but, despite the reasonable Lib Dem showing, it felt more like a Conservative rally than a debate of any kind. Even one or two people who said they had come along only to see what all the fuss was about turned out, when we asked, to be habitual Conservative voters. However, even in the new political landscape of summer of 2008, several of these people still looked vaguely sheepish about admitting that they voted Conservative. As far as we could tell there were no floating voters present at all.

The candidates got up to speak in alphabetical order, with

Chris Adams, the UKIP candidate, going first. His speech was the standard UKIP blizzard of terrifying and questionable statistics. Adams said that '75 per cent of all Britain's laws are now made by Brussels' – which was 5 per cent up on the figure we'd been told at the UKIP crime conference in Woodbridge. At this rate, we calculated, roughly 1,000 per cent of British law would be made in Brussels before the next general election.

'We are losing control of our own dear country,' Chris warned the audience, practically in tears. 'The country is on a knife edge, so think before you vote,' he continued. 'The EU is rele-gating our country to the status of Luxembourg on the world stage.' Amid all this apocalyptic scaremongering he kept repeating 'and this isn't alarmism' and, at another point, 'this isn't scaremongering'. Chris ran out of time and the lady vicar simply turned his mic off in mid-sentence, then gave him a brisk telling-off for exceeding his allocated three and a half minutes. He tried to carry on regardless, but the vicar shouted him down and told him to shut up immediately and go and sit down. Which he did.

The vicar had announced earlier that there would be 'no applause' and 'no shouting', so when John Howell moved up to the pulpit and the Tories began to cheer their man, she shushed them loudly with the microphone. Howell's speech focused, uncontroversially, on the fact that he had lived in the constituency all his life. He also managed to mention that he liked to play the piano and the church organ. Simply describing all that soaked up a fair bit of his allocated time. Beyond describing his musical skills he hammered home his rock-solid Nimby credentials, claiming to have saved part of the constituency from 'the menace of open-cast gravel mining'.

'There is a revolution required to bring back power to local people,' said John. That got a round of applause from the Tories in the audience, but the vicar quickly told them to stop. John struck us as a chinless wonder rather than a revolutionary, and we reckoned that the most revolutionary thing he was ever likely to do was order new types of low-energy light bulbs for his accountancy business.

'We've got to keep Labour on the run,' John added, beginning a trundle through the standard Conservative Party gripes about the tax burden, climaxing with a super-gripe about petrol prices and road taxes. 'This government does not understand that in the countryside a car is not a luxury, it is a necessity,' he said. There was a muttering of approval at this. From what we'd seen, most of the cars nestling in the driveways of Dorchester-on-Thames were, in fact, luxurious by anyone's standards, including, as they did, a number of massive vintage sports cars and restored vintage saloons that, presumably, consumed huge quantities of petrol. John finished his talk on time and got an approving look from the vicar.

Facing such an overwhelmingly hostile audience Stephen Kearney of the Liberal Democrats was on the back foot from the start. Like John Howell he kept things pretty vague, pitching himself as being driven by a passion for overcoming social injustice. Another motivation was the hope of one day overcoming Henley's apparent binge-drinking problem. Stephen's keyword was 'key' – for example, as he told it, it was a 'key problem' that there were three thousand drunks on the streets of Henley on a Saturday night. According to the last census the total population of Henley town was 10,631, including children. If Stephen's figures were correct then half the population of Henley rampaged drunkenly around the place every weekend. To match his hyperbole, Stephen made tremendously disproportionate hand gestures and wore an intense, agonized look on his face – as though the entire weight of Henley's problems rested on his shoulders. Despite this, he was very dapperly dressed, and, with his ostentatious love for his fellow man, came over as a cross between Mahatma Gandhi and double-glazing salesman.

Richard McKenzie, the Labour Party candidate, decided that the best tactic was to play the Christian card. He groped for a personal connection with the ecclesiastical surroundings, pointing out that he played saxophone in a 'faith band' at his own church. Then, self-deprecatingly, he told a story about how a Tory activist had boasted to him, 'We don't count the Conservative vote around here, we just weigh it.' McKenzie's charm got him through the first minute, but then the more committed Tories in the audience started to give him a bit of barracking when he began talking about education policy. A group in the front row started waving a Tory campaign newspaper with an article about education on its front page. But the lady vicar unleashed a full-strength glare at them and they packed it in. When McKenzie finished there was an uncomfortable, silent pause and then, a few seconds later, his handful of bussed-in supporters began clapping furiously, their efforts echoing sadly around the cavernous space.

The Common Good Party candidate, Dick Rodgers, seemed to struggle to fill his allotted three minutes. 'I want us all in Britain to care passionately about making the world a better place for everybody,' he said, then hesitated and seemed to lose confidence, before adding shyly: 'I know it sounds twee and idealistic . . . but . . . the basis of life is not consumerism – and certainly not Islam – it is Christianity.' Stephen, the Liberal, nodded in furious agreement with all this. 'I won't get elected,' the Christian added brightly, and with a beatific smile, 'but every vote counts and no vote for me is wasted. Every vote will send a message to those in power.' There was some muffled applause for Rodgers, perhaps because his message chimed with the church surroundings. (In the event he was to get 121 votes, seven less than the Miss Great Britain Party candidate, Amanda Harrington.)

There followed a series of questions from the audience which ended with a man who had a cut-glass Oxford accent and looked every inch a Conservative. He looked set for a good Nimby spiel or some other country-going-to-dogs type complaint, but, to everyone's surprise he asked, in exasperated terms, how on earth political parties could expect to increase social equality if they were planning to abolish inheritance tax. The panel, even the Labour Party man, seemed to have trouble understanding what he was getting at. Social equality? What's in that for us? John Howell got it completely wrong and turned the question around to brag that 'David Cameron's initiative in abolishing inheritance for everyone except millionaires has been a major vote winner'.

A week later John Howell won the seat with 19,796 votes, with the Liberal Democrat candidate Stephen Kearney trailing in a distant second on 9,680. The Labour candidate lost his deposit. The Green candidate came third and increased his vote slightly.

Howell had therefore been spot on about the popularity of the promise to abolish inheritance tax. Between them the people sitting in the pews must have owned dozens and dozens of valuable homes in Henley and the surrounding villages. Houses were, at the time of writing, so expensive in Oxfordshire that the home of the average hustings-goer must have been around £500,000, and up to a couple of million in many cases. Doing a back of an envelope calculation, you were looking at the owners of maybe between £50 million and £100 million of residential property. The abolition of inheritance tax was probably worth £20 million or so just to the people in the abbey for the hustings, and possibly £100 million in the village of Dorchester as a whole. When you added it up across Oxfordshire and then across the country, the Conservatives were putting a mountain of money on the table if you voted for them.

Not far away from Henley the politics of housing and house price money was making an impact in a different way. A few weeks before the hustings David and I had turned up at a village hall meeting in Weston-on-the-Green, called to oppose the building of large numbers of modern houses for poor people on an airfield next to the village. The proposal was part of a national scheme to build a series of 'eco-towns' in the south of England.

This was bad news for the couple of hundred inhabitants of Weston who enjoyed the golden combination of thatched dwellings in green surroundings fifteen minutes' drive from the supermarkets and mod cons of central Oxford. Houses here were much in demand and worth a fortune. Life was good and everything in the garden was – quite literally – rosy. Then, one fine morning in the spring of 2008, the villagers of Weston woke to read in the *Daily Telegraph* that the government had chosen a disused Ministry of Defence airfield next to their Saxon church, village green and post office to build an eco-town. That's eco-town to you or me, but was seen, not unreasonably, as a vast and badly thought-out new overspill housing estate into which the homeless, bedsit-dwelling or otherwise badly housed and problem-ridden proletarians of the inner cities and the skuzzier bits of Oxfordshire could be dumped.

The villagers were not going down without a fight, however, and found themselves a leader in the shape of tennis star Tim Henman's dad – Tony – who lived in a large squire's residence near the church. Given the fact that the villagers had so little chance of winning you couldn't help but wonder if heroic failure was somehow in the Henman bloodline and ran between the generations like the Blackadder dynasty.

Tony's campaign strategy was to rally as many of the locals as possible and get them to pay for a process called judicial review. This would probably not defeat the proposal, but it would slow it down. If they could hang on until after the next general election the Conservatives would get in and the whole concept of building houses for poor folks would be back off the agenda, at least – Tony reckoned – in the Tory heartlands of rural Oxfordshire.

But how to get the locals onside? Tony told the *Daily Telegraph* he had at first thought of calling his protest group WOG OFF (WOG standing for Weston-on-the-Green) but had decided against that because of the curse of Political Correctness. The proposed new town, Tony observed in the same newspaper interview, was to be called Weston Otmoor. That, he said, was ridiculous. It would be better to call it Motown. In the end Tony called his protest group The Weston Front.

The village hall was crowded on the evening of the protest meeting and Tony dominated the proceedings. There must have been two hundred people crammed into the hall. It was raining outside and the room was overheated. David and I had arrived separately and whereas I just cruised in saying, truthfully, that I was not local but that I was 'interested in the whole eco-town thing', David had more of a problem. He reckoned that was because, first of all, he was black – which also meant he was definitely not local – and, second, he was the only black person at the meeting.

The meeting got under way and the atmosphere in the packed hall was, I thought, more one of intense bewilderment and fear than of anger. The whole thing was being treated more like a natural catastrophe or an enormous stroke of bad luck than a political movement. Some of the villagers looked very upset indeed, especially the older ones. It was as though they had just been told they had cancer or something. There was a look of preoccupied terror etched on some faces. They were investing a lot of hope in Tony and were ready to clutch at any straws he had to offer.

Tony sat at a table at the back of hall, flanked by advisers and members of the Front committee. He looked like he meant business and had about him the air of a retired political leader, military man, Wild West sheriff or vigilante chief persuaded to strap on his Magnum one last time in order to 'take out the trash' – or in this case to stop the trash arriving in the first place in a series of removal vans and beat-up transits from the notorious Blackbird Leys council estate in Oxford or other ASBO hotspots around the county (such as, apparently, the hapless town of Didcot, which kept getting a mention as though it were a particularly lawless and pirate-infested province of Somalia).

When you looked at Tony there was a definite touch of the Clint Eastwood gunslinger there, except that he spoke precisely, in short sentences. Everyone in the hall seemed to know who he was and was deferential. Whether this was because of some previous service to the community, or that a perpetual source of national sporting disappointment had sprung from his loins, we could not tell. When somebody asked Tony a question he tended to lean forward and start lecturing, peering through his spectacles as he read, and raising his eyes over them when he spoke. He called the meeting to order with a broad and some-what pompous review of the national political situation – like a military commander briefing his junior officers.

Tony's big idea was to subvert democracy and bog down the process of planning approval for the new town with a series of legal challenges and filibusters. He was pretty clear that these legal objections were unlikely to succeed because, frankly, the plan had a lot going for it. The population was growing. New houses were needed right across the South and, when you looked at the proposal objectively, a disused airfield in some low-value farmland on the edge of a big city right next to a huge motorway junction was as good a place as any to build them. But while the objections might not succeed, they would buy time. Tony was 'absolutely certain' that the Conservatives would win the next general election and that the new Conservative government would scrap the eco-town plan.

After giving this overview, Tony introduced a variety of experts – including councillors and council planning officers – who were there to help him. The meeting cheered up when it was explained that, according to its own rules, the government would have to make sure that existing local plans for provision of things like water supply, sewage disposal, schools and transport did not clash with plans for the new town. That would take time. But then he said he was working with his opposite number at the neighbouring Oxford City Council. Mention of this body's involvement sent an agonized ripple of alarm around the room. An elderly couple sitting near me looked at each other with a look of real fear on their faces: 'That proves it. It's an overspill estate for Oxford!' The audience was aghast, literally gasping, as the council officer explained that the secretary of state could force the social housing development through despite Cherwell council's opposition. 'We can't, at the end of the day, go against national planning permission,' he said, adding: 'If they want to build it, nobody can stop them.'

Tony introduced his next expert, Michael, a Conservative councillor from Cherwell Valley Council and the chair of its planning committee. He warned everyone that the plan would be hard to defeat because 'this part of the world is designated as an area of "extreme housing stress"'. At this point one man shouted out in a really distressed, upper-class elderly accent: 'But why here . . .?' There was an understandable and perhaps natural view that while new houses might be needed some-where in the country, they should be built in somebody else's back yard.

Councillor Michael's speech took on an even more sobering tone: 'We are backing you as much as we can. But remember the housing is being presented as a national priority eco-town – both an ecological move and providing affordable housing. Those are the two big objectives at the moment. And that gives it, I'm afraid, a lot of advantages in the planning process.

'Because it is being imposed from the top,' he continued, 'our existing local plans will have to be rewritten to fit in with it. That will hold things up a bit. Oxfordshire will have to look at the implications of the schools that will need to be built, bus services, sewage farms . . . everything.' At the mention of schools, the elderly couple near me looked at each other with real dismay. Sewage! Bus stations! Who the hell uses bus stations?! And schools!! Bog-standard comprehensives full of feral kids bunking off Media Studies to go joy-riding around what remained of the village lanes, doing handbrake turns in front of the post office before robbing it.

A plump man with white hair stood up and identified himself as a Conservative councillor from another part of the county and made a frankly party political pitch. 'The fact is,' he said, 'we are going to have a Conservative government in two years. David Cameron is coming to Weston, and when he comes here, we have to make him commit to not going ahead with the new town . . . that's the way we can do it. That's the only way to do it.'

Next up was a slightly scruffy man in an off-white jacket with patches on the elbows. He made a little speech in the form of a question directed at the planning officer. He summed up what was really at stake – that the new social housing project would probably see new people arriving in the area *en masse*, new people whom some of the locals present in the hall probably wouldn't like very much. 'When you put in your report to the government, I hope you will point out that these proposals will completely transform the traditional socio-economic composition of this area for good,' said the man. 'That's what this is really about.' There was an emotional round of applause.

But when the cheers died down, the Conservative councillor warned the villagers to stay away from what he called 'the emotive issues'. This seemed to me to be a euphemism for the meeting's evident desire not to have any unfamiliar poor people living near them. The councillor then reminded them that they had recently seen off a proposal to build a centre for housing asylum seekers in Oxfordshire by sticking to technical planning objections and 'avoiding the emotive issues'.

'Don't worry about being called Nimbies, by the way,' he said out of the blue. 'That does not matter. Just stick to the planning process, and raise as many detailed, technical objections as you can . . . tie them up in knots, pull the proposal to pieces.' There followed a range of detailed and eager straw-clutching suggestions about things which could be complained about – including questioning whether the motorway bridges would be able to safely carry extra traffic brought about by the new development. Then it was suggested that they could all object on archaeological grounds, which got the vicar's wife very excited. She turned to her husband with a nudge-nudge look on her face – maybe there was an argument about damaging church property which could somehow be used to help gum up the works.

The desperateness of this got to me. These people were going to lose a lot of money in terms of the value of their property if the new town was built. More than this, their view of themselves as quaint country dwellers enjoying the good life and never having to meet anyone they didn't know would be destroyed. The lifestyle they enjoyed, to be sure, was not like something out of a Thomas Hardy novel – they were, after all, three minutes from the M40 motorway and all had satellite dishes and plumbed-in drains. But many would have invested a fair chunk of their life – maybe all of it – in their quest to retire to a country cottage with roses around the door where they could quietly die and leave a bag of House Price money to their children and grandchildren. These people were almost exclusively white and middle class, and were used to exercising power in one way or another. It seemed to cause actual physical shock for some of them to be powerless, their lives determined by the decisions of others.

Henman then began to sum up, saying that what he had heard was all very well, but pressing for a judicial review was really the way forward (a judicial review is a legal challenge to the planning proposal which could in theory defeat the government's right to override planning objections). It was by no means certain, or even especially likely, that The Weston Front would win in the courts. And if they lost they would have to pay all the legal costs which would run, possibly, into hundreds of thousands. But the key thing was that the social housing development could not go ahead if a judicial review was under way, and that would buy them time.

Henman promised to think how money could be found for that. In the meantime The Weston Front would continue drawing up petitions, distributing leaflets, doing PR work with the press and joining in with other anti-new town groups to organize demonstrations.

'What makes me angry is that if this goes ahead in October there's no turning back,' said Henman. 'It is only a third of the electorate that voted in this government . . . once they have planning permission it will be virtually impossible to get that overturned. Once it begins and they start pouring concrete in, it won't go away – I find that an horrendous prospect.'

The meeting broke up and I went with David to the Chequers, a pub about half a mile away, just outside the village. The Chequers was almost deserted but there we found a group of three or four locals who knew about Henman's meeting – they were discussing it – but had evidently decided not to attend. They were already fairly tipsy. A few minutes later another group, led by a very elderly couple and a middle-aged woman who might have been their daughter, arrived at the pub, and we recognized them from the meeting. It seemed they knew the non-protesting drinkers, and a heated argument broke out almost at once.

Those who had attended the meeting chided the drinkers for missing it. The drinkers took umbrage, and one of them, a woman, slurring her words slightly, testily began telling a story about a friend of hers who had found it impossible to sell her house because of the uncertainty over Weston Otmoor. The woman's friend was angry with Henman and his group because she thought that the new town would bring new schools, roads and supermarkets and their arrival would actually increase the value of her house. It was only Henman and the others who lived in the old part of the village, the woman said, those who lived in the fancy thatched cottages, who would lose out. It was the 'retired people' who were against the development, and all they were interested in was making sure their houses were worth lots of money. She objected to all the posters along the road saying that the new eco-town should not be built because it would 'destroy the countryside'. 'This is not the f***ing countryside,' she said. 'It's right next door to a f***ing motorway and you are ten minutes from Oxford.'

The old guy who had been at the meeting disagreed. He said that the value of his house had gone down since the proposal had first been published. If the new town was built the area would be full of 'scum'. It would turn into a slum and he was going to 'lose a fortune'. The slurring woman reacted angrily: 'You're all right – you've made a fortune! What about us? It makes me sick. You are like Henman in that massive house. And you all bow down to him!'

In July 2008 Tony Henman got the judicial review he was seeking, paid for with public money in the form of a grant from the Conservative-controlled Local Government Association. The Labour housing minister Caroline Flint conceded that the legal arguments would slow down the planning process, and might even delay a decision until after the next general election.

In January 2009, however, judges ruled that initial consultation by the government had been adequate and that the planning process could continue. The delay had in the end been slight.

On the same day as the judicial review was granted an official report into housing policy in the countryside was published. It found that 'countryside communities risk being destroyed by the huge gulf between house prices and local incomes' – in other words, people who had grown up in the countryside were unable to buy houses in the same area, because rich newcomers had pushed house prices up, and not enough new homes had been built.

The report added that, as ever, cities were becoming more crowded, and a whole generation of young people were likely to be inadequately housed or financially crippled by overextending themselves to buy somewhere to live. Social tension was mounting in the towns and inner cities, said the report – and a lot of that boiled down to competition for increasingly scarce housing stock. Meanwhile, villages the length and breadth of England were becoming, in the words of the report, 'exclusive enclaves of the elderly and wealthy' who lived in a world of their own.

# SIX

# *Floral Jam – Basingstoke, Hampshire*

To an elderly woman in a motorized wheelchair a six-inch wooden step can seem like the north face of the Eiger, especially after a couple of glasses of Pimm's. The small step was all that separated the woman from the inside of a large white marquee – where a lavish cream tea lay in wait – but she was having some difficulty negotiating it. Two leading members of the Hampshire Women's Institute wondered aloud whether she needed a push. But their wheelchair-bound sister simply slammed her motor into reverse, then flipped through the gears – her head snapping back violently – causing the chair to leap forward and bound over the step. After making the wheelchair equivalent of a handbrake turn, she spun round to her chums with a look of triumph on her face.

'She did a wheelie!' shrieked one of the women from beneath her wide-brimmed hat, before breaking into a gale of jolly laughter. She watched with a smile as the wheelchair lady disappeared inside the marquee. Lifting her head to reveal a bubbly face, the hat-wearing woman – resplendent in a floral frock – turned to us and said: 'Are you the gentlemen who have come to sort out Englishness?'

When talking our way into the Hampshire Women's Institute's gathering at the Audleys Wood Hotel, near Basingstoke, over the phone, we had told their officials that we were on a quest to find the essence of conservative – with a small 'c' – England.

We had said we wanted to come and observe Middle England in its natural habitat and there seemed no better place to be than among the ladies of the Women's Institute. What made them tick? What did they believe? Why had they banded together?

'Good!' the hat-wearing woman replied briskly, as though she were talking to a couple of emergency plumbers. 'You have come to exactly the right place,' she continued. 'You can't get more English than this – a brass band and the Women's Institute on a hot summer's day.' She then made a grand, sweeping gesture with one arm, taking in the perfect blue sky, the manicured lawns and the flower beds, along with the gardens, crazy paving and neoclassical architecture of the hotel and its grounds. In the distance beyond the hedgerow, ripening wheat waved gently, while before us stood the white marquee, which held a forest of enormous hats, their wearers' conversation tinkling out and across the grounds.

With the countryside in all its glory, the members of a police brass band in their Trumpton-style uniforms, the tables decorated with flowers and set for a tea of tiny triangular sandwiches made with bleach-white bread, butter scones and jam – could there be a more quintessentially English summer scene? As a couple of smelly (male) hacks, we were outside the marquee both literally and metaphorically, looking in through the entrance like a two curious schoolboys.

The woman taking care of us during our visit to the Women's Institute tea party was Lynne Andrews of Locksheath WI. Lynne, the First Vice Chairman of the Hampshire County Federation of Women's Institutes, was, to echo a phrase we heard over and over again during the day, 'really lovely'. The ladies of the WI seemed to use this expression even more frequently – and with about as much consideration – as the UKIP people (those we had observed, at least) came out with 'utterly horrendous'. Thus, the flowers in the hotel garden were 'really lovely'; so too the reception the Women's Institute members had received from the hotel staff. The weather was 'really lovely', as were even more abstract notions such as the idea of holding the gathering in the first place.

Lynne had a round and friendly face framed by a fancy white straw hat with a black trim. She was short and buxom and looked as if she was in her forties: she was thus one of the younger ladies at the event. Of the two hundred women there, most looked as though they were well into their sixties, with a smattering of fifty-year-olds, septuagenarians and even octogenarians. As we arrived, Lynne and some others were making a fuss over the longest-serving member of the Hampshire Federation's seven-thousand-strong collective. The woman was sitting on a bench on a wide lawn outside the marquee and was being interviewed, with a video camera, by a young female reporter from the local newspaper. The frail but still animated woman was to be awarded a long-service medal later in the day, having been a member of the Institute for sixty-one years. Her birthday in fact coincided with the foundation of the Hampshire WI. They were both ninety years old, so this was cause for a double celebration.

Lynne had joined the WI after originally attending an 'information day'. The sense of companionship appealed to her, but she decided to join a branch that did not do handicrafts (which meant sewing and knitting). Branches varied considerably, she told us. Some of them were mostly about cooking and baking and crafts; others were more like discussion groups or keep-fit classes. The most recent branch to be set up in Hampshire was called the 'Kitchen Dancers' of Winchester, which was formed by a group of women who felt they were starting to get on a bit. The joke was that they liked dancing on their own, but the only place they could do that now – to spare their blushes – was in the kitchens of their own homes.

Lynne was quick to point out that the Women's Institute was

'strictly non-political'. When asked whether any of the members might have any political affiliations, she flinched, sucked her teeth and took a short but dramatic step backwards. She agreed that an alliance with an organization of seven thousand members in Hampshire alone, many of them pillars of their local or village communities, would be a tremendous prize for any political party. But Lynne was adamant: 'They just wouldn't dare.' That was especially true after the Tony Blair slow-handclapping incident of 2000, which, she explained, was not done to demonstrate that the WI was anti-Labour, or would swing behind the Conservatives or the Liberals. What sparked it, she said, was that Blair had completely misjudged the mood of the WI. 'He thought he could show up with his nice smile, and all these little old ladies would just love him,' Lynne said, 'but it didn't work out.' Lynne thought that those present might even have agreed with everything he was saying, but they simply wanted to tell him that they did not want a party political speech on their patch. The reason for this, she said, was simple: politics within the WI would divide its membership, and pit one member against another. When they had their WI hats on – which at this gathering was literally true in the case of almost every member – they put political, religious and any other sort of difference aside.

'The Women's Institute isn't all jam and "Jerusalem", you know!' Lynne said, trying to stress the organization's more radical side. There was, however, plenty of homemade jam on sale. And the most emotional moment of the afternoon came when, in a show of sorority and nationhood, all two hundred of the guests rose as one to sing from the top of their voices, a cappella, the WI anthem 'Jerusalem'.

The WI had always advocated social equality and in the 1930s it had campaigned in favour of equal pay for women. Recently, the WI had championed or spread the message about HIV/AIDS and safer sex, and it had debated climate change, pensions and domestic violence against women. In 1951, Lady Elizabeth Brunner, the head of the WI, had launched the 'Keep Britain Tidy' campaign, one of the country's most emblematic public awareness campaigns (which eventually morphed into the 'Big Tidy Up' movement with six thousand nationwide groups). The way Lynne described it, the WI sounded like the active service wing of Radio 4's *Woman's Hour*.

After a while, we were joined by Pat Marshall, who was the overall WI chief in Hampshire. She wore a badge of office, a substantial brass chain like something a mayor might wear, with a pendant featuring the WI symbol picked out in rubies and diamonds above the motto of the WI, 'For Home and For Country'. It turned out that the pendant had been made as a brooch by her father in the 1930s. Like almost everyone else present, Pat wore a large hat, in her case one made of straw, and loose-fitting clothes.

Pat began to tell us how radical and up to date the WI was, illustrating this by saying that the Hampshire group had recently passed a resolution in favour of better and safer working conditions for prostitutes – highly relevant in a county in which soldiers and sailors are so numerous. Beyond this, they had sent one of their members – sixty-two-year-old Jean Johnson, aka 'JJ' – on a fact-finding tour around the world paid for by Channel Four television, which was making a documentary about it all.

Right on cue Jean turned up to chat. 'Here's our lovely brothel lady,' Lynne said. There followed an animated discussion about how the Channel Four filming was going, and it seemed Jean was having a great time. She had just come back from a stay at a 'bunny ranch' in California, and a spell in a brothel in New Zealand. She had visited the red-light district in Amsterdam where she had sat in a window, as is the custom of the local tarts – 'not that it did me any good'. But before we could explore all this much further an old lady, not a day under seventy-five, came towards the marquee holding a tall glass of what looked like Pimm's. Jean stopped in her tracks. 'Hello, how are you?' she gushed. 'God, you're drinking again! Disgusting behaviour!' Jean teased her friend with generous, mock-bawdy humour.

The big white marquee in which the event was being held looked like the sort that would be hired for an overpriced wedding. It was carpeted, with places set for around two hundred. It had curtains and furbelows at its plastic windows and outside there were luxurious mobile toilets.

When everyone was seated, Lynne gave a short speech in which she cheekily remarked, à propos of the police band, 'It's very comforting to have so many strong arms of the law here.' The ladies were then addressed briefly by the Lord Lieutenant of Hampshire, Mrs Mary Fagan JP, who, as guest of honour, was representing the Queen. There was a raffle, with prizes of supermarket wine and chocolates. By this stage in our journey, we knew that conservative England – whether with a small 'c' or a big 'C' – was addicted to raffles, often with prizes that looked suspiciously like unwanted Christmas presents.

During tea the ladies were serenaded by the thirty-strong Hampshire Constabulary Marching Band, who were making a hell of a racket, the French horns straying especially badly. The play list comprised light classical standards, showstoppers and TV and movie theme tunes including, at enormous length, the entire *Star Wars* suite. At one point, when the band played the 'Light Cavalry' overture by Franz von Suppé, the WI women started pony riding in their seats to the energetic 'da-da-da-da-da-da-da-da-da-da-da . . .' beat.

The police band had brought along its own photographer; he was hanging about on the fringes looking bored, and having a technical conversation with the local paper reporter about digital photography. He explained his job to us as being, essentially, that of 'producing propaganda for the police' – lots of images of jolly coppers out there in the community, doing the right thing. This touchy-feely *Dixon of Dock Green* material was, he explained, designed to counteract the less cuddly pictures of the police in newspapers and on the national news, and the ridiculous representation, as he saw it, of the police in TV drama.

The fact was, he continued, there was hardly any crime in the villages of Hampshire. 'You might get one crime once every twenty years,' he said. But people still wanted a policeman on the beat in their village, the snapper explained, not because that would make any difference to crime levels but because it made them feel better. So a show of force at events like this, he reckoned, did everyone a lot of psychological good without costing too much. The presence of the police band here at the WI event sort of implied, he said, that the police were every-where – on patrol in peaceful and safe places, such as villages and country hotel gardens, just in case things started to kick off – which, of course, they were not likely to do.

The police band leader was Major James Burcham M.Mus., PGDip. (TCM) LRSM, a staff officer with the Royal Marines Band Service at the Royal Marines School of Music in Portsmouth. 'He's off to Afghanistan soon,' whispered one of the band members, a short, fat Laughing Policeman type in his early sixties who had retired, with his policewoman wife (also in the band), to the South West from London. The band had been going for more than 110 years, and, in the foyer of the marquee, there were old photographs of the band playing from the 1920s. They were, it turned out, happy to play for pay anywhere – birthdays, weddings and bar mitzvahs were not a problem, hence their WI booking. More sombrely, they had just been to France to perform for the British Legion as part of its Somme anniversary, and were going on tour to Malta later in the month.

Another of the band members, this one in his mid-sixties with greasy, slightly Teddy boyish black hair, talked to us about the war in Afghanistan. He said the way to stop the Taliban, and thus the importation of drugs into the UK, was to carpet-bomb the parts of the country with the poppy fields, if not the whole country. While we were at it, we ought to bomb Iran as well, since they were obviously up to no good. We ventured that the Taliban would just hide in their caves until the bombing was over, and then emerge to start growing poppies again once the coast was clear. He looked momentarily puzzled, as though this idea had never occurred to him. Then his face brightened: 'Well, we'll just bomb 'em again . . . and keep on bombing 'em until they get the message.' He said the heroin trade was paying for international terrorism and was the cause of 'all your serious crime'. We just had to go in there and fire-bomb the entire country, as though it was a Rentokil pest infestation job, but on a vast scale.

Such heavy politicking and gung-ho banter was somewhat out of step with the floral, feminine and festive nature of the afternoon's event. But it was not entirely out of place, especially in Hampshire – very much the military heartland and historic fortress of England.

When the Women's Institute was established in 1915, Hampshire had been one of the poorest and most backward parts of the country. The Industrial Revolution and imports of cheap food from the Empire had in the nineteenth century destroyed the agricultural economy, and impoverished the local aristocracy and farm workers alike. As a way out, many emigrated to Canada and Australia while others joined the navy in Portsmouth, on the south coast, or the army, headquartered at Aldershot in the north of the county. The county regiment lost thousands of soldiers in the Afghan Wars at the end of the nineteenth century. Many women went into domestic service in London.

In the First World War, Hampshire's sacrifice in blood was characteristically disproportionate. The county produced thirty-six battalions and the military historian W. J. Harris has written that the county and its regiments suffered 'an appallingly high rate of casualties' and brought death and widowhood to practically every family in the county. The Hampshire regiments took part in ninety-two battles during the First World War: they were concentrated in the battles of the Somme at Passchendaele and the catastrophic Dardanelles landings. Part of the original role of the WI was to train women to help in the war effort and at the same time to provide a network of support while the men were away. In times of war the WI were always knitting socks for the men at the front, or making jam to supplement their rations.

Many things have brought modern Hampshire back to life. The most significant boost to its economy, however, as the county's economic development unit coyly acknowledges, is a dependence on military spending and arms production. £60 billion a year is spent by the government on the armed forces and on the procurement of defence equipment – or, if you prefer, weapons. The Ministry of Defence is the biggest employer in the county, apart from the County Council itself which represents in economic terms another way in which the government channels millions into the region.

Apart from the ex-soldiers in the police band, the county's military connections were no longer immediately apparent at the WI gathering in Basingstoke. On the surface everything was, well, lovely. And unless the ladies of the WI were going to apply their ingenuity to knitting body armour and armoured cars (said to be in short supply on the Afghan front line), there was little they could do to help.

When we discreetly enquired, we found that many of the older women were widows, just like generations of previous WI members before them. This was not because of war, but rather the impact of ageing. It is a simple fact that women live longer than men – and in the near future they may outlive men by almost an entire additional lifetime. By 2011 there will be, for example, on current trends, more than 10,000 women in England over one hundred years old. Nine out of ten will be widows, because only one thousand men will reach that age.

What we discovered was the sense of solidarity, mutual caring and practical help the women provided for each other. They were a voluntary branch of the welfare state, and the service they provided simply in keeping tabs on and maintaining the morale of the elderly was probably worth millions. In this way they were a perfect example of one of the 'little battalions' of society which the intellectual Tory's favourite philosopher, Edmund Burke, famously described as the essence of free and civilized human society.

In a way we had come close to discovering Burke's 'civilized human society': we had found the 'essence of conservatism' right there in Basingstoke. All the values Burke praised were there – modesty, good manners, civility, respect for authority, voluntary effort and, above all, a sense of calm and orderliness. Even the aristocracy (which Burke thought to be far superior to democracy, especially after the horrors of the French Revolution) was present in the presiding form of the Lady Lord Lieutenant of Hampshire, Mary Fagan.

We had seen the future of Conservatism – and indeed of the whole country – right there in a big tent in Basingstoke. The future was old. And the future was female.

# SEVEN

# *Cecil Rides Again – Belgravia, London*

As we ferreted around in Conservative Britain, we increasingly began to realize that we needed to search for the legacy of the most dominant Conservative figure since Winston Churchill – Margaret Thatcher. David Cameron and his aides, we guessed, must regard her as a mixed blessing. On the one hand, nearly twenty years after being ousted as Prime Minister she still inspires fierce devotion among diehard party members and symbolizes, more than anyone else, a tough, uncompromising Conservatism that still appeals to some of the electorate. On the other, her hard-bitten approach saddled the Conservatives with the reputation – hard to shift – of being, in Theresa May's phrase, the 'nasty party'. Since the 1990's this reputation has probably lost them tens of millions of votes.

More than ten years after New Labour swept to power, just how deep was the affection among grass-roots Tories for Margaret Thatcher? Who were the Thatcherite true believers – were they, like the Boys from Brazil, hunkered down in some secret bunker, optimistically developing fresh plans for world domination? Or were they, like the last, pathetic remnants of a once all-powerful army, simply cursing their fate and drowning their sorrows, as their numbers dwindled due to old age? In our hunt for the answers we decided to attend the annual dinner of Conservative Way Forward, a pressure group formed when Thatcher left office. The idea of Conservative Way Forward was, and still is, to honour Thatcher's memory and to ensure that her kinds of policies are still being promoted.

The dinner was held in the banqueting suite of an expensive hotel in Mayfair. The tickets cost a lot of money, and we'd been concerned that we might have to wear tuxedos, but, in the event, we managed to get by in suits. When we arrived, the first thing we noticed was that the whole thing had a naughty, furtive and slightly conspiratorial feel about it. The fall of Thatcher had been a momentous event, and here we were among the most deeply committed members of her tribe. They were the survivors, now completely at odds with New Labour's politically correct and touchy-feely Britain, and they seemed to relish a sense that they were outlaws, keeping the old symbols alive and speaking in codes only they really understood.

The second thing we noticed was that, as a group, they were very like the UKIP people we had met in Woodbridge – the same overwhelming sense of grievance and betrayal, and a feeling that they were simply trapped in an 'I told you so' loop, fighting the battles the rest of the world had long since stopped caring about, or even understanding. They were mostly, but not exclusively, old and white. The Way Forward people were all members of the Conservative Party but some, we discovered, had informal links to UKIP and voted for them at elections. This was a profound breach of protocol and added to the air of transgression which seemed to hang over the event.

Compared to the UKIP shindigs we had seen, though, the Conservative Way Forward dinner was a far more upmarket affair. For a start, tickets for the dinner cost £75, and Conservative Way Forward offered fund-raising methods vastly superior to those mustered by UKIP. Where UKIP offered a raffle with cheap, bog-standard prizes, Conservative Way Forward had an auction rather than a raffle and the prizes included a holiday for two in the Dordogne, a trip in a vintage aeroplane and a signed copy of Margaret Thatcher's memoirs – the latter went for £400. Conservative Way Forward guests weren't the super-rich though: they appeared to us to be more like bank managers, property dealers, retired solicitors and minor company directors.

Before we tucked into dinner, the master of ceremonies requested us to stand for grace. We were asked to remember those in Zimbabwe who were going without food because of 'the communist dictator Robert Mugabe'. We were asked to pray for 'a return of loyalty within the Conservative Party'. No one seemed to know whether to say 'Amen' or 'hear, hear'.

After dinner Cecil Parkinson – Thatcher's former Industry Secretary and once one of her closest allies – stood at a lectern and began to speak softly into the microphone. He still had his famous mop of hair, now snow-white, and wore a light blue suit and a yellow tie, which contrasted fantastically with his tangerine perma-tan. Cecil kicked off with a few jokes, and told a story about a judge who had once asked him to summarize his achievements: 'How can I possibly summarize my life story and achievements in just ten minutes,' Cecil had complained, to which the judge replied: 'Speak slowly.' This prompted raucous laughter and thumping of tables, especially from one seating some of the younger people in the room. They looked like students, men and women with an air of fogeyness about them combined with a Bullingdon Club-type brashness.

Once he had warmed up his audience, Cecil launched into a long and emotional tribute to the late George Gardiner MP, one of the prime movers in the setting up of Conservative Way Forward. Gardiner was best known for having called John Major a 'ventriloquist's dummy' when acting in the interests of the EU. Major had responded by naming Gardiner as one of the 'bastards' in the senior levels of the Conservative Party who had undermined him. The overriding belief among the party faithful was that Thatcher had never been defeated by the enemy, and that she had never lost at the polls. Rather, she had been stabbed in the back by members of her own party – which was why the dinner had started with everyone standing and praying to Almighty God for the return of loyalty within the party.

After his fulsome praise of Gardiner, Cecil moved on to venerate the late Eric Forth, another relatively obscure back-bench Tory MP, and a former leader of Conservative Way Forward. A colourful character, Forth had once got into trouble for saying that his job as an MP was to represent the 'white, Anglo-Saxon and bigoted' in Parliament. He had been a 'rent-a-quote' MP for the tabloids, always ready to say something right-wing and outrageous in return for publicity. As well as being a vocal supporter of the death penalty, he had backed apartheid in South Africa and objected to the NHS spending money on care for AIDS victims. His justification for the latter was that all AIDS victims were either homosexuals or drug users and that they therefore deserved their fate. Forth's views could hardly have been unfamiliar to the people sitting at our table, yet there was a murmur of pleasure at the mention of his name.

As Cecil spoke warmly of Eric Forth's funeral, his voice dripped with sentimentality. Everyone at the funeral, said Cecil, had been surprised to hear Elvis Presley's 'Are You Lonesome Tonight?' at the end of the ceremony. What the mourners didn't realize, Cecil said, was that Eric was a great Elvis impersonator and that the song had been recorded by Eric and was now being sung to the mourners by him, as it were, from beyond the grave.

After his hammy homage to Gardiner and Forth, Cecil really got into his stride, and moved on to talk about how he had been debating the Lisbon Treaty – which would see greater European integration – in the House of Lords. He did not say much about the treaty itself – it was disposed of with a knowing shrug – the implication being that this additional measure of European political integration was so wrong-headed that there was little point in trying to discuss it. He moved on instead to a routine denunciation of the Labour Party, hanging this on the fact that the evening coincided with the first anniversary of Gordon Brown's appointment as Prime Minister.

Cecil said that Brown had been 'brilliant for the Conservative Party' because he was so inept. He then ran through the Labour cabinet, lampooning them. 'Ed Balls – I won't make the obvious joke,' said Cecil, adding of Hazel Blears: 'I could sell her a whole kennel full of puppies.' Wandsworth Conservatives received a glowing namecheck: 'If you want to know why it is you are right to be in the Conservative Party,' said Cecil, 'if your faith ever wavers – then just spend some time in Wandsworth. It shows that a low-taxing, low-spending local authority can work and the people of Wandsworth have voted us back in time after time.' That got a big round of applause.

Cecil had now praised several minor gods in the right-wing Tory pantheon. Then, almost as an afterthought, he tossed in a far more famous name, one seldom mentioned in public with approval these days – Enoch Powell. Apropos of nothing Cecil suddenly mentioned how Powell had once come up to him in Parliament and said, gnomically: 'Cecil – never underestimate the power of inertia.' The Conservative Way Forward guests pondered this one for a moment as Cecil paused for comic effect, then he added: 'Well, what does one say in response to a thing like that? "Well, yes, Enoch, I will bear that in mind"? But that was Enoch for you, making these types of profound statements.' The room rocked with appreciative laughter. Some found it so funny and, at the same time moving, that they had to wipe a tear from the corner of their eye.

After Cecil's speech it was time for a question and answers session, with the great arch Thatcherite himself providing the answers. This, to us, seemed no more than an excuse for the Conservative Way Forward members to sound off with bracingly right-wing sentiments, and it even seemed to have a competitive element, as if everyone was trying to out-right-wing each other.

At the Bullingdon table the young bucks wanted to know: 'Should the Conservative Party be more assertive about the role Britain should play in the world?' Cecil used the question to focus on Mugabe, whom he described as 'the incarnation of evil'. He said that, after losing the election in Zimbabwe, Mugabe had claimed that 'only God could remove him' from office. 'Well then,' said Cecil, 'maybe the SAS could become the angels of God.'

Cecil broadened the subject a little by saying that Ian Smith, the last leader of the whites-only minority government – in the days when Zimbabwe was known as Rhodesia – had been a wise and good leader and that it was a shame that Britain had abandoned him. We were surprised to hear such a prominent politician praise, even in retrospect, white-minority rule, but it got a cheer and it was in keeping with the transgressive mood of the event. Gloria, one of the people on our table, even shouted, 'Ian Smith was a brilliant man!' Cecil then told us how he had once gone to the Rhodesian capital Salisbury – now Harare – and discovered that the bank rate was 1 per cent, and hadn't shifted from that in six years. Rhodesia, said Cecil, had been 'a beautiful, civilized country'. On the same African tour, he remembered, he had ventured over the border into Zambia, which had a black-majority government. Zambia had been 'ramshackle and run down and there was poverty everywhere'. Now Zimbabwe was much worse than even Zambia, he concluded.

Perhaps sensing that all this was going down well, Cecil moved on to the history of black-majority rule throughout Africa. 'The whole of Africa is a tragedy,' he said, and then told a joke which, he said, summed up his feelings about the continent: 'God decided to create the most beautiful, the most perfect continent on earth – wide rivers, fertile land, beautiful countryside, astonishing wildlife and every kind of natural resource you could wish for. An angel said to God – if you make a place like that then it will completely dominate the earth. And God said – wait until you see the people I am going to put in it.' And that was that. No more questions.

After Cecil's speech David and I had a glass of wine and chatted to the two women at our table, Margaret and Gloria, both of whom seemed to be in their sixties. Gloria was a widow and had been an air hostess before marrying an airline pilot. Now she was retired, living in Wandsworth, and made money from property dealing. Gloria thought Cecil's speech had been really great value, but a bit restrained and, generally, not right-wing enough for her tastes, especially on the European Union. She seemed to like the idea of sending a death squad to kill Robert Mugabe, though.

While the four of us were talking, an elderly Tory with a bald pate and bushy hair at the sides came over to greet Gloria and Margaret and – it seemed pretty obvious to us – to ogle their décolletage. Both Gloria and Margaret were dressed very glamorously, and used plenty of make-up and wore out-rageously snazzy clothes in order to roll back the years. The bald man seemed to know 'the girls' – as he called them – already, and jokingly asked whether they were making an effort to look especially gorgeous because they knew Cecil would be attending. 'Because we all know what Cecil is like, don't we?' said the man.

As we chatted I took a good look at Gloria; it was hard not to, because she had really gone to town that evening. She was wearing a very low-cut, skin-tight dress, in emerald green silk. The amount of cleavage on show was a bit disconcerting – she had enhanced the effect with what looked liked brightly coloured foundation and glitter – and had further gilded the lily with a mass of jewellery. Her eyelashes were elongated and spiked with mascara, and at a glance – and at the risk of sounding unkind – resembled a couple of furry spiders at play. But Gloria's crowning glory was her hair – a mountain of bright orange locks with the apparent texture of fibreglass. It was held in place by an elaborate arrangement of copper wire, which was decorated with small green jewels, which matched her dress. A large green glittering scroll sat on the top of the whole arrangement, like an artificial flower.

Gloria had a strange accent, which seemed to alternate between cut-glass RP and rasping cockney. She was a Eurosceptic and this, she said, was her 'main thing', at least politically. As we had discovered, many grass-roots Tories took the same view, but bit their tongues because party bosses had said it was a divisive issue which made the party look, in the eyes of the public, old-fashioned and self-absorbed. Gloria said she always voted for UKIP in the European elections, reasoning that, because MEPs were elected on a list system, there was a danger that a vote cast for the Conservatives might result in the election of a Europhile Tory. 'You don't know what you get when you vote for a Tory any more,' said Gloria, who thought there were too many Europhiles in the Conservative Party and that they ought to leave it. Europhile Tories were, she said, 'traitors' both to the party and to the country, with Edward Heath being the arch traitor. Gloria believed that Margaret Thatcher had been 'got rid of' by her party not because of the poll tax fiasco, but because pro-European Tories had conspired against her in order to hasten the march of a European super-state.

As I was absorbing all this, David was chatting to Gloria's friend Margaret, who was active in the Hyde Park branch of the Conservative Party. Like Gloria, she dressed to impress, but in a more restrained way. She wore a short black dress, with a tight band of pearls around her neck, and a short greying-blonde hairdo in a Margaret Thatcherish style. She wore rimless spectacles, rolled her eyes quite a bit and had a very good manicure, with mauve nail varnish.

Margaret said that she too had made money from property. She talked about Syed Kamall, a Conservative MEP who was present at the dinner, a rare non-white presence at a Conservative gathering. When David asked why she thought people like Kamall wanted to serve as MEPs, she said with frank incredulity: 'They're on £350,000 a year – and they make £850,000 if they've got a wife.' This did not make much political or mathematical sense. But having established that Margaret was single, David asked if she was thinking of getting married to an MEP. She responded in kind, and soon she was openly flirting with him. The riff was: 'You be Dave the Tory MEP and I'll be your Tory wife and we can be on the gravy train together.' Later, Margaret dragged David off to speak to Kamall with the idea of starting the process of being selected and promoted as a Tory MP, claiming that she had direct contacts in Conservative Central Office who 'could make things happen'. Kamall, however, did not seem very interested. He simply gave David his card and told him to give him a ring. 'Maybe we can talk . . .'

While David was away chatting to Kamall, Margaret leaned over towards me and said, wide-eyed: 'Your friend is amazing. And he's the only black person in the room.' I took this to mean that, if he wanted to, David could exploit the situation in any way he liked. She seemed very excited about it all, rather like a promoter who had just spotted some new, raw boxing talent. Later, when Margaret thought I wasn't listening, I saw her get Gloria's attention, nod towards David and mouth: 'He's perfect. Central Office would love him. He's got absolutely everything.'

With the dinner over and people beginning to drift away, David and I sloped off to the hotel bar downstairs for a quiet drink. The Bullingdon mob had got there first, and were sprawled over the bar stools, drinking cocktails from bizarrely shaped glasses. The men were wearing smart James Bond-type suits and the women little black dresses, and it appeared that they had booked rooms. For them, we reckoned, Cecil's speech and the formal dinner had been part of a rich kid's naughty night out – a bit of non-PC stand-up entertainment, followed by a posh supper, a few cocktails in the hotel bar and then upstairs to a luxurious room. They had clearly been putting it away, and they were not in the least bit interested in us. As we settled down on a low sofa, out of earshot of the young bucks – our conversation masked by piped jazz – I marvelled that David had managed to stay in character and not become annoyed. I had been taken aback by Parkinson's remarks about Africa – especially his talk about the continent having been a Garden of Eden that had been destroyed by Africans – specifically black Africans – in spite of the efforts of Ian Smith and sundry other white supremacists and Wild Geese-type mercenaries. In my naivety I thought that David might have been a bit freaked out by that, not least because, as Margaret had remarked, he was the only black person in the room. When I put this to David he shrugged and smiled, and sat there picking at the complimentary peanuts and shaking his head. He said that when Cecil launched into his eulogy of Ian Smith he just thought, 'Here we go again.' He didn't feel especially threatened or angry. The moral, philosophical and political stance of the Tories was hopelessly predictable, David thought. For the best part of forty-one years he had endured the daily grind of racial prejudice, on a sliding scale from institutionalized discrimination to open abuse and threats. You had to know when to pick your battles, he said, otherwise you found yourself in a fight all the time, and that would be both exhausting and self-defeating.

But David and I wondered why Parkinson had zeroed in on Mugabe in that way. He was a former minister of the crown and clearly a well-informed man who had seen a lot of the world, and knew that it was a complicated place, not a simple Punch and Judy Show of good leaders versus evil leaders. Mugabe was a monster, but you couldn't help think he was being singled out because he was a black monster. And if he wasn't there, Africa was so messed up by its colonial history that there was no guarantee that somebody better would come to the fore if Cecil's wish came true and he was assassinated by an SAS death squad. Zambia had been thrown in, surely, just to create the idea that Africans – all Africans – could not rule themselves. What were the implications of that? Restrict the right to vote to white people only? Bring back the British Empire and the slave trade? That wasn't on any sort of practical agenda and, anyway, the EU wouldn't allow it, as UKIP would have been keen to point out. The truth was that Parkinson was probably no more than a hack who felt that he had to earn his fee (if he charged one) as an after-dinner speaker. He probably could not see the point of developing any fresh or original thoughts, especially if he was going to deliver them to a bunch of people as inflexible in their thinking as Gloria and the rest. He was simply stroking them and pushing their buttons in order to give them a good time. Mugabe was perfect for that: he was in the news at the time, and hatred of him allowed people to exercise their moral self-righteousness (he was after all a mass murderer) while denouncing such folk devils as international communism and black nationalism. Some people on the right wing of the party had at one time defined Nelson Mandela as a terrorist who ought to stay in jail or perhaps even be executed. Mugabe was a version of Nelson Mandela that it was still OK to say you wanted to hang. Sticking metaphorical pins into Robert Mugabe and then praying for his death was like voodoo for white people. It was their way of having fun.

Most white people, David said, were unaware of racism because it didn't affect them; maybe they even benefited from it. Why should they care about it anyway? On the other hand, how could Gloria say that Smith had been a 'great man' – even if she thought that – when she was sharing a table with a black person? But she wasn't going to let us spoil her evening. Ian Smith was a figure from the 1960s – a rebel against the Labour government of the day – and she probably had a soft spot for him simply for that reason.

Rather than show your anger, it was important, said David,

to keep your powder dry for when you got pulled over in your car for absolutely no reason at all, or when the local school suddenly decided your kids were far less intelligent than they actually were. If you kicked off every time you got a funny look, or got taken for the hired help when you went into a building for a business meeting, you weren't going to get very far in life. If you went down that road, pretty soon you would drive yourself crazy, and get a reputation for being difficult or even dangerous and violent. For David therefore, who was used to dealing with such things regularly, Cecil Parkinson's views were not very high on his personal agenda.

This was David's survival strategy. You had to take the personal beliefs of people such as Parkinson and those cheering him on as no more than that – just nonsensical and unpleasant things they happened to enjoy thinking. David could see the attraction of picking up a bottle of wine from the table and hurling it at Parkinson's head, but he had trained as a boxer. He knew that the best way of combating such attitudes was to stay light on his feet, keep his guard up and only attack when he was sure of winning. The best strategy in life was to hang in there, roll with the punches and try to win on points.

# EIGHT

# Glastonbury for Squares – Stoneleigh, Warwickshire

The English countryside clearly has a far greater tendency towards conservatism than England's cities and towns. The countryside might be England's green and pleasant land – despite the 4x4s charging all over the place – but there's much less ethnic diversity and country people are noticeably more resistant to change. With the advent of Labour's anti-hunting legislation, which had seen widespread protests by country folk, the divide between country and city people had become harder than ever to ignore.

We picked out the Royal Show – held at the headquarters of the Royal Agricultural Society, near the Warwickshire village of Stoneleigh – as the best place to check out the strength of the bonds between conservatism and the countryside. Stoneleigh is in 'Shakespeare Country' but it's close to Coventry and not far from three motorways – the M40, M6 and M1 – and the society even has its own motorway exit sign. Approaching the Royal Agricultural Society on show day we found it sitting amidst rolling fields and trees as far as the eye could see. Police traffic diversion signs and stewards directed visitors to park in the surrounding fields.

We followed a path downhill from the car park, through the neat rows of highly polished, mid-range family saloons – and the odd Range Rover – towards a bright blue bridge made of iron girders, placed, temporarily we presumed, over a sluggish stretch of the River Avon. Tractors and horseboxes were crossing the bridge and filing into a marshalling ground for exhibitors, an area of concrete and compacted, brick-coloured mud. With a few metal fences, turnstiles and stewards in high-visibility bibs, it felt a bit like approaching a football match, but with a much thinner crowd. Those attending the show looked pretty much like your average urban Saturday afternoon shoppers, with only the occasional person who might pass for a refugee from *The Archers*.

The stewards manning the turnstiles included a fair number of turbaned Sikhs, joking with each other in thick Birmingham accents as they tried to flog overpriced official programmes. These turned out to be little more than a page of platitudinous guff from the boss of the society and lots of dull advertisements. Once clear of the programme sellers, we headed up the other side of the valley, at the top of which were parked two huge digger trucks, their front wheels in the air and the extended shovel arms leaning on each other, creating a triumphal arch through which you entered the main show area. A sign advertised digger-driving lessons at £300 a day.

The Royal Agricultural Society, which provides training for farmers and conducts research into selective breeding of cattle, among other things, is an educational institution. As we learned from the programme and the people around us, its annual show was aimed mainly at people in the farming, livestock and horse-breeding industries. Although the Society and its show are resolutely non-political, the Countryside Alliance – which is extremely political – had a large official presence at the show, and had been granted its own small arena near the entrance. A number of groups with links to the Countryside Alliance had tents and stalls surrounding the arena, among them many I hadn't encountered before, such as the National Gamekeepers' Association, the National Organisation of Beaters, the National Ferret Welfare Society and the Fly Dressers Guild. Also touting for business beside the Countryside Alliance arena was a one-man mole extermination service and a stall selling wickerwork deer.

The Gamekeepers' Association was very quiet. Its display consisted of a powerful looking quad bike with a piece of gun-holding equipment mounted on the front. It looked like a military assault vehicle, capable of some pretty serious anti-social behaviour, and with its big go-anywhere off-road tyres this machine could cut across a ploughed field or crash through woodland if you found yourself caught in a traffic jam. In January 2008 Nicholas 'Fatty' Soames, the Conservative MP and Countryside Alliance stalwart, was prosecuted for driving one illegally – i.e. on a public road without insurance – while three young children, unhelmeted and unrestrained, perched beside him. Some years ago, Ozzy Osbourne nearly killed himself by driving one of these things into a tree.

More intriguingly, the Gamekeepers' Association was selling a pin-up calendar of various duchesses and female landowners, fetchingly photographed in hacking or hunting garb. Some of the pictures also featured whips, jackboots, guns, knives, swords, racks full of guns, spears, suits of armour, deadly battleaxes, hooks and the like. The whole effect was like a *Country Life* 'girls in pearls' feature crossed with a slice of Max Mosley's imagination. The women were photographed looking glamorous and interacting with their gamekeepers in a way I found very suggestive of *Lady Chatterley's Lover*.

The Fly Dressers' Guild had a table at which members were sitting making decoys and lures for fly fishing, with the intention of selling them on the internet. The National Organisation of Beaters' tent was empty and there was nothing really to see in it other than a banner reading 'National Organisation of Beaters'.

In the Countryside Alliance's arena the main action was provided by a group of three or four men in bowler hats and white coats, who were chasing about twenty bloodhounds around the fenced-off area and controlling them with heavy whips made out of thick rope. The dogs were huge slobbering creatures – a bit like 'The Hounds' which Montgomery Burns regularly sets on Bart and Homer Simpson. Apart from David and me, hardly anyone stayed to watch and we began to feel conspicuous. The bowler-hatted men tried to keep the dogs under control with shouts and toots on a little hunting horn that sounded like a kazoo. But basically the dogs, with no particular scent to follow, were spinning off in all directions, bounding around and gushing saliva. A man on a microphone gave a very patchy and rather bored commentary, describing the pack of hounds and where they came from. Every few minutes he fawningly thanked the 'Master of Hounds for allowing the dogs to be displayed'.

After a few minutes the men tried to get the hounds back into a cramped cage but one or two escaped, causing the bowler-hatted men to run after them and attack them quite severely – it seemed to us – with their heavy whips. Once the animals were safely in the cage a passer-by – an average looking man with a pot belly – asked one of the handlers to explain the difference between a foxhound and a bloodhound. The handler had piggy eyes and a hat that came right down over his head so that it rested loosely on his ears. He seemed intensely annoyed by the question. He replied, with a heavy note of sarcasm, 'Well, for a start they's a totally different shape and they's gorra sense of smell which is about thirty times stronger. But apart from that, not much.' A woman dog handler chipped in. She sounded like a member of the Grundy clan from *The Archers*: 'They can follow the scent orra man fur up to three days, they can.' 'Are they used to hunt people?' asked the pot-bellied man, at which the handler chuckled to himself and looked at his colleagues from beneath his bowler hat. His expression seemed to say, 'Here we go – bloody townie.'

Next to the arena and its bloodhound display stood the main Countryside Alliance tent, a large marquee with a display about the activities of the group, with a banner reading 'Fight Prejudice'. Despite this, the Alliance, as far as we could see, was very much an all-white outfit. It was hard to see how an interest in keeping bloodhounds – which, we later learned, were originally bred to hunt down slaves escaping from plantations in the southern United States – was likely to enhance the Countryside Alliance's reputation for fighting prejudice. Inside the Alliance tent we also found a man with a bird of prey perched on a glove on his arm, and an area where people could sign petitions or join the organization. But there was very little going on and the whole thing was very overstaffed.

With little else to do, a Countryside Alliance functionary approached my teenage daughter, who had come along for the trip, and asked, 'Do you ride?' She thought about this and replied with a cheeky grin, 'Well, I've got a bike', and asked if that counted. The man raised his eyebrows and said, with a faintly sinister smile and a country accent, 'No, that's not a country sport.' At this point more Countryside Alliance officials, some wearing the ubiquitous bowler hats and carrying pamphlets, began to gather near us. We accepted the pamphlet thrust upon us and beat a hasty retreat, melting into the larger crowd of people heading towards the main part of the Royal Show.

If you listened to the National Farmers' Union – one of the most effective pressure groups in the country – you might have thought the rural economy was on the brink of ruin. But from what we saw at the Royal Show there still seemed to be plenty of money sloshing around in the countryside. A large area of the show was devoted to the display and sale of new cars, with car manufacturers proudly exhibiting their top-of-the-range luxury 4x4s, family saloons, amphibious-looking jeeps and quad bikes. Video screens attracted the punters, showing shiny vehicles roaring and bouncing across fields and plunging through rivers. A few gentleman farmer types – wearing green wellies, flat caps and hacking jackets – were comparing the various luxury jeeps and four-wheel-drive cars. Nearby displays of tractors and farming equipment were, to a great extent, being ignored.

The most crowded area of the show – in fact the only crowded area – was the huge section devoted to food and drink. If the idea was to display the best of British food, all it seemed to do was show the causes of obesity. The food hall was the size of an aircraft hangar, and dotted about it were market stalls and various areas designated for eating. In the largest of these, diners were entertained by a man playing a Yamaha organ, very much in the style of Edward Heath, our piano-playing former Prime Minister. Outside, each of the major supermarket chains had a large and semi-permanent looking tent. These were attracting really big crowds, especially for the live displays of cookery – such as how to make the perfect (very high-fat) steak sandwich – which were done on little stages with amplification. The whole experience was exactly like watching a cookery show on daytime TV.

Next to the supermarket tents was another eating and drinking area, this one about the same size as the indoor food hall. People were tucking in to what was basically junk food – pork pies, roast lamb sandwiches, lots of 'farm fresh' (whatever that meant) ice cream, honey, jam, pastry and handmade fudge. And sausages – what seemed like hundreds and hundreds of different types of speciality sausages. As far as we could tell all the food on display contained very high levels of fat, but there was a sort of implication that because the people dishing it up were wearing straw boaters, and because the food was being eaten in industrial, semi-agricultural surroundings, with various prize-winning blue ribbons and rosettes in evidence, it was somehow wholesome. There were a lot of fat and unhealthy looking people sitting around trestle tables. It seemed that for more than a few of them eating was a hobby, and they were sampling food from all the produce stalls, working their way around them one by one.

Despite all this dietary unhealthiness, the National Vegetable Society did have a stall in the second most popular part of the show – the garden centre. Here a woman was dispensing advice in the style of *Gardeners' Question Time* – 'Me courgettes – in me vegetable bed – me courgettes were getting five inches long, then they turn yellow and die. What can I do about it?' 'That happens,' said the person from the society, with a thick Brummie accent, 'that happens sometimes. Don't worry about it. It'll put itself right. The plant's probably not big enough yet to support 'em. But it'll put itself right.' The questioner seemed to be satisfied by this piece of ancient wisdom and shuffled off. What was worrying was that even the people who made the effort to grow vegetables looked unhealthy. More so that they were defeated by the task of growing courgettes, which, as I understood it, was only slightly more difficult than growing mould on the side of a damp wall.

Outside the food hall and garden centre hangars the crowd initially thinned out and then became noticeably more healthy and wealthy as you moved towards the equine part of the showground. It quickly became evident that this was a private scene for those involved with horses, and that what they were doing was showing off in front of each other. There were two large display areas, each with a small grandstand and a commentary box. In the first there was a display which involved girls of ten years old or younger sitting on pet ponies, dressed in child-size fox-hunting gear and being led around the arena by women in elaborate Victorian circus ring leader costumes. The little girls wore crash helmets, navy blue jackets and yellow trousers and jackboots and some even had double-barrelled names. The PA speaker boomed away in a cut-glass female accent – 'It's a very prestigious event this . . . Henrietta has won this event – she's only six years old – what a great start in life. And the prize is being given by her grandmother. How proud must she be. What a tremendous thrill that must be, ladies and gentlemen, and a better start in life than that is hard to imagine . . .'

In another part of the showground cows were parading in a special cattle display arena in front of a grandstand that was probably about two-thirds empty. Judging from the non-League football matches I have attended, there were probably no more than five hundred spectators. The commentator here was hyper-active and not as posh-sounding, explaining at one point that his normal job was as a stock auctioneer. He rattled his commentary off in a repetitive, high-speed percussive stream of consciousness: 'British cows British food and British milk – complete quality all the way ladies and gentlemen all the way through to our very generous sponsors Marks and Spencer and we are certainly very very grateful to them and they are supplying this great quality food ladies and gentlemen to you the consumer in your home and for you to consume and that is right and long should it continue as I am sure it will.' The cows were led around the arena to desultory applause. To me it somehow resembled a sort of Hindu fundamentalist beauty contest, except that the contestants here (to my untrained, townie eyes at least) looked fabulously ugly – gigantic biotech machines for producing excess protein, fat and milk, the bulls with nightmarish, slobbering mouths and faces which looked as if they had been smashed into a wall and reassembled in the wrong order. And cows – lots of different shapes and sizes but all with terrifying and pendulous udders the size of spacehoppers. I didn't stay for long.

In the general 'quality living' section of the showground there was a furniture shop called Betta Life which seemed to be selling kitchens. The saleswoman was standing alone in the middle of her large tent and complaining into her mobile phone in a Yorkshire accent, 'There's abserlootely norbuddy 'ere at all. I haven't had anyone come in all fooking day.' Next door the Christians in the Countryside Mission tent was similarly bereft. My daughter and I looked around their tent, reading a display of signs, one of which made the incorrect and needless boast that Christians had invented medical care. As we were loudly denouncing this insult to Islam (the Muslims invented medicine and that's a fact) a slightly creepy bloke wearing sandals and a Terry Waite beard (and general demeanour) came up to us and said, 'Would you like a cup of tea and a chat?' We made our excuses and left.

It was equally deserted in the International Zone which was dominated by a huge tent erected in honour of the Falkland Islands. The tent had no punters, but there were six bored officials who leapt upon us as soon as we showed an interest. One of the officials tried to sell us the idea of taking a holiday in the Falklands – which failed on the twin grounds that it would cost £3000 to fly there and, once you arrived, there was nothing to do other than look at penguins and bits of old wood. The official countered this objection by giving us a list of 'Falkland Islands Events' which, we noted, climaxed with the celebration of Margaret Thatcher Day (10 January).

Strangely, the Falkland Islands tent was in the same row as one erected by Argentina, and separated only by Ukraine, whose display of agricultural produce was restricted to about thirty different types of vodka, some plastic bottles of greenish-orange cooking oil and some unhealthy and unappetizing Swiss roll presented in cellophane with gaudy Cyrillic writing on it. All this stuff was just plonked artlessly on a plastic bench, except for the vodka, that is, which was in a glass case under lock and key. There appeared to be a vast number of Ukrainian officials inside the tent, but they were chatting away to each other, laughing raucously and drinking vodka as though the idea that anyone would want to come and do business with them had evaporated hours ago, if it had ever existed in the first place.

As we were leaving, desperate looking officials were promoting the August Bank Holiday 'Festival of the Countryside'. This event, held on the same showground, was aimed more squarely at the mainstream urban population. Judging from the publicity material it conformed to the widespread suburban view that the countryside is just one big motoring-based adventure park suitable for 4x4 off-roading, quad-bike riding, monster truck racing, 'classic car' appreciation, demolition derbies and the occasional competitive displays of gigantic digging machines, tanks and other military equipment.

That was for the men. To make the 'Festival of the Countryside' a family event, and not just a national convention of Jeremy Clarkson impersonators, women could be parked in the all-weather, indoor garden show and antiques fair. For the kids there was the usual disappointing offer of petting zoo, face painting and worksheets, functioning as a thin conscience-salving crust on the reality of junk food and overpriced fun fair rides.

Driving back to London the long way (out of sheer boredom, down side roads and avoiding the motorway), I decided that the English countryside was really pretty unattractive, at least outside the National Parks. I am reluctant to write this down, because it might be held against me as a sort sacrilege against nature or evidence of insanity. When you examined it carefully almost the entire countryside was really just a glorified suburb, much of it a type of low-density sprawl of soulless 'executive' housing developments serviced by supermarkets, with identikit barn-like exterior cladding and ersatz clock towers, weathervanes and what have you.

The marketing power of 'the countryside' was still powerful, though, a symbol of the good life and of high social status. On the evidence of our foray into Warwickshire, however, every crummy and industrially produced junk food joint in every motorway service station in the country seemed to be called something like Country Kitchen; and there was the Harvester restaurant chain. And every middle-class person seemed to aspire either to having a little cottage out there in the country, or maybe to retire there. Yet the reality was fields of luminous yellow oil seed rape, and scrubby, neglected land on the margins of cities. When it came down to it, village life was a matter of isolated strangers living in their second, or retirement, homes and staying indoors.

If I was on the track of Conservative England I reckoned I was not going to find it in what passed for 'the countryside'. The Conservative Party (not quite the same thing as Conservative England) had wielded political power in the shires for generations, and also at a national level for most of the twentieth century. If it was the job of Conservatives to conserve, they had not been doing a very good job of it.

# NINE

# The Heart of Clarkness – Kensington, London

The parliamentary constituency of Kensington and Chelsea has iconic status among Conservatives. It contains some of the richest households in the country, it is one of the safest Conservative seats and many Conservative movers and shakers live there. At the time of our visit to a summer party held by one of the Conservative Association's ward organizations, the seat was held by the slightly dull Malcolm Rifkind. Before Rifkind, the MP had been Michael Portillo, and before him the entertaining Alan Clark, scourge of modern PR people, focus groups and image consultants and a man who was very far from afraid to speak his mind.

Clark had been non-PC in almost every imaginable way. He was a serial adulterer, described by his long-suffering wife as 'a shit' after it was revealed in the *News of the World* that he had conducted an affair with the wife of a South African judge *and* his two daughters. When Clark complained that the three women ('a coven of witches') had sold their story to the tabloid, his wife had little sympathy: 'Well, what do you expect when you sleep with below-stairs types?' she reportedly said. He was also a bit of a hero in Tory circles for having been caught driving his Porsche at 99 mph while he was a cabinet minister, and admitting to being drunk while making a ministerial announcement in the House of Commons.

But there was a darker side to the eccentric and caddish

persona which Clark revealed in his best-selling diaries (drama-
tized in 2004 by the BBC). He mocked the idea of independence
for African countries, saying that they might as well be called
'Bongo Bongo Land'. He had expressed anxiety to friends that
the Prime Minister Margaret Thatcher was being overly influ-
enced by Jewish Conservative activists and voters in her north
London constituency of Finchley, and that, because of this,
there were 'too many Jewboys' in the cabinet. He had once
described himself to an astounded interviewer, with no apparent
irony, as having gone beyond Conservatism to become a
convinced National Socialist, which is to say a Nazi.

But, as if to show that the Conservative Party was a broad
church, the current MP, Malcolm Rifkind, was Jewish. In his
diaries Alan Clark described Rifkind as 'a weasel'. The
constituency party also selected Michael Portillo as candidate
– he inevitably became its MP – knowing that the former
Defence Minister had admitted to gay relationships in the past.
Clark feared homosexuals and was on record as saying that he
would never drink from the same glass as a known homosexual
in order to avoid the possibility of catching AIDS. However,
unpredictable to the last, he had also turned up to support
events run by pro-gay rights pressure groups.

This year the Kensington and Chelsea Conservative Party had
chosen a near-perfect venue for its annual summer soirée – the
Queen's Club on the west side of Kensington, towards
Hammersmith. Every June, Queen's hosts the Stella Artois tennis
championship, which functions as a warm-up tournament
before Wimbledon. Tennis buffs claim the grass courts at
Queen's are the best in the world.

The summer party had been organized by the Queen's Gate
ward branch of the Kensington and Chelsea Conservative Party,
and took place in a function room on an upper floor of the
clubhouse. The room had French windows leading out onto a

balcony overlooking the tennis courts. On the floor below there was a larger balcony with views of the courts, where Queen's Club members were milling about in pristine tennis whites and drinking gin and tonics, all straight out of *The Great Gatsby*, with jumpers and racquets casually slung over their shoulders. It was, fittingly, a warm, tranquil evening.

David and I arrived independently, and at slightly different times, so that we could observe any differences in the way we were treated. David got there first. As the only black person, it seemed, in the entire club – let alone seeking admission to the Conservative function – he immediately attracted attention. The man on the door, a stiff chap wearing a very well-cut grey two-button suit, greeted David in a perfectly pleasant but guarded way. His name was Robin and he was the MC for the evening.

'So, what brings you here?' Robin asked. David explained that he was interested in hearing the guest speaker – the professional explorer and adventurer Colonel John Blashford-Snell, who had lately returned from visiting a tribe called the Wai Wai in the South American jungle. Robin seemed unconvinced, and continued in clipped and quizzical military tones: 'Do you live in Queen's Gate ward?' The subtext seemed to be: we know who lives in the ward; if you lived in the ward we would have noticed you, so what are you up to? David replied, truthfully, that he lived in Battersea, and then let slip that Wandsworth was his local authority, suggesting he was connected to the shock troops of the Wandsworth Conservative Party. At the mention of the magic words, Robin visibly relaxed, and he seemed both delighted and amused to receive a visit from this new acolyte of the famous Labour-crushing operation just south of the river.

David elaborated on why he had turned up: he was especially interested in Blashford-Snell because the Wai Wai tribe lived in Guyana. David's family came from Guyana, so he was naturally drawn to the subject. Also, although David did not let on, we were interested in the fact that Blashford-Snell had taken a piano up the Amazon and donated it to the tribe, seemingly as a way of introducing them to the delights of Western civilization.

My own entry was far more straightforward. I just showed my ticket and was directed along the corridor with no fuss, no questions asked. By the time I reached the room where the talk was due to take place David was well embedded, leaning against a wall with a drink and looking a bit disgruntled. There were about 150 people present at the gathering, and the room was crowded. David was very smartly dressed and looked to me like a well-off businessman, which meant that he didn't stand out as much as he might have done. As he told me more than once, the higher he rose in the social hierarchy, the more he found that the only colour that mattered was the colour of money.

Although many of those present were getting on in years, the proportion of young people was higher than I had seen at similar Tory events. This crowd was all about old money, good grooming and sophistication – with expensive taste and education in evidence all around. It was *Spectator* territory, the *FT* and the top end of the *Telegraph*. Not many of your non-U, middle-brow *Daily Mail* Tories, and probably no *Sun* readers at all. It was all very public school, Oxbridge, good suits, Jermyn Street shirts and handmade shoes.

Blashford-Snell entered from a side door and began sorting out his PowerPoint presentation on a screen at the far end of the room. He had about him an air of the Groucho Marx character Captain Spaulding, the African explorer. Disappointingly, the parallel only extended so far – he hadn't arrived in a sedan chair smoking a cigar, carried by four burly African bearers in grass skirts. Robin the MC called the meeting to order and the colonel bumbled into action.

His talk had something of a military briefing about it, and he made me think of Fowler, the RAF character in the film *Chicken Run*. If he didn't have the complete attention of his audience at this early stage, Blashford-Snell soon enlivened the lecture with holiday snapshot-type slides of himself and his team at various points in their adventure. When he finally reached the part where he met the Wai Wai, the colonel mentioned the South American native women 'who welcomed us as only South American native woman can', which was taken as an Alan Clark-like boast that sex with the local women was on offer to the colonel and his team. This went down well with the youngish audience – especially a small knot of men in their early twenties, decked out in Young Fogey suits and looking like chubby public schoolboys. In fact, the Young Fogeys found the speech riotously funny, and cheered and jeered at the appropriate moments throughout. One of them had a peculiar Edward Heath shoulder laugh, his whole body quaking as he hooted away.

Ignoring the laughs, the colonel's face took on a dreamy look and he proceeded to draw a connection between the native women of South America and black women in inner-city London. Speaking without notes, he said: 'You know, it is rather similar with the Black People in Brixton . . . you have these tremendous bossy black women down there who organize the community.' Like the tribal matriarchs of the Amazon jungle, the black women of Brixton were tremendously resourceful, according to the colonel: 'They look after their community and you have to see it – they organize things in their garden sheds.' He had done some charity work in south London. The bossy black women, he had found, could do 'something useful' with almost any old tat they were given. He had supplied them with some redundant computers and they had 'worked wonders' with this equipment. Then, without much conviction, he called on the people in the room to consider heading down to Brixton, find a bossy black mother – perhaps in a shed somewhere – and present her with similar hand-me-downs. It seemed to me that precisely nobody in the room would bother to do that.

The colonel returned to his PowerPoint lecture. As an aside, he related how Queen Victoria had been annoyed by the government of Bolivia and demanded that a gunboat be sent to teach them a lesson. On learning that Bolivia was landlocked and there was no way of getting a boat up the river, she had simply ordered that the country be removed from all British maps of the world. And this is exactly what happened, the colonel said: 'Bolivia didn't appear on British maps for many years'.

After telling this story – which got another rousing cheer – he told his audience how he had made a boat out of straw and bamboo sticks and, rather like the *Kon-Tiki*, sailed up a river with a crew of natives. When the colonel then described how the boat had fallen to pieces going over some rapids, nearly drowning the crew, there was more laughter; and the place itself fell apart as he described how he patched the boat up and finally donated it to the Brazilian navy.

Returning to a more domestic agenda, the colonel moved on to talk about the threat to the health of young people caused by lack of sport and fitness. The much earlier Conservative policy of selling off playing fields so that, as he put it, council houses could be built on the land, had been 'a disaster'. Sport and physical activity, he believed, were the answer to a swathe of problems faced by young people. Margaret Thatcher, he said, had agreed with him on this. Twenty years earlier, Mrs Thatcher had given him 'two thousand youths to take up to Fort George in Scotland, so I could straighten them out'. And it had worked. Presumably somewhere in Britain there are two thousand straightened-out forty-year-olds who still bear the scars. Perhaps they will at some point set up a Victim Support Group and appear on *The Trisha Goddard Show*.

But there was more. The colonel said that the charity he ran had a pair of sail-assisted tug boats that were used to take youths in danger of straying into a life of crime out to sea for two weeks of uninterrupted 'straightening out'. After that he returned them to dry land, presumably more than ready to become model citizens, or, it struck us, self-employed pirates. 'I can do five hundred a year,' he claimed. If you took the UKIP estimate of 130 million crimes a year, and assumed that most of these crimes were committed by the sort of youths the colonel had in mind, and at the rate of one crime per youth, then it would take a mere 260 million years to solve society's problems in this way.

After the lecture I struck up a conversation with an unusual looking man dressed like a dandy in bright red trousers and a waistcoat, with a pocket watch on a sturdy gold chain. I liked his style, I told him. 'Oh yes!' the dandy replied, delighted that someone had noticed his appearance. 'Me red trews . . . I'm glad y'like 'em.' He explained that he dressed that way because he had 'dressed like a funeral director' all his life, so now he thought he would have some fun. He asked me where I was from; when I told him Richmond his face fell and he changed the subject. He pointed out of the window, across the balcony to the lawn tennis courts where several matches were in progress: 'Look at all the tennis people. Aren't they marvellous? I was no good at rugger, cricket, ball games. No good at team games. My thing is sailing. But I'm not like Blashford-Snell, though. I don't want to go anywhere that's hot, got creepy-crawlies or slime.'

The dandy's wife (or partner) liked the colonel's anecdote about Bolivia being expunged from the map. Mrs Dandy suggested, perhaps teasingly, that syphilis had originated in Bolivia. The dandy then started eyeing up Blashford-Snell, clearly planning to chat to him. He told me in hushed tones that the colonel had a strange party trick: 'He goes round to people's hizzizz and pulls all the stuffing out of their sofas and then stuffs it back in again. It's his hobby.' The dandy and his wife moved over towards the colonel, trying – and failing – to shake me off.

'Don't I know you?' the colonel said to the dandy, through narrowed eyes, as he approached. 'You do!' the dandy teased in a sing-song voice. The colonel was slightly stumped. 'Were you in the army?' he ventured. 'Nope!' The dandy then put the colonel out of his misery by explaining how, twenty years earlier, they had been at the same party and the colonel had taken the stuffing out of a sofa. 'Ahhh, yes,' said the colonel, looking extremely perplexed. 'It was one of those parties.' The dandy disappeared, leaving behind him a queue of women waiting to thank the colonel politely for his speech.

'Why do they do all this, with the knives?' asked one woman, referring to the colonel's work with the black matriarchs of Brixton and among young people in general.

'It's because they're bored,' the colonel said without hesitation and with complete conviction. 'It is as simple as that.'

'How do we fix this?' the woman asked.

'We make them not bored,' the colonel responded, which, if you accepted his premise, was a pretty logical argument. 'We give 'em . . . you know . . . playing fields, games, money to buy books, and . . . y' know . . . computers . . .' and he flicked a hand to emphasize what he was saying.

The colonel remained remarkably consistent with his line of argument. Boredom was the problem – the root of all evil, as it were – and these problem youths with knives just 'needed to be kept busy'. One stray person, a middle-aged bloke – perhaps trying to be funny – asked, 'but why are they bored?' The colonel, previously so categorical, was now lost in thought. He paused for a very long time, swaying back and forth on the balls of his feet as he mulled over the problem. Finally he pronounced: 'It is because they haven't got anything to do.'

'Isn't that because they've got no money?' the middle-aged

man replied. 'Surely,' he continued, 'if they had a load of money, they wouldn't stay bored for very long . . .'

David, meanwhile, was finding all this hard to put up with. He told me he had been far more provoked by Blashford-Snell and all this talk of black women in Brixton than he had been by all the Vera Lynn-era Empire loyalism of Cecil Parkinson at the Conservative Party dinner in Belgravia. He felt he had to move away from clusters of conversation, in case he just opened up. Despite his well-thought-out survival strategy, he felt that this time he was in danger of losing his temper and getting into a slanging match.

David is one of the most sociable and friendly men I have ever met. It can sometimes be a problem going to a pub or a petrol station with him, because within minutes he'll be jawing with some total stranger. Several times during our journey, David had apparently clicked with some of the Tories, probably because of his charm and easy manner. But at Queen's people seemed to be immune to this, at least in the room in which the colonel was speaking. There was nobody in there David thought he could speak to, and the other people, seeing him on his own, didn't bother to talk to him. It looked as if he might end up talking to the Polish serving staff, but, if anything, they were even more wary of him.

At Queen's we felt that we were in the company of people who actually exercised power of some sort, and they were younger and appeared to be much better educated and more sophisticated than some of the Tories we had met. And yet they were still prepared to give Blashford-Snell house room, to revel in his stories of playing the great white chief lording it over the darkies with their risible straw boats, their child-like musicality and lack of pianos. Even if some of the Billy Bunter student types appeared to be laughing at the colonel, rather than with him, David really could not stomach it. It had got to him. And it was hot. All around was the rhythmic sound of the tennis matches in progress, the swirling, psychedelic pattern of the carpet – pygmy Tories with PowerPoints, sausages on sticks instead of skulls, red trousers and, probably, poison blow-pipes. The Horror! The Horror! – The Heart of Clarkness.

David made the break for it through the French windows and onto the balcony terrace where there was a different gaggle of guests, about ten in all. They were all men and they were young, mostly in their thirties. There was a double-take when David recognized one of the group as a fellow member of his local boxing gym. They chatted briefly, and it turned out that the man was a stockbroker who had been invited along by business contacts. He wasn't very political, and liked to attend Queen's for social and sporting reasons. He wasn't the least bit interested in listening to Blashford-Snell, whom he regarded as something between a curiosity to be pitied and an idiot to be ignored.

David felt much more confident with these younger guys. They were very interested in money and, to a lesser extent, physical fitness and sport. They did not seem to give two hoots for the Conservative Party of the white man's burden and so on. Exporting pianos to South America? Sure, they would probably think, but only if there was a 500 per cent mark-up on the supply contract. They were fun-loving gym-attending young bucks with City connections, and they pointedly ignored the colonel and the proceedings inside the room, to and beyond the point of rude-ness. They chatted to David about the gym and about boxing, and they spoke intermittently into astoundingly expensive-looking mobile phones which looked as if they were made of something like lacquered titanium and ivory and were as thin as credit cards.

When you got down to politics with these people they thought the Conservative Party was pretty hopeless, narrow-minded and nowhere near global enough in its thinking. In their world, race, nationality and skin colour had ceased to matter long ago. They spent their time in swish offices, on aero-planes, and at elite sports events, the latter an industry in itself, functioning as a continuous year-round convention for those who successfully created, traded and invested money. On a weekday evening the Queen's Club only just made it onto the map of that world, a very minor portal, a tiny satellite on the furthest rim of wherever the real action was taking place.

The gathering at Queen's that evening re-emphasized in miniature what seemed to us to be a fundamental fault line on the political right. On the balcony terrace you had the libertarian free-marketeers who weren't interested in ideas about nations and race. Deregulation and free trade, they said, had led, and was always bound to lead, to the fading away first of the power of the nation state, and finally perhaps of a national identity itself. Entire industries, among them farming, coal mining and fishing, had been destroyed by unrestrained market forces. And free trade on a global scale had led to the phenomenon of mass migration, as people followed wealth and jobs, something they had always done throughout history and throughout the world.

Inside, hiding from the evening sunshine and listening to Blashford-Snell, were people who seemed, to us, whether or not they were aware of it, to represent the other side of the Conservative movement – the people, now generally older, and with less power and money, who valued ideas of nation and tradition above all else. It was this wing of the Conservative Party which was more likely to take a keen and not necessarily approving interest in immigration, which was more likely to stand up when the national anthem was played, and which wanted to preserve its idea of the countryside and generally keep things the way they had always been.

For the time being at least, both these broad types of people – global-view neo-liberals and traditionalist Britishers – were happy to be associated with the Conservatives. But, as we found out during our visit to the Queen's Club, they were not necessarily happy to stand in the same room as each other.

# TEN

# This Land Is My Land –
# Blenheim, Oxfordshire

At the Royal Show at Stoneleigh, Warwickshire, I had encountered Countryside Alliance types and their friends; now it was David's turn to take the lead in meeting them. Accordingly, he attended the fiftieth annual Country Landowners' Association (CLA) Game Fair at Blenheim Palace in Woodstock, just outside Oxford. A Baroque masterpiece designed by Vanbrugh, with gardens laid out by Capability Brown, as well as being the ancestral home of the Dukes of Marlborough, Blenheim was the birthplace of Sir Winston Churchill. Once there, David found his way to the Countryside Alliance tent where he discovered celebrity chef Clarissa Dickson Wright, the staunch Conservative, red meat-loving, ex-alcoholic, former co-presenter (along with the late Jennifer Paterson) of the TV series *Two Fat Ladies*, poking out from behind a large pile of books on a small table at the edge of the tent.

Clarissa had four separate titles for sale in front of her but not many takers. She was chatting away to a rare passing punter, reminiscing about her years of boozing and gorging which she seemed to have enjoyed. Those years, and the passage of time, had left her now looking distinctly unhealthy, if her pale, waxy skin and bloodshot eyes were anything to go by. She wore an ill-fitting black polo shirt bearing a pro-hunting slogan, 'DAMN THIS BAN', and she looked somewhat uncomfortable in the mid-afternoon heat.

After a while a youngish man with close-cropped hair, who looked as if he had had a bit too much to drink, walked up to Clarissa and said, 'All right, love . . . How's it going?', as he pumped her hand vigorously. 'Fine,' said Clarissa, turning with discomfort and distaste to get a better look at him. He wanted her to know that he was right behind her and the campaign. Then he hurried off, as though on an urgent mission.

Next up was a portly, middle-aged woman in a wide-brimmed lime-green sun hat. She was grinning like the Cheshire Cat and wanted to know more about Clarissa's plans for the future. Was she intending to do any more television work? 'No, I can't be bothered with it,' Clarissa replied. 'The fees are the same as they used to be years ago. You can't afford to take on enough people to do it properly.' This led on to a discussion about the woes of the country in general, and the possibility of change of government.

'Do you think this lot are finished, then?' asked somebody else in the small queue which had now formed in front of Clarissa. 'Oh, I'd say so,' she replied without much enthusiasm. 'Definitely, definitely,' yelped the woman in the lime-green hat. Clarissa turned deadly serious: 'I don't actually do politics. I'm happy writing at the moment . . . and campaigning. But it is very good. We're really getting somewhere, especially with this silly hunting ban.'

With a membership of some 36,000, much like the Countryside Alliance the Country Landowners' Association has a simple mandate: to protect the rights of country folk. Well, country folk who happen to be private landowners, that is. One of the CLA's chief priorities for 2008 was to 'defend private property rights in England and Wales and insist on compensation when private property rights are diminished in any way'. This point, at the head of their policy agenda, went to the heart of a 'campaign to minimize the impact of statutory public access provisions and promote the benefits of an incentive-led voluntary approach whether this is access to coastal areas, rivers or woodland'. In other words the CLA's *raison d'être* is, 'Get off my land!'

In contrast to the Royal Agricultural Show, which focused mainly on farming and food production (with some horse-rearing on the side), at the CLA Game Fair farming was a sideshow. While the CLA did have legitimate concerns about the state of the British farming industry, a relatively small amount of the countryside was actually given over to farming. What seemed to me, on closer scrutiny, to be at the very core of the CLA's existence was the issue of cordoning off vast tracts of beautiful rural land for the exclusive use of a very few extremely wealthy people, to the exclusion of everyone else.

David Cameron had visited the CLA Game Fair the evening before David's visit and, according to a statement issued by the organizers, he had been 'thrilled by what he saw'. Cameron was quoted as saying: 'The CLA Game Fair is bigger and better than ever – it's a good day out. I am delighted it is taking place in my constituency of West Oxfordshire.' Before Cameron rebranded himself as a trendy Notting Hill dweller, following a fashionable, modern lifestyle and ostentatiously riding his bicycle, he had ridden with the Heythrop Hunt in his constituency. Hunting was so close to his heart, he devoted a large chunk of his maiden parliamentary speech to the subject: 'There is a long tradition of hunting in west Oxfordshire, originally based in the royal forest of Wychwood, where Ethelred II established the first royal hunting lodge more than nine centuries ago. I will always stand up for the freedom of people in the countryside to take part in country sports.'

At the fair there was a mind-boggling array of stalls, stands, concessions and displays of varying sizes, all dedicated to that other most English of pastimes: shopping. There was a Hawkshead country casual clothing stand, arts and crafts stalls, cane sellers, hippy chic outfitters, even a massage tent . . . One woman was selling mini fans with built-in water sprayers for £2.99 outside a makeshift toyshop. 'You can even keep the dog cool,' she said, demonstrating its efficacy by spraying a yelping Yorkie being held by a middle-aged couple.

Down Gunsmith Alley and Air Gun Alley there were yet more stalls selling shotguns, air guns and all manner of shooting paraphernalia. In London, anyone walking around with guns slung over their shoulders would arouse the interest of the general public and the police. But not here. Beyond the rows of gun and archery retailers it started to get noisy, and you needed to wear ear protectors to be able to move comfortably along the line of clay pigeon-shooting operators and trainers. It was all laser clays and paintball alleys, pseudo shooting designed to teach kids how to handle weapons and to educate them into the way of the gun, country style. In the archery section, where people stood in shooting galleries (another popular feature of the fair) firing off arrows at rubber animal targets – deer, rabbits, badgers etc. – Bear Grylls, the gung-ho adventurer and television presenter, though he wasn't there in person had a small stall selling survival equipment. "Ere, it's all 'alf price,' shouted a fat woman to her boyfriend as she walked away from the stall. 'That's cos it's crap,' mumbled the boyfriend. They laughed loudly. The guy manning the stall looked out glumly after them from beneath his cammo hat.

For the kids, there was also wakeboarding (sponsored by Fat Face, the 'outdoor lifestyle retailer') and quad biking. For the big kids, there was the Volvo Challenge, which seemed to entail little more than driving up a short dirt track in Volvo's latest 4x4 and then balancing the car on a sort of seesaw, to the amazement of onlookers. On a small patch of grass cordoned off by a white picket fence, a man had laid out an array of plastic birds on the grass and was picking them up individually and asking his rather lackadaisical audience if they could identify them. 'What's that?' he said, holding one up.

'A blackbird,' cried a woman in the crowd. 'Well, it's a bird and it's black but actually it's a carrion crow,' said the bird man. Then he started banging on about shooting birds, the best time of year to catch them, and the joys of pigeon and rook pie. 'Do you know that 250,000 wood pigeon are shot every year?'

At a stall run by Corbieton Enterprises, a Scottish company specializing in deer-stalking equipment and other such accessories for game hunting, a small crowd had gathered. They were watching three synthetic rodent decoys on stands vibrating as they emitted intermittent electronic squawking, yelping and screeching noises. These were the 'Screaming Quiver Rabbit', the 'Ultimate Predator Decoy II' and the 'All Call', which, as the literature boasted, 'lets you put your electronic calling sounds right at the decoy where they'll be the most effective'. This trio of decoys proved irresistible to a balding punter with a Jack Russell. As the furry robot critters shook, rattled and bawled, the dog went spare. His owner thought this was hilarious: 'I know you want them,' he kept teasing, laughing maniacally until the dog was practically foaming at the mouth.

Everywhere there were dogs. Occasionally, a pair would face off, snarling and growling, and their owners would look daggers at each other as well, convinced the other was in the wrong. Sometimes face-offs would turn into a humping session, though, which usually diffused the tension. As at the Royal Show in Stoneleigh, there were plenty of dogs officially on show, including packs of hunting dogs, even though foxhunting was officially banned.

The CLA Game Fair at Blenheim also provided us with a brush with that essential ingredient of English Conservatism – deference to the Royal Family and to the feudal order it still represents. The Duke of Edinburgh was there, we saw his brilliant white panama hat bobbing about as he met members of the British Olympic shooting team and the chairman of the National Gamekeepers' Association.

The Duke looked, among the more smartly dressed country-side types, to be in his element. It struck us again that the countryside, no matter how many National Parks and public bridleways there might be, consists largely of a playground for the rich and well-connected, with their estates, shooting parties and hunts; armies of beaters, gamekeepers and kennel-people and packs of dogs. The Game Fair was a celebration of all that – and all the baffling social ties and distinctions that came with it.

ELEVEN

# *The Grouchy Club – Mayfair, London*

At 69 St James's Street, Mayfair, stands the Carlton Club, a hallowed Conservative institution. Next door to the Carlton Club is William Evans, the gun and rifle makers. There are, however, no guns on display in Evans's window. Instead the windows display the preferred uniforms of wealthy Tory males which we had already seen throughout our travels in both town and country. That is to say white shirts with big blue checks; gilets; flat caps; thermal socks; corduroy trousers in very loud colours such as pink, purple and mauve; brown moccasins; green wellies; duck-print ties; blue blazers; white trousers; hacking jackets, walking sticks and lots and lots of green and brown. Metaphorically speaking, Evans is a dressing-up box for the rich, silver-haired members of the Carlton Club.

From the outside, the Carlton Club is as discreet as a grand neoclassical building can be. With no polished brass name plate by its front door, from the street you'd be hard-pressed to work out what goes on inside. In the nineteenth century, the Carlton was effectively the headquarters of the Conservative Party, long before Conservative Central Office was established in Smith Square. The Conservative Party HQ was recently shifted to Millbank, the modern media centre established by the likes of the BBC, ITV and Sky News for their coverage of Parliament and politics in general. But the Carlton remains today as a

161

prestigious gentlemen's club, and a cathedral to conservatism, where its members can enjoy long lunches, dinners and drinks receptions in surroundings which reflect the building's long association with the Conservative Party. Irresistible, then, to people like David and myself, trying to find the heartbeat of Tory Britain.

The St James's entrance to the Carlton is, it turns out, technically the back door. The actual front of the building, which is much more palatial, looks out over the green sward of St James's Park. There is no obvious security – no heavies on the doors, for example – but we guessed that security is tight but covert, dating back at least to the IRA bombing campaigns in London of the 1970s and 1980s. In June 1990 the Provisional IRA exploded a bomb in the building, injuring more than twenty people.

We visited at teatime in the middle of a week. Parliament was sitting and the club was not very busy, its spaciousness emphasized by the absence of people. We had managed to get into the place as members of a group of about twenty-five Conservative activists from Tatton, in Cheshire, who were enjoying a day out in London (earlier that day we had all been to the Houses of Parliament). As part of our jolly with the Tatton Tories, tea was scheduled in the club's grand Churchill Room. Once inside the club we found we could wander fairly freely, but we had no access to the main lounge, which was for members only. Until very recently women were not admitted to the Carlton, though an exception was made for Margaret Thatcher when she was Prime Minister: she was regarded as an honorary man. When women were finally admitted in 2008, Theresa May, then the Conservative Party Chairman, commented: 'I'm just sorry that it took them this long to join the twenty-first century.'

Despite the Carlton Club's recent lurch towards sexual equality, the place still had a musty, masculine feel to it. Above the fireplace in the lobby hung a Giles cartoon depicting Alan Clark surrounded by Tory grandees fawning over his diaries, and under a huge gilt-edge mirror there was a bust of Denis Thatcher. (From a distance he looked a bit like Eric Morecambe.) Even though they are now both dead, Denis and the Alan Clark cartoon offered the only apparent connections between the club and the modern world. Everywhere else there were gigantic oil portraits of scowling Victorians. Benjamin Disraeli's portrait sat directly above Benjamin Disraeli's chair, which was in the place it had always been, but was now carefully covered with a sheet of Plexiglas to protect it from unwelcome buttocks. For a moment some members of the Tatton group stood mesmerized before the chair, marvelling at how much wear to the red leather upholstery seemed to have been caused by Disraeli's bottom.

I'm not much of a club person myself, on the basis first sketched out by Groucho Marx that any club desperate enough to have me as a member probably isn't worth joining. Not too far from the Carlton is a trendy private members' club for media and advertising folk called the Groucho Club, named in honour of Groucho Marx's line. But, judging from the ferocious looks on the mutton-chopped faces in the oil paintings that lined the Carlton Club, this place was more like the Grouchy Club.

The Churchill Room was a large function room – or possibly a small ballroom – with tall windows and a high ceiling, decked out with tables widely spaced apart. This was the ultimate luxury in a city like London where space is at a premium; it guaranteed one of the principal attractions of the club – privacy. It was possible to spot people and to recognize them in the room, but it was not possible to hear what they were saying. We found the place strangely uncomfortable, not only because we were interlopers but because it was hard to decide if we were in a museum or a restaurant.

The club's interior décor was certainly distinctive and I had seen something similar, particularly in the houses of older Tory activists in Richmond. One classic example was a small, modern house just off the Green in the centre of the town. Inside, the elderly activist's house was an unbridled carnival of chintz. There were flowery curtains and furbelows, Georgian-style chairs, gilt-framed prints of Renaissance architectural drawings and Grecian urns, a few genuine antiques here and there and cut flowers everywhere. If one motif dominated the place, it was that of the cabbage rose. Overall the house was a symphony of good taste in matching and cascading shades of blue satin, a concentrated slice of Versailles spoiled only by the odd bit of Old Person Tat.

The décor in the home of the elderly activist and in the Carlton Club was of a piece: Elysian, neoclassical-to-Georgian, and largely at odds with the world outside. Tea at the Carlton Club was a silver service affair and, as usual, the staff seemed to be mainly Polish, though some were from South Asia. They were obsequious in their white gloves and crisp blue uniforms, ensuring no eye contact was made unless acknowledging a request. When they were not carrying things to and from the tables they loitered in corners of the room like sentries, scanning the tables and waiting to be summoned.

Conversation among the Tatton Conservatives was uncomfortably stilted and largely non-political. Lisa, who was a constituency organizer, her fella and a second, rather glamorous lady with long, dark hair sat impassively, preferring to talk about walking their dogs around Tatton Park or the advantages of shopping in Manchester or Birmingham rather than what direction the Tory Party ought to be taking. They became animated only when talking about London and the South in general, the consensus being that the capital was 'dirty, noisy and overcrowded'. Lisa had tried living there for a while, she said, but failed to break the back of it. She worked for the Tories in Tatton but she actually lived near Crewe, which she described as 'grotty' and a 'horrible little railway town in the middle of nowhere'. Her bloke, who had a quiet, thoughtful air about him, pondered this for a while. 'Well, there's only one good thing you can say about Crewe: it's not Stoke.'

Tea came and went in rather mean quantities. It was not even served on bone china, but regular mass-catering crockery. Tea and scones is traditionally English and here we were enjoying it in a bastion of historic, Conservative, traditional England, under a glowering oil painting of the Duke of Wellington or somebody similar. But the crockery could easily have been from a motorway service station.

With the tea beginning to cool, the star turn arrived. George Osborne, shadow chancellor of Her Majesty's Loyal Opposition, poured himself into the room with a liquid charm and looking a bit effete in an ill-fitting dark blue suit, blue tie and white shirt. If the latest betting was to be believed, George would soon be the second most powerful man in the country. In June 2001 he won Tatton back from the independent candidate Martin Bell, with a majority of 8611. In May 2005 he increased his majority to 11,731. Tatton was solidly Tory once more, and the smooth hand of George could soon be on the Treasury's tiller.

George was kicking back now, working the room and flattering the visiting eccentrics and stalwarts from his constituency, perhaps thinking that it was a good idea to keep in touch with the grass roots. 'Where's me cup of tea then?' he shouted jauntily as he arrived. There were a few mild chuckles and signs of nervous expectation. George's attempt to come across as Mr Ordinary was amusing because he was about as far away from a man of the people as you could get – St Paul's School and Magdalen College, Oxford, followed by scholarships at grad school in the United States and a spell working in the Conservative Research Department. He was fresh and new – young wine in a very old bottle – and the living, modern incarnation of the grandees and magnates displayed in oils on the walls all around him.

Some of the group, which had been sightseeing around Whitehall and the West End earlier in the day, had seen George in a car with William Hague. Hague was still a favourite with the Thatcher wing of the party because of the way he made his promise to reject the euro when he was leader during the 2001 general election.

'William and I had been with George Bush,' he said, the words cascading from his lips like melted chocolate.

'Really? What's he like?' asked one of the group, wide-eyed.

'He's really a nice chap. Not at all as he's portrayed on television . . .' (that's to say as a nitwit with the IQ of a monkey). No matter who the punters were or wherever they hailed from, George had an opinion or a comment. It was all rather painful, really, because the Tatton Tories did not have much to say. Then, just as suddenly as he had arrived George was gone, to be replaced by Nicholas and Ann Winterton, husband and wife MPs for the Cheshire constituencies of Macclesfield and Congleton respectively, in the south Manchester equivalent of the stockbroker belt, not far from Tatton.

Ann Winterton paddled round the room like a clucking mother hen, then stepped up to our table. 'Have you had a lovely day?' she asked, her gaffe-o-meter turned up to full blast, assessing the danger since there were strangers present, and one of them was – probably unusually for the Carlton Club – black. Back in 2002, the then Tory leader Iain Duncan-Smith had sacked Ann as his agriculture spokesman after she made a 'joke' at a rugby club dinner which featured an Englishman throwing a Pakistani off a train because they were 'ten a penny' in Britain. Winterton had apologized but had refused to resign. Two years later, in February 2004, she was again in trouble after telling a joke at a Whitehall dinner party. This time the joke was at the expense of the twenty-three Chinese cockle pickers who had lost their lives in Morecambe Bay. The joke evidently featured a couple of sharks, who were fed up with eating tuna, saying to each other, 'Let's go up to Morecambe Bay for a Chinese.' Initially reluctant to show contrition for this gaffe, she was suspended from the party; only after she eventually apologized was the whip restored.

'Do you go up to Congleton at the weekends?' a woman from Alderley Edge asked. 'Yes,' said Mrs Winterton, she did. She drove up there on Thursdays to avoid all the traffic. The consummate politician, she told them exactly what they wanted to hear: that London was a terrible place, dirty, overcrowded and polluted. Aye, it were great to get up to Cheshire and breathe that good clean Cheshire air.

Because the Wintertons, like turtledoves, worked best in pairs, seventy-year-old Sir Nicholas soon made his way over to our table as well. He wore the regulation dark blue suit, but he had customized it rather nattily with a luminous green tie and matching handkerchief that burst exuberantly out of his top pocket. Curiously, he also had a gold pound sterling symbol brooch on his lapel, which looked exactly like the UKIP logo. At the point when he decided to speak to our table, the talk had somehow moved on to Battersea Power Station. Like a child desperate to jump on a speeding merry-go-round, he dived headlong into the conversation. 'Are you in the building trade, connected with Battersea Power Station or a developer or something?' he asked David, trying to get a fix. 'No,' came the reply, followed by some diversionary talk.

'Do you know, I am very keen on preserving our heritage,' Winterton said, cautiously, 'but I think that maybe buildings like that [i.e. anything non-Victorian or modern] are not really part of a heritage that is frankly worth protecting.' Everyone half-heartedly agreed. Suddenly somebody asked, 'Why is the Carlton Club called the Carlton Club?' Winterton said he didn't know, but he could find out. And off he rushed, asking around, but nobody seemed to know. He returned after a while with the explanation that the name came from the original site of the club, which used to be in Carlton Terrace. He seemed tremendously pleased that he had come up trumps and successfully answered a question.

Days later, however, Ann and Sir Nicholas had some more pressing questions to answer, namely that they had 'unwittingly' broken MPs' expenses rules by claiming an allowance for a second home owned by a family trust. In 2002, they had trans-ferred their second home (a flat in dirty, overcrowded, polluted London) to the trust, to which the taxpayer paid rent of £21,600 per annum. The Commissioner for Standards had said the Wintertons should have known that the rules on second-home allowances had changed. The Wintertons had been among a group of only six Tory MPs to reject David Cameron's demand to publish their expenses in full. The Tory leader described their abuse of the Commons allowances system as 'indefensible'. But Sir Nicholas hit back in unequivocal terms, telling his local paper, the *Macclesfield Express*, that he had been the victim of an 'illegal ageist campaign' by unelected advisers whom he described as 'pedlars of lies'.

'In some quarters there is a group of people who want to see the back of me and Ann,' said Sir Nicholas. 'They may well be David Cameron's sort of mafia that you get around a leader.' He added, 'If David Cameron hasn't got the courage to speak to me personally then I don't think that reflects very well on him.'

The Wintertons moved away to work the rest of the room and I tried to gently steer the conversation towards politics. The Tatton Tories wanted to know where I came from and whether I had a connection with the North West. It was a chance to do my Mancunian nationalist act, and, hoping it would play well and prompt some more exciting conversation, I boldly slagged off the New Labour strategy of trying to regenerate

Manchester by promoting gay rights and hen nights, which had turned Manchester's central canal area into the North's premier boozing and party zone. Instead of rising to the bait they all looked a bit shocked and vaguely disgusted. I can't be sure, but once again I got the sense that Tory minds were wondering whether David and I might in fact be a gay couple.

Looking around at the huge, gloomy oil paintings of Victorian grandees that hung on the walls of the Churchill Room, I had another brainwave. New Labour had also sought to get regeneration going in the North by throwing taxpayers' money into snazzy galleries full of modern art, and had also plonked plenty of modern art sculptures around the North, Antony Gormley's *Angel of the North* being the prime example. Surely bashing modern art and profligate public spending in one go was bound to get the Tatton Tories glowing with pleasure. For good measure I went on about how Manchester had been ruined by the socialists with all their high taxes, unionized dustbin men, human rights agendas and anti-motorist legislation. But the strongest reaction all this prompted was one of the female Tattoners observing that Manchester 'got a bit crowded on Saturdays'. The women knew this because they often went from Tatton to Manchester to shop, like Victoria Beckham once did, in the expensive shops on King Street. I got the impression that, in the main, the Tatton Tories weren't really interested in politics, but perhaps saw involvement with the Conservatives as just a chance for a few drinks parties and days out, like the one they were currently enjoying.

In a last-ditch effort to get a conversation going I went for – in Tatton terms – the Nuclear Option: I gingerly mentioned Neil Hamilton, the disgraced former Conservative MP for Tatton, who had been vanquished by Martin Bell, the independent anti-corruption candidate, in the 1997 general election. Looks of horror suggested that this wasn't a topic the Tatton Tories liked to discuss. But one woman said she had recently seen

Martin Bell talking on the BBC's *The One Show*. 'He was still wearing his white suit,' said the woman, 'or an off-white sort of crème colour I suppose you'd call it.'

Soon after, the gathering had broken up. David and I had been in the company of Conservatives in one of the Conservative Party's most hallowed places, but the whole thing had been strangely non-political. The Tatton Tories didn't seem to have any real passion for politics. Maybe they were more guarded than usual because David and I were there. Or maybe going on an expedition to the Carlton Club was, to them, really no more or less meaningful than a visit to a National Trust property, a civic art gallery, or Manchester's better shops. Or perhaps we had unwittingly touched upon an Important Thing about Conservatism – that many Conservatives, and the Tatton Tories seemed to be among them, want less politics rather than more, because politics might change things, and they wouldn't really like that.

# TWELVE

## *Polo Minted – Chester, Cheshire*

A helicopter circles and descends from a cloudless, dazzling blue sky above Chester racecourse. It lands on the far side of a polo ground, near the tent but well away from the race course's main stand and the large crowds gathering for the evening's entertainment. The arrival attracts the attention of a languid gaggle of middle-aged men in ties and lightweight summer suits accompanied by women in hats and floaty, floral summer dresses.

'Hey, I recognize that helicopter – its Colin's,' says a short, chubby man in a straw fedora, sunglasses, grey suit and a pink tie, the shade of which matches his complexion. He takes up a pair of field glasses so that he can get a good look at the registration number. Then he punches some numbers into a mobile phone and begins an animated conversation: 'Yeah . . . yeah . . . [chuckle] . . . I thought it was your Robinson because I see the call sign . . . Yeah . . . yeah . . . I am looking at it now . . .' The chubby man is beaming with delight. He is talking loudly with a slight Liverpudlian accent and has silenced the rest of the group.

'Yeah . . . yeah . . . where's you come down from? Oh – 'ow long did it take . . .? Thirty-five minutes? . . . Anyway, I just saw your Robinson? And I thought I bet that's Colin's so here we are talking about it . . . what a world. Eh? Heh heh heh . . . OK, mucker, I'll see you soon.'

The chubby man folds his mobile, picks up his drink, takes a good glug and starts boasting that he had come down from the same place as the helicopter and it had only taken him an hour in his car but it had taken the helicopter guy thirty-five minutes: 'Said the wind was against him.' Everyone thinks this is a hoot. He turns to the woman next him, possibly his wife, and says: 'The next time you say I want to spend too much money on a car remember that fella's got a helicopter and it cost him three hundred grand.' A little later we see the same man approach somebody – possibly Colin – and say: 'I saw you in a magazine recently . . . was it the *Telegraph* . . . no, it was *Staffordshire Life*, wasn't it? . . .'

'Really? What was I doing?'

'Fishing.'

'Fishing? I haven't been fishing for years?'

'Oh – perhaps it was somebody else. But I was sure it was you.'

As part of its campaign in the summer of 2008 the Countryside Alliance's Cheshire and North Wales regional branch had organized an open-air summer afternoon and evening event at Chester racecourse in the historic city of Chester. The invitation, which was open to the general public, offered a free glass of Pimm's, access to a polo match and the suggestion that supporters should bring their own picnic and be ready to stay drinking and carousing into the night. The Alliance had set out their stall next to the polo ground on the far side of the racecourse.

Apart from those arriving by helicopter, most had turned up in expensive cars which had been allowed to park inside the ring of the racecourse itself, over towards the polo ground. Most of the cars were powerful 4x4s or other such status symbols and few, if any, carried political stickers. One of the cheaper looking cars (a newish Volvo estate with what looked like genuine country mud on its wheel arches) displayed allegiance to the British Deer Association; another had a 'Scrap the Act' sticker demanding the legalization of fox hunting, the very issue which had led to the formation of the Countryside Alliance in the first place. There were plenty of Range Rovers with tinted windows – big flashy silver ones, one or two with significant looking personalized number plates – but there were no Land Rovers or farm vehicles. In fact, none of the cars looked as if they were driven by anyone who wasn't either wealthy or status-conscious, and the only vehicles which looked like they had a connection with rural pursuits were the massive, purpose-built horseboxes for moving strings of polo ponies around the country. They were remarkable: custom-made combinations of horsebox and team coach.

The polo ground itself was enormous – at least the size of two or three football pitches – and fenced off with rope and wooden edging to stop the ball from disappearing. That evening two teams of four riders were up against each other – Rathbone & Co. against Donaldson & Co. – an event sponsored by the Queen's bank, Coutts, and by Boodle, one of England's oldest and most expensive jewellers (the company regularly advertises in the *Spectator*). There were a couple of hundred people at the event, clustered around a pair of marquees where they were buying glasses of Pimm's at £4.50 a pop. Some had lined up along the rope fence while others were sitting on the sidelines on picnic rugs. Nobody seemed to be watching the match, which would have been difficult anyway without binoculars since the action was taking place so far away. Many of those present had field glasses, formidable looking pieces of kit and almost certainly very expensive, but they seemed to function only as accessories. Apart from the pink man checking out his friend's helicopter, I didn't see a single person use their field glasses.

Commentary was being broadcast over a mobile PA system, with a man inside a portable glass cubicle giving explicit warnings whenever the ponies came thundering towards the spectators. From time to time he would try to prompt his audience into taking an interest – or at least to turn their heads in the direction of the action. 'Oh, and that was a terrific effort, ladies and gentlemen,' he would opine, and a few of the ladies and gentlemen would applaud weakly. When one of the teams did eventually score a goal, the applause was so desultory and feeble that it was unlikely the players could have heard it anyway. The commentator's other stock expression was: 'Oh, and he's failed to quite get hold of that', which he said whenever the ball was not under control – which appeared to be almost always. It was good to see that the world of polo had its own set of commentary clichés.

Prominent among the spectators was a gang of seven elderly men wearing what looked like uniform blazers, double-breasted with brass buttons. One or two also wore panama hats. Their ties bore polo insignias, suggesting that they were more connected with the sport of polo than with the Countryside Alliance. They sat just outside the marquee in a row of collapsible chairs, impassive, long-faced and staring into the distance, their hands resting on spread knees. They resembled samurai or, perhaps more appropriately (this being Middle England), Cavalier cavalry commanders at their field command HQ. One was grumbling to his companions out of the corner of his mouth about the cost of insurance for horseboxes and the proposed increase in road tax: 'That's what's wrong with this country – there is simply too much red tape.' He said this without much conviction and the other old boys didn't seem to be paying much attention to him. Otherwise engaged, some nodded and grunted with approval, others winced and screwed up their faces in response to events taking place far away on the other side of the polo ground. Were they the equivalent of football match referees? They were probably more like line judges. I knew nothing about polo whatsoever and was not really in a position to ask for a quick tutorial now.

The people taking the most interest in the polo were gatherings of young women in their twenties sitting on the edge of the field having picnics on their picnic rugs, chatting and casting occasional glances at the match under way. At least one girl in every group, it seemed, was going out with one of the polo players; and she had brought along two or three girlfriends, perhaps so that she could boast about the fact that she had managed to bag a man who could afford to play polo, and perhaps to suggest that they too might be able to meet and nail such a man themselves. They had serious, expensive looking picnic gear, and at least one of them had one of those rectangular wicker hampers lined with gingham, with internal leather straps to hold small plates and tiny little forks and spoons in place. They wore flowery cotton summer dresses, in restrained pastels – blues and muted greens – and they wore plimsolls and flip-flops. All were white, and almost all blonde, their hair mostly long and carefully cut. Theirs was a natural, wholesome country look. In fact, they looked incredibly healthy, sort of bursting with vitality and cleanliness. Walking along the line of the picnicking girls, we picked up conversations about horses, of course, but also about clothes and shopping – including finely honed insults, designed as elaborate compliments, on the wisdom of each other's handbag-buying strategies – all delivered in plummy Sloane Ranger accents.

If there was solid wealth on display in the shape of helicopters, expensive cars, huge horseboxes and gold wristwatches, apart from that there was no bling at all; well, except, that is, for the women's sunglasses, which were pretty flashy with designer logos picked out in gold and silver. The women weren't wearing big Ascot day-at-the-races hats and, with one exception, didn't look as if they had made much of an effort to dress up at all. The exception was a woman sitting in a deckchair wearing a very severe navy blue dress suit with polka dots and a big hat and matching hatband; she looked as if she had been bound for the wedding of some minor member of the Royal Family and had got diverted to the Countryside Alliance by mistake. She didn't look simply annoyed about that: she looked absolutely ferociously so and kept throwing dagger-like X-ray glances in my direction.

After a final burst of enthusiasm a hooter sounded and the commentator announced that the match was over. Donaldson & Co. had won. The ponies looked absolutely knackered and were snorting heavily, or coughing, as they trotted back. Once they were out of the way, the riders lined up near the Pimm's tent for the awards ceremony, each step of which was lovingly described by the commentator over the PA system. One of the picnicking women with long blonde hair mirthlessly presented the winning captain with a magnum of champagne which, thankfully, he did not shake madly and spray over everybody.

The way the Countryside Alliance people focused on horses and dogs was extraordinary, even given the nature of the present event. You'd pick up snippets of conversation and, by the care and concern being expressed, would assume they were talking about their children – even if some of their offsprings' names or nicknames did sound a bit odd. 'How is Nobby doing these days?' they'd say, or 'Is Socks behaving himself any better now he's had his operation?' It turned out they were referring to horses, or dogs, or the mounts of mutual acquaintances. Some did discuss the merits of various public schools – Shrewsbury and Manchester Grammar appeared to be the local ones – but conversation was mainly about sport, and they seemed to take pride in the various injuries their boys had sustained playing rugby. There was an almost competitive element as they talked about all the near fatal head and spine injuries they had endured and, as the Pimm's continued to flow, they laughed like drains.

In what might have passed for a male version of the

handbags conversation that had been going on among the blondes at the margins of the field, one proud father asked another if his son was thinking of taking up polo, now that he had reached a certain age.

'No, no,' boomed the father, possibly covering up for the fact that there was no way he could afford to support a polo habit on top of everything else. 'He's really not "into" polo. He does three-day eventing, though . . . he's more "into" that . . .' he added, looking a bit crumpled.

The father of the teenager about to be inducted into the world of polo, on the other hand, looked triumphant and said in a tone of mock sincerity: 'Ahh . . . eventing . . . I seeee.'

The rest of the group – and all the other gaggles – talked incessantly about upcoming horse-related social events with a desperate sense of one-upmanship.

'Are you entering this year?' . . . 'Nooo . . . well, it is such a difficult course . . . rillllly difficult . . . you would have to have a rilly good horse for that course . . . Rilly tough.' . . . 'I have heard that that one is a really difficult course, rilly tough.'

One particular trio of women standing off to one side were indulging in particularly snobbish behaviour, discussing 'good families' in Staffordshire: 'The Fergusons and the Hendersons live practically next door to each other, and the problem is that they keep an open house and if anybody turns up there and asks for anything, they get it.'

Another member of the trio chipped in: 'If she has a fault it is that she is far, far too generous . . .'

'. . . that's it absolutely, exactly . . .'

'Do you know she lent . . . to . . . and I said, well, she'll never see that again, then yaaars later she realized she needed it, and she asked for it back, but she didn't get it. But she didn't seem to mind. So that is her all over . . . oh, absolutely . . . frightfully, frightfully sorry . . .'

Once the race and joyless awards ceremony had come to an

end there was the slightly bizarre sight of a group of young Asian men in headdresses strung out across the polo ground, walking slowly, with heads down, staring at the grass. They looked like policemen carrying out one of those inch-by-inch searches, looking out for evidence at the scene of a murder. They were in fact pushing down the divots in the polo ground thrown up by the ponies' hooves.

This got the attention of the women.

'Who are these people? . . . They are Sikhs.'

'That's very diplomatically put,' one slightly drunk man said. Then he became informative, which enabled him to make a connection with the man who had organized the event. 'You know, Robert has got a man who gets them up from Birmingham in gangs to do this job. They are absolutely marvellous . . . they do it much cheaper than local people.'

'Well, that's the trouble with English people,' the woman said, 'they complain and complain and complain, but they won't do these jobs, will they?' – interjections of 'No, no' – 'they wouldn't be happy bunnies if they were asked to do that . . . So Robert knows a man and he gets them up from Birmingham and they are happy to do it.'

'More than happy I should expect.'

'You know, these chaps are marvellous, aren't they . . . really, really marvellous . . . you simply couldn't have an event like this without them . . .' the squiffy man said, his tone suddenly reflective, even slightly emotional.

'You are absolutely right,' said one of the elderly women. 'They are marvellous. Look at them . . . Absolutely marvellous.'

# THIRTEEN

# Rubber Chickens –
# Watford, Hertfordshire

Rowena Gordon, an upper-class young English girl, and Topaz Rossi, a feisty American, meet and become best friends at Oxford. They are members of a social elite. Both are determined to succeed in their chosen careers, Topaz as a journalist and Rowena as a scout in the music industry. But their friendship turns to rivalry when they fall out over a man. From then on, Rowena and Topaz are determined to do each other down, as they battle against each other in both their personal and private lives. This is the gist of the blurb for Louise Bagshawe's first novel, *Career Girls*, described by *The Daily Express* as 'stylish, sexy and throbbing with vitality'.

Based on the solid and sensible commercial premise of transferring the *Sex and the City* type action and characters from New York to London (or Oxfordshire), plus a few layers of local culturally specific gloss, the book sold well. For somebody as intelligent as Louise, this process presented few intellectual challenges. But there was one snag. The market for undemanding women's fiction of this sort – 'chick lit' – was highly competitive. With so many books of similar style on the market it was hard to stand out, at least without spending millions on advertising.

The easiest and cheapest way to do this was for the author to have an interesting back story, and the good looks and sort of perverse reversal of roles from her main character that would get her written about in the colour supplements, in women's magazines and, more importantly, onto television chat shows. Louise Bagshawe was born in London in 1971, and her family moved to the country when she was seven. She attended local Catholic schools and went up to Christ Church College, Oxford, in 1989 where she read English with, according to her Conservative Party biography, 'a special emphasis on early English literature – and a bit of Old Norse!' She was Secretary of the Oxford Union, and Young Poet of the Year at eighteen. Louise published *Career Girls* when she was twenty-two and she has since written twelve novels. Her previous publisher Orion stated on her author biog that she 'lives with her husband in New York'. She now lives in the UK, but the couple do rent out five properties in the US. She is now the Conservative candidate for Corby, the former steel-producing town not far from Watford, in the East Midlands.

We met Louise at a political luncheon she was addressing in the banqueting room of an incredibly dowdy suburban golf club near Watford, a gathering which provided one of the more surreal moments of our entire journey. This was truly a clash of two worlds – or three if you included our own – the modern, energetic marketing hype of Planet Bagshawe, and the bewildered existential numbness of genuine Tory grass roots. The event had the ostensible aim of raising funds for the Hertfordshire area Conservative organization. Why they should have bothered with this was a mystery since it was well known in the ranks that Lord Ashcroft (or 'Lord Cashcroft' as the Tories were apt to call him), the Deputy Chairman of the Conservative Party, would pick up the tab for any campaign where there was the remotest chance of either winning or losing a seat. Like a host of these functions it seemed to be mainly a social ritual, a bunch of old friends getting together for no good reason other than having a lot of time on their hands.

The golf club where the event took place was precisely the

kind of joint that no Louise Bagshawe heroine would ever find herself in – boring, suburban, conventional – full of nondescript middle-aged blokes, nearly all of them white – and playing golf in the middle of the week. The banqueting room was exactly how you would expect it to be, right down to the uPVC conservatory windows at one end of the room and the gigantic heritage-style wooden plough hanging incongruously on one of the blank halogen-lit ultra-hygienic looking walls. There were no golfers in the banqueting area, only Tories. As was usual at these events they were, in the main, remarkably old, with one or two younger people present, such as Louise herself.

Not surprisingly, Louise looked extremely uncomfortable in such surroundings. We were early and were standing at the bar when she breezed in and started scanning the room nervously. Then she clocked us and offered a beaming, searchlight smile with just a hint of fear in her eyes. She seemed about to say something, but then thought better of it. She fussed and hovered, looking for somebody important. She was clutching a plastic bag tightly.

Unlike the gushing *Daily Express* review of her book, on this occasion Louise herself was neither vital nor throbbing; nor did she look particularly sexy. In her PR photographs she appeared as a tousle-haired Stevie Nicks rock chick lookalike, but for the golf club do she had gone for a strangely androgynous look. Her shortish blonde hair was tied back and held in place by a black bow and she wore a simple black trouser suit, with the trouser bottoms flapping about well above the floor. The suit, hair and bow made her resemble an eighteenth-century figure – a female George Washington or Pitt the Younger. She was quite small, too, so there was also an element of a Battle of Trafalgar-era midshipman or – more appropriately – pantomime principal boy about her. Her mannerisms and speech were remarkably eighteenth-century as well – all very traditional in style, with appropriate rhetorical flourishes:

'I am a Thatcherite, ladies and gentlemen, and I make no apology for that . . .'

Louise didn't mention her writing career nor, indeed, did she say anything about herself at all during her speech, which was addressed to about forty people seated around five circular tables in groups of eight. The speech was brief – little more than a routine denunciation of 'the socialists' and Gordon Brown – 'What a ghastly man he has turned out to be, ladies and gentlemen.' As a crowd-pleaser she threw in the fact that the Conservatives were popular in the opinion polls – that's to say that they were less catastrophically unpopular than the Brown government – and therefore on track at that moment to win the next general election. For good measure she added: 'Gordon Brown has a reputation as having been a good Chancellor, but let me tell you, ladies and gentlemen, that he was one of the very worst Chancellors we have ever had.' As with her non-apology for being a Thatcherite, such remarks seemed a bit pointless in a gathering where everyone was bound to share her opinions. They didn't even bother to applaud and Louise seemed a bit panicked by the flat reception.

One questioner raised the issue of the Conservative Party's education policy. Normally at such gatherings this took the form of a demand for the reintroduction of the eleven-plus selection system across the board, but this particular questioner offered a variation on the theme. He thought the main problem with education was that teachers were not paid nearly enough. Did Louise agree with that? 'Absolutely,' she said, nodding her head with such vehemence that her bow nearly fell off. 'We believe in markets and we believe in choice – and if that is "Thatcherite" then so be it, ladies and gentlemen – I make no apologies for that!' She then switched seamlessly to more socialist-bashing, with a dash of name-dropping as well: 'Michael Gove has plans to bring forward a market solution to education that I can tell you have the Labour Party quaking in their socialist boots.' She added to the early Georgian feel of her performance, matching her style of dress and her mannerisms with a reference to 'Adam Smith's hidden hand of the market'. She repeated: 'Yessssss . . . that is our radical and Thatcherite education policy and Labour are very, very afraid of it.' Here Louise adopted a high-pitched version of a Churchillian growl, skipping even more frantically from one foot to another and moving her head from side to side for brief eye contact with everyone present.

Whatever you thought about Louise you could not accuse her of failing to give the punters what they wanted to hear, either in her novel writing or speechifying. The other Tories on our table visibly warmed to this stream of totemic Pavlovian words. One of them, a rather bumptious man called Ian, scanned our faces for any signs of adverse reaction to the 'hidden hand of the market' reference. We tried to maintain our inscrutability. Louise carried on, still skipping as she spoke, outlining a plan whereby parents could choose any school they wanted, anywhere in the country. Under this scheme, she said, 'the money will follow the pupil' meaning that less popular schools would get less money; while popular schools would get that money transferred to them.

'What is the proportion of National Income that should go on defence?' another elderly person on a far table asked. Louise shot back with a vague crowd-pleaser: 'Well, a lot more than now!' It was strange to watch this. The audience was not trying to grill Bagshawe at all, or find out where she was coming from: in cricketing terms they were just lobbing her gentle full tosses so that she could whack the ball out of the ground. It was hard to tell if the crowd was enjoying this performance, or whether they were bored by it. Certainly there did not seem to be much warmth, and Louise was clearly not connecting with her audience in the way that Cecil Parkinson had done at the Way Forward dinner in Belgravia. Louise kept at it, though. She said that the lack of spending on the military was a 'national disgrace'. She added: 'Gordon Brown has not changed. He is an Extreme Socialist, ladies and gentlemen, who hates and detests our armed forces.'

Questioned rather coldly about Conservative prospects for winning the next general election, she stated categorically: 'We are going to win, and win well. We have a really excellent candidates' list.' She elaborated further: 'And we are going to win a series of victories in this area, in many adjoining constituencies. David Cameron is an excellent leader who means what he says and I hope that my friend and colleague here will be joining me on the green benches – he will make a superb Member of Parliament.' This was a reference to Ian Oakley, the candidate for Watford, and the man who was sitting at our table. Oakley smiled modestly, lowered his eyelids and nodded his head in a remarkably smug manner. Watford was a 'three-way' marginal which he could take for the Tories on the slightest of swings to him from either Labour or Lib Dem, or from both. But what we couldn't get away from, if we were reading the vibes right, was the absence of any real warmth or feeling of goodwill towards Louise. It was hard to see why they had invited her, really.

But it did not matter too much what a group of mostly elderly grass-roots activists in Watford thought about Louise Bagshawe. More importantly, the nation's style and fashion journalists, natural novelty seekers, had taken to the idea that the Tory Party had been reinvented as a body which was not only non-toxic, but positively brimming with gorgeous, multi-racial, high-achieving bright young things whose legions had suddenly appeared, appropriately enough, out of the blue. They started with Cameron himself and his attractive wife, Samantha, and then went on the hunt for other glam and fashionable right-wing women. Throughout 2008, and reaching a climax in the middle of the year, there had been a welter of 'It's cool to be a Tory' features in the broadsheet colour supplements and in style and fashion magazines. Blue was the new black.

Just before people took their seats for lunch, we overheard Louise boasting to the organizer of the event that she had recently appeared on the important *Question Time* TV programme. 'I would never have got on that if it wasn't for the books,' she said. 'And at the same time that appearance really, really helped with the sales of the books. So the two things go together really . . . they help each other . . . really.'

Ian Oakley, the Watford candidate, was our nominal host during the lunch and presided over our table with all the subtlety of a pub bore. And, since Louise spoke only briefly, we spent a good deal of time listening to him rattling on about various subjects. Ian was an unhealthy looking individual, fairly young but with a double chin and bags under eyes which darted around a fair bit behind cheap spectacles as he spoke. He had about him a distinct air of David Brent: his rapid eye move-ment, constant cackling and unnecessarily forceful way of speaking contributed to a mildly deranged, overfriendly and hyperactive character.

The first thing he did on meeting us was to pull some beer mats from his pocket, spilling them across the table as he offered them to us. They were round and featured a needlessly un-flattering close-up of Ian and his chins; around the portrait ran the UKIP-like slogan: WE WERE PROMISED A REFERENDUM ON THE EU CONSTITUTION . . . I WANT ONE. DO YOU?

The beer mats were, he explained, his secret campaign weapon. He went round pubs leaving them on tables. He seemed to like the implied naughtiness and deviousness in this, since it was highly unlikely that the pub companies would allow such blatant political advertising. Ian was up against the Lib Dems who controlled Watford Council, and whose tactical votes had denied the Conservatives the parliamentary constituency which the C1/C2 *Sun*-reader demographics had determined was rightly his. His eyes seemed to revolve with hatred at the mention of the Lib Dems. We discussed in our usual neutral way the nature of the 'Lib Dem Problem' in Richmond, where 'the yellow peril' held a 'natural' Conservative seat. Ian absolutely loved my use of the phrase 'yellow peril' to describe the Lib Dems, something I'd picked up on a political programme on Radio Four. I couldn't believe that he had not heard it before, but at its mention he went totally David Brent, laughing so hard that I thought he would injure himself. When he had calmed down we explained the neutral line that we had been told to adopt by the ancient Tory ladies of the Richmond Conservatives: the Lib Dems were good local campaigners who had a foothold in the area because there were lots of wealthy left-wing bohemian intellectuals (i.e. gays) and greens and loathsome media and publishing types and so on – the kind of people you might also find in Hampstead or Islington. Ian lost it again at the mention of 'relatively large numbers of gays', corpsing and squawking with laughter: 'Is that why they are the yellow peril then . . . peril, eh. Eh?'

Then he got control of himself again and said with mad relish: 'I don't have that problem round here . . . it's all White Van Man on my patch.' And there was that demonic cackle. Mention of green politics and the popularity of environmentalism in the Richmond constituency seemed to set off a chain of thought in Ian's head, related to David Cameron's adoption of feel-good 'green' politics . . . bicycles, windmills, green and blue tree-based party logo and all: 'It's amazin', innit,' he sneered: 'Last year it was all green this, and all green that . . . all that bollocks. Then petrol goes up by a couple of quid and suddenly you don't hear any of that crap any more . . . People just want lots and lots and lots of cheap petrol. And we are going to give it to them. That's how you win . . .'

\* \* \*

Apart from all the other oddities, the Watford gathering was notable in one other respect. We saw for the first and probably the only time an illustration of genuine Tory ethnic diversity. There appeared to be a number of Jewish people at the golf club that day, as evidenced by a sort of performance over the menu and people being asked to choose either kosher or non-kosher dishes. David, who had close relations who were Jewish, also reckoned that the style of dress of some of the older and middle-aged women present owed something to that of the well-established north London Jewish community. At our table there was a Jewish man called Harvey and a woman we presumed was his wife. Harvey wore a yarmulke, a skullcap. He was an organizer for a group called Conservative Friends of Israel and, in addition, was a councillor and was thinking about putting himself forward as a parliamentary candidate.

Ian Oakley and Harvey interacted quite a bit, as though they were old friends. Ian kept up a pretty constant stream of racially based banter, sprinkled with Bernard Manning-style jokes: 'Why were the Jews in the wilderness for forty years?' he quipped. 'Because they bought a sat nav from Alan Sugar.' Ian was also a fan of the bad-taste American animated sitcom *South Park*, and he kept quoting from it. For some reason, as he was ribbing Harvey about Jewishness, Ian started on a theme about Barbra Streisand and *Yentl*, and he quoted a *South Park* episode which featured Streisand as a giant, all-devouring, child-torturing monster robot. This led to a discussion about Israel in which Oakley said that, once he had been elected MP for Watford, he planned to get on as many foreign affairs committees as possible, so that he could have lots of fact-finding freebie trips, and get drunk all the time in sunny climes. Warming to his theme, which we – charitably – guessed was meant to be amusing, he said he hoped to make many trips to Israel where, in a further aspiration, he could take a machine gun and a flame-thrower and destroy a good many Palestinian villages, just as the Israelis did.

Following up these staggeringly oafish riffs, Ian also claimed that some people thought he might be Jewish: 'Of course, I've got a way of proving that I am not . . . But I won't do it here.' When the conversation seemed in danger of lapsing into good taste Ian soon put things right. At one point he said: 'You know, one of the problems that politicians should do something about is hunger throughout the world. There are just too many starving people' – at which point he ordered a second helping of baked salmon from the Polish waitress – 'and my contribution is to make sure I am not one of them.'

There then followed a discussion – seemingly intended to be comic – of how people (taken to mean the entire population of Watford), in Ian's experience, thought that Jews were terrible people, but the general public (every last person in Watford) did not realize that the Ashkenazi-type Eastern European Jews were OK and it was only the more oriental-type Sephardic Jews who were irredeemably murderous and it was they who caused 'all the problems'. 'Yes,' quipped Harvey sardonically, 'we Jews would only be half the people we are without the Sephardi.' We reckoned this remark was probably aimed at shutting Oakley up, but to be honest, we were quite baffled by this conversation.

After Louise Bagshawe had finished her speech Ian asked her a question about the British National Party, which he described as 'a disgrace'. He wanted to know how the Conservative Party should go about countering them. Louise's reply was that those who voted for the BNP were decent people who felt that their fears about immigration were being ignored. A Tory government would 'get control over immigration' and then there would be no need for BNP supporters to vote BNP any more because the Conservative Party would do the job. Ian seemed happy enough with this. Soon after that there was a raffle. As usual we didn't win anything, but a very old Scotsman on our table carried off the top prize of a bottle of supermarket wine, complaining that he had no real need for it because he did not drink and, it seemed, tragically, had nobody to share it with. He looked at the bottle in a sad way as if he found handling it embarrassing and physically awkward. But he was too polite to give it back.

A month after the Louise Bagshawe lunch we read in the *Daily Telegraph* that Ian Oakley had resigned from the Conservative Party following his arrest in connection with a campaign of harassment he had waged against local political rivals. When his case came to court, Louise Bagshawe's 'superb candidate' was said to have slashed the tyres of cars belonging to political rivals and to have wrecked the shutters at the Liberal Democrat headquarters in Watford. He was also accused of making anonymous silent phone calls to the female Lib Dem parliamentary candidate for Watford. All of this had taken place over a period of eighteen months. The court also heard that Oakley had arranged for gay and lesbian magazines to be sent to the same candidate under her name at her workplace.

Ian had dished out equally bizarre and upsetting treatment to another, male, political rival. Over a period of six months he daubed graffiti on his home, marking him out as a 'perv', and sending letters to him and his supporters wrongly accusing him of being a 'child abuser'. Ian's fingerprints were found on envelopes containing poison pen letters and a CCTV camera had caught him in action during one of the graffiti attacks. Adjourning the case for psychiatric reports, Barry Northrop, chairman of the Watford magistrates, had told Oakley his offences were 'very, very serious indeed, so serious that custody would be an option'.

Oakley pleaded guilty and asked for sixty-eight other offences to be taken into account. He was ordered to compensate the people whose tyres he had slashed and to pay prosecution costs of £80. By anyone's standards he got off very lightly.

## FOURTEEN

# *A Right Boules Up –*
# *Cheltenham, Gloucestershire*

The Cheltenham Conservatives' summer boules tournament had been advertised on the internet. Open to anyone willing to pay the extortionate £10 entrance fee, it was to take place in the beer garden of an ancient red-brick, thatched real ale pub in the heart of a chocolate-boxy Cotswold village not far from Cheltenham. It was Rodmell all over again – full of ivy- and rose-clad cottages set, this time, around a stunningly beautiful Saxon church. Everything was thatched in the village: not just the pub and the cottages but even the local quickie-mart general store. As well as the thatched roof, the pub also flew a vast Union Jack and an Irish tricolour, the latter in honour of the nearby racecourse where, every March, the Cheltenham Festival attracts punters from the Republic in their thousands. Had there been a telephone box or bus stop in the centre of the village, I am sure that would have been thatched as well.

Inside, the pub itself was pretty typical of its kind: low ceilings, quaint nooks and crannies, special hatches through which you could order your beer, but the beer garden was enormous – roughly the size of a seven-a-side football pitch, with acres of space between the tables – manicured and surrounded by tall hedgerows full of birdsong. The boules pitch was at the back, fenced off with a hedge, but jutting out into farmland on the edge of the village.

Keen to see another slice of Conservative rural life, I headed through the open gate and into the boules compound. I was in the county for a meeting the next day, I told the organizers, I was deeply interested in the Conservative movement and I had previously been involved in party campaigns in London. If I had come to Cheltenham with a fairly open mind as to how the day would pan out, I had also been drawn there because, a number of years ago (1992, in fact), there had been an enormous fuss about the selection by the party of John Taylor (now Lord Taylor of Warwick), who was a black candidate. This had split the local Conservative Association and it was probably the last time that Conservatives had, in any great number at least, been seen to be overtly racist. Taylor was not selected, and it was therefore no great surprise to find that the boules tournament was an all-white affair. There were about thirty people and most of them were old.

As usual with such events, most of the organization seemed to have been done by elderly women, yet another reminder, I concluded, that the female grip on Conservative Party grass roots was tightening. As society and party members aged, and because women tended to outlive men, so that grip would only get stronger.

The woman in charge of the boules tournament – elderly (of course), snow-white Margaret Thatcher-style hairdo, lots of make-up, hawk-like features – seemed sceptical and a bit nervous about my presence. I seemed to be the only stranger at the gathering and I didn't fit the demographic at all. Still, she was happy enough to relieve me of my £10 and directed me to the food laid out on a rickety table in a miniature white marquee. The food vaguely reminded me of the birthday parties I had attended as a toddler in the sixties – dried-up triangles of sandwiches on Mother's Pride, those horrible little cold baby sausages on sticks, streaked and spotted with fat, warm orange cordial, crisps, and shop-bought Victoria sponge plonked artlessly on a piece of silver foil.

I piled up a paper plate – with crisps, mostly – and was paired off for the boules competition with Penny, a retired NHS nurse who was now a Conservative councillor for Cheltenham. Penny was extremely friendly, with a kindly face, and, in contrast to the general frostiness, she had a delightfully relaxed and welcoming manner. Blonde and just a little podgy, she complained that she did not really like the summer because she always got attacked by insects. She had been so badly bitten once that her legs had swelled up.

Penny was mildly flirtatious in the way that some Tory women of a certain age can be, and attracted plenty of slightly smutty comments and innuendo because of the fact that she was consorting with a 'young man' (i.e. me), and a stranger to boot. In its bluntness, it struck me that Conservative men were not in the least bit charming and many of them didn't seem in the slightest bit interested in talking to women. They preferred to ignore them or make jibes about them. Married couples arriving for the boules immediately split up into segregated groups, the men talking about men's stuff – cars, property, the failing careers of various rivals, council business – the women about womanly or family things – health, births, marriages and deaths.

Penny and I chatted comfortably, she in a non-political and highly sensible way about the recent flooding that had affected the local area so badly. Penny was on a council committee which was looking at all that, planning improvements to streams and drains so the streets wouldn't get flooded again. She admitted that being a councillor was really a full-time job, one she could never have managed when she was a nurse. It was interesting and kept her busy and active in her retirement. There was a flash of steel at the mention of the Lib Dems, who had just taken back control of Cheltenham Council at the May elections, after running a 'very negative campaign'. I sympathized, offering the neutral if tautological 'Yessss . . . the Lib Dems can win seats if they run a good campaign . . . hmmmm.' She agreed, and added firmly: 'But they are so negative, very, very negative.' Once again it turned out that the elderly grass-roots activists hated the Lib Dems far more than the Labour Party. Obvious, I suppose: in Tory 'heartland' areas like Cheltenham you probably didn't see a Labour activist from one decade to the next.

Apart from Penny, most of the people at the tournament were elderly, with the notable exception of an aggressive looking younger man called Tim, greying hair fashionably cut, who swaggered about in a pink shirt unbuttoned at the neck and tight jeans. His friend was similarly dressed and they had a couple of younger, fashionably dressed women in tow. Penny identified him as a new recruit. Later, as I was leaving the pub, I overheard him in heated discussion with a woman about council business. She was complaining that tenants in social housing were constantly demanding repairs and that, as soon as these were done, they demanded more. At the same time there was a lot of vandalism. Tim said that the tenants she was dealing with ought to be grateful that she did not simply put them all in caravans, which was all they deserved.

After a while a man, probably in his forties, came over and actually began talking to Penny, breaking the gender divide. He asked to be introduced to me, as though he thought that I was her partner or boyfriend. When Penny told him I was from out of town, he started going on about how the village was the most haunted in England. Various apparitions had been spotted over the years, he confirmed: 'There's supposed to be a headless huntsman who rides through the village blowing his horn. What I want to know is how he blows the horn? What part of the anatomy does he use?' and he guffawed coarsely. 'Maybe the horn is somehow wedged into the hole in the stump of his neck . . .' I answered facetiously, getting a suspicious look for my pains.

The hawk-faced woman then called us all to order, standing on a soapbox to demand silence and to issue instructions. There was, of course, a raffle but, unusually, it was held first, before the boules tournament began. The prizes, true to form, were bottles of booze and a box of chocolates. A woman sitting near me won the chocolates. She looked miserable, lumpy and dumpy in a baggy T-shirt and generally shapeless clothes; she brightened slightly when she saw that her luck had changed, but made the mistake of saying optimistically to her husband: 'That's good.' He quickly cut her down: 'Huh! They've been trying to get rid of those for years.' The lumpy woman said bitterly that she was going to give them to her mum, as it solved the problem of what to give her as a present. The exchange was like something from a bad seventies sitcom about marital discord.

The organizer, now wobbling slightly on her soapbox, moved on from the raffle and explained the mechanics of boules in a very bossy, no-nonsense way. 'We are not playing by Normandy rules,' she said. 'These are our own Cheltenham rules . . .' That prompted general uproar: 'Hurray – we don't need the bloody Frogs!' somebody shouted jokily and there was more hilarity. 'You are all complaining that it's French, but at least that means we'll annoy the Germans,' one old boy shouted, a remark which didn't seem to make much sense. When the woman asked him to explain himself he just blustered and said, 'Well, there's too much sucking up to the Germans . . . isn't there? . . . that's what I say. What?' He had a blue open-neck shirt and shoulder-length white hair, swept back. Despite that, he looked a bit like Michael Howard.

The noisiest person present was an obese, bald-headed man in a polo shirt who looked like a Sontaran from *Dr Who*. He spoke, or rather shouted, in a thick cockney-cum-estuary accent, which made him stand out from the rest even more. Without exception, all the other men seemed very panama-hatted middle class. The fat guy issued a constant stream of teasing and insults, but all done in a cheerful, friendly way, and cackled from time to time like Sid James in a *Carry On* film. It was as though a stray *Sun* reader had gate-crashed a – well – a boules tournament attended by *Daily Telegraph* readers, which of course was exactly what had happened. Innuendo was his speciality and, since we were playing boules, this led inevitably to lots of remarks about 'throwing your balls about', 'make sure you give your balls a good polish' and so on. He got a lot of mileage out of one woman in particular, young enough not to have white hair. She was very fat and had enormous breasts. When she bent forward slightly to throw the ball he shouted: 'Don't lean over too far, darlin' . . . they'll pull you over!'

Penny and I did OK at boules, a game which to me in my ignorance seemed to require a lot of luck and relatively little skill. Its big advantage was that it needed no real effort and could safely be played by anyone – including old right-wing people – even when drunk. Well, by almost anyone. The Sontaran *Sun* reader was a menace. On his first go he threw the heavy ball – slightly bigger than a golf ball and solid steel – high into the air, apparently by accident. It could easily have landed on somebody's head and killed them. 'Oh bollocks!' he shouted and tried to laugh it off, but some of the others were really alarmed. He went a bit quiet after that.

One old man with enormous jug ears was evidently the treasurer of the local Conservative Association. He was paired with a woman called Sally. Sally was very good at boules. Though she looked well into middle age, she was one of the younger participants. She had big, big orange hair, bulked out and probably back-combed, and wore a fitted pink woollen jacket and black slacks. She smoked constantly. She looked a bit like a 1960s Australian (or perhaps Cheltenham) housewife. She seemed to be coming from a particular place in terms of fashion, but it was hard to work out where exactly that was. Was she being ironic, like the punk rockers and New Wave art school students of old, who used to dress in a way that was so out that it was in? Or was she just much older than she looked, in stylistic terms trapped like a fly in amber? Sally and the treasurer won the competition – for the second year running apparently – and they both seemed immensely proud of their victory. The treasurer then took his seat at a bench alongside a man called Sid who, Penny told me, was ninety years old and had been 'tortured by the Japs' during the Second World War.

Many of the elderly women were on sweet sherry. 'I like Harvey's Bristol Cream,' one of them said. 'I have it with my dinner sometimes. It brings out the flavour of soup.' Another looked tremendously old – she was certainly in her nineties and possibly even a hundred – and was sitting in her chair and taking it all in. She seemed very on the ball and was chatting in an animated way to some of the other younger striplings, i.e. those of sixty or seventy. There was an elderly woman with flyaway white hair, quite small and with a hunched back whom people seemed to be avoiding. She wore a cardigan, even though it was a boiling hot day, and complained constantly and unrestrainedly to nobody in particular that the boules tournament was a stupid idea, adding scathingly that it was very badly organized: 'We are going to be here until midnight unless somebody organizes this properly,' she rasped again, adding: 'Stop talking and chatting and get it started!' The others ignored her, Penny rolling her eyes in a way that seemed to suggest that the woman was a notorious pain in the backside and that it was best just to blank her.

On the next table, on the other side, there was an elderly woman with dyed red-brown hair; she had been engaged in a heated political discussion about the credit crunch just as I arrived. Oddly, she resembled the late Barbara Castle. 'Blair knew all this crisis was coming, and that's why he got out,' she said with an air of great authority. The group around her agreed enthusiastically. It was all a plot, the Barbara Castle lookalike explained sagely: 'The socialists have ruined the country and then we will come in and fix it and then give it back to them . . . That's what's happened in every election since 1936, when I was ten,' she said and her audience all heartily agreed and tut-tutted. Then she added a surprising rider, sympathizing with Gordon Brown: 'You can't blame the government, though. It's the people who vote them in. That's the trouble.' There was more deep agreement: 'Yes, that's right, you're right there . . . they always let you down . . .' Later this woman changed the subject to her family, how they never phoned her and how she had all these strategies to catch them when they were in. She knew when her son got up and went to bed, when he had a nap and when he went to the pub. She could cross-reference all this with her daughter – his sister – and, by triangulating, surprise them with a call they were bound to pick up. She chuckled as she explained all this and I felt guilty about my own lack of zeal in keeping in touch with my aged parents.

Then she moved on to news concerning various members of the local Conservative Association – who had died of old age, who had what illness. There was a poignant moment when she said that a friend of hers had just lost her son – he had died of old age. So, a ninety-year-old mother had lost a seventy-year-old son. I pondered on that and to people watching me carefully because I was an outsider I must have looked a bit distracted. It was bad enough, I thought, for a mother to lose a son for any reason; but to have him die of old age . . . that was very strange, and struck me as almost unbearably sad. It really hit me. I was getting old myself.

On the subject of death, I noticed that several of those present were heavy smokers and it was clear that one or two liked a drop of drink as well. Penny, my boules partner, was not drinking much, but she did admit that when on holiday she liked to 'put down an anchor every evening and drink like a fish'. There was one particular elderly woman, thin as a rake, in a Chanel-type suit, with what appeared to be heavily coloured honey-blonde hair, and a lined face and tightly stretched features; she was actually chain-smoking, lighting one cigarette after another from, on at least one occasion, the smouldering stub of the previous one. As the afternoon drifted into evening, I had the palpable sensation of being in a cloud of smoke, even though we were outdoors. Pubs were like that in the old days. I hadn't experienced this in ages. It was like being transported back in time.

And so, as the evening darkened and the blue clouds of fag smoke wafted over us, the Sontaran man honked on with his double entendres; the married couples bickered among themselves; the complaining woman continued to complain – and to be ignored; and the hundred-year-old sat bolt upright, staring into space, with the rictus of a smile on her face. And when the drink took over, the entire event began to resemble a shambolic outing from a disreputable old people's home.

# FIFTEEN

# The Charlatans – Hammersmith, London

It's the summer party of the Conservative Party's Hammersmith branch in west London and there are about two hundred people in attendance at a town house in Brook Green, a smart area of the borough. As at any Conservative gathering almost everyone present is white. An exception is Shaun Bailey, who is black, and who is the prospective Conservative parliamentary candidate for the newly created Hammersmith seat. He has with him a female friend, also black and, like Shaun, young and extremely good-looking. She is expensively dressed, with an elaborate ringlet hairstyle and lots of make-up. She looks like a hip-hop diva.

In the split-level designer kitchen of the town house Shaun is regaling three prosperous middle-aged blondes – the sort of women who might well send their daughters to St Paul's Girls' School on the other side of Brook Green – with tales from his life as a youth worker among the disaffected and knife-carrying black youths of Shepherd's Bush. The rest of the gathering – senior lawyers, City big shots, PR people from Conservative Central Office and so on, appear to be ignoring him. They are in the main part of the house, talking about money and power; the comings and goings of people in Whitehall departments; and multinational property and financial companies.

So Shaun is there with the wavering attention of the blondes who are now openly ogling his powerful masculine physique.

Most of the men here are dressed up in suits and ties, but Shaun is in his gym vest and tight trousers, six pack visible through the clinging material, bull shoulders and arm muscles on naked display. He has one polished anecdote after another about life on the streets. These stories will be familiar to you if you have listened to the radio profiles on Shaun, or read the mass of newspaper and magazine articles about him. He has a practised patter, weaving the media-friendly mean streets micro-dramas with anthropological stuff about the importance for black people, of matriarchy and of boys obeying their mothers.

'I've got this lad and he was a killer. A stone-cold killer,' he says in an attempt to shake the blondes from their semi-comatose condition. 'When he was in prison they just could not control him at all. Not at all. One word from his mother and he did what he was told.' And he laughed. But the women weren't buying it. One of them asked: 'Well, if his mother's influence was that important, why didn't she use it to stop him committing a murder in the first place?' And she began looking at her wristwatch with an air that said – I've had enough of this guy's bullshit.

To keep them interested Shaun introduced a shock prison story that I had not heard him use before, thus suggesting the possibility that he was making it up as he went along.

'If you go into Holloway women's prison you have to share your knickers with other women,' he told the blondes. But they didn't really bite on that either. A girl who looked as if she might be fifteen or sixteen wandered into the circle. It seemed that she was the daughter of one of the blondes and was checking on whether or not it was time to go home yet. Bailey was onto her straight away, warning her that she shouldn't have sex with boys, because they would not respect her for it. The girl looked embarrassed and said nothing.

Bailey then went on to outline a strangely conspiratorial theory: people in the entertainment and media businesses had conspired to create the idea of the teenager, and to foster divisions between children and parents which could be exploited to make money. Essentially, he felt that Britain should go back to the early 1950s, and Africans especially should go back to 'traditional societies', such as those found in West Africa. The girl looked at him as though he was mad and obviously wanted to get away but – having failed to absorb the teenage-rebellion-is-poison message – she had the good manners to realize that it would be rude to do so while Shaun was still unburdening himself. Bailey, who wasn't drinking because of his standing as gymnast, body-builder and health fanatic, then began berating the girl about the need to avoid getting a sexually transmitted disease, warning her that if she had a baby it would ruin her chances of going to university. The girl giggled nervously at this point. She clearly came from the sort of family who had probably put her name down for a good school at birth and nothing at all on God's great earth was going to ruin that. She was the kind of intelligent, good-looking and – above all – rich chick who could probably afford to be very picky-choosy and non-traditional in the boyfriend and lifestyle department. If she did have an abortion, a dose of Glastonbury scabies and a few daft lost weekends of booze and soft drugs, it was more likely to increase the advance for her first Louise Bagshawe-type novel than put the kibosh on her carefully planned progress through academia and the professions.

In a desperate attempt to get away, one of the women finally interjected: 'This is all really marvellous. And I do hope somebody is paying you for all this work you are doing for us on top of your ordinary work.' Shaun smiled broadly and nodded his head slowly and conspiratorially: 'Yes, yes, somebody is looking after me . . .' And then he became inscrutable and wandered off, still grinning and nodding. Was Bailey in receipt of 'Ashcroft money' – part of a multimillion-pound fund established personally by the Conservative Party

Deputy Chairman Lord Ashcroft to finance candidates in key Labour seats, such as Hammersmith? It seemed likely. The whole topic of 'Ashcroft money' was a sensitive one.

The circle around Shaun began to break up and he headed into the main part of the house where the more influential guests were gathered. The owner of the house, and host of the party, introduced Shaun to a slightly sinister looking bald-headed man wearing expensive media glasses and a Nehru jacket. He looked like Dr Evil. Then, right on cue, the host said: 'Shaun, let me introduce you to our friendly, local arms dealer . . . these guys have a lot of money and they throw it around, as you'll find when you get into Parliament . . . Only joking!' The bald-headed man turned out to be the owner of Purdey guns, a local manufacturer of handmade clay pigeon and hunting shotguns. Bailey quipped, as part of his inner-city hard man act: 'I'm good with a shooter . . . but not clay pigeons.'

The man making the introductions was Simon Walker, chief executive of the British Private Equity and Venture Capital Association. A dapper man, Walker looked as if he was still in his forties. The BVCA was essentially a trade organization promoting the interests of banks which specialized in lending money to public organizations under the terms of private finance initiatives. Before that he had been chief executive of Reuters and before that head of PR at British Airways and Buckingham Palace. He had also worked at No. 10 Downing Street as part of John Major's policy team. In other words, he was a heavy hitter in the world of professional politics, PR and money. On the day of the party Simon had been representing the BVCA at a trade union conference. The unions tend to dislike private finance in the public sector. He had been counter-ing the unions' PR line that private finance initiatives were just a way of cutting public sector wages and diverting taxpayers' money into the coffers of the banks through high interest rates.

The unions, Simon thought, had a good case along these lines. It was a tough job, in PR terms, to put the other side of the argument.

Simon's house was very fashionable, more in the Scandinavian or Italian style of radical chic Islington or Hampstead than your more traditional gilt mirrors, shot-silk chairs and chintz of conventional Palais de Versailles Carlton Club-type Conservative Edmund Burke-approved décor. This place was tricked out like a modern art gallery – with lots of white walls, polished hardwood floors and little halogen spotlights everywhere. The kitchen was a wonder of hi-tech cooking equipment organized around a vast blue enamel cooker with several eye-level ovens and lots of marble and granite food preparation surfaces everywhere. The idea here seemed to be that a house is a machine for living in. There was a lot of plausible looking modern art – generally abstract post-expressionism – everywhere, as well as groovy ethnic artefacts such as African tribal masks. There was also a large framed speech by Martin Luther King with a non-ironic arty drawing of his face. It was the sort of house you could imagine Peter Mandelson living in; a little bit of New York transplanted to West London. The house was almost certainly worth a fortune: a smaller one in a less fashionable street was on a local estate agent's website for £2.5 million at the time. At one point, before the majority of the guests arrived, I overheard Simon discussing the chances of getting planning permission to put in more floors downstairs, beneath the already developed basement. At the time I had volunteered to slice up the olive bread, and so, ignored as hired help, had a brilliant 'What The Butler Saw' vantage point. Simon had spent a lot of money on the party. He had even hired a string quartet, but did not call on them in the end. They were just hanging about in tails and bow ties with violins, 'on standby', and ended up sitting in the largely deserted upstairs living room, playing cards and looking faintly insulted.

The guests fell into two clear categories – the old and retired, and young go-getters, many of whom appeared to have jobs with the Conservative Party or closely related firms or think-tanks. They came from Hammersmith and surrounding areas like Kensington, Chelsea, Notting Hill and Ealing. Some of the older ones had been very senior lawyers (perhaps even judges) and were discussing internal goings-on in different law firms with offices right there in the Inns of Court, big multimillion-pound international law firms like Denton Hall. It was a warm evening and the men were mostly down to shirts and ties (there were relatively few blazers) but there was one guy present, old, tall and tremendously thin – he had been a high-ranking officer in the forces, maybe a general or air vice-marshal or something – who knew a lot about the intelligence services. He was discussing the day's big news story that a secret dossier on Arab terrorism had been 'lost' and that this had been put down to incompetence. He doubted that; it was probably deliberately leaked, he reckoned, deliberately because it contained disinformation that would put the terrorists off. He claimed that British intelligence did that a lot during the conflict with the IRA. It was routine. When you had, for example, worked out the exact command structure of a terrorist group, you had to put out some disinformation saying you hadn't. It was basic spy stuff, he said. The public didn't get it, and thought the intelligence services were inefficient. But the public were wrong – and so were journalists who, in his opinion, were in the main 'simpletons and idiots' who could be manipulated by intelligence services at will. It felt strange listening to all this since I was myself an enemy spy – of sorts – even if for essentially comic purposes. But he didn't seem like your usual foaming-at-the-mouth spy and military history nut. He could have been the former head of MI6 or the KGB for all I knew. His wife was an elderly blonde wearing a floaty, tent-like white dress. He pretty much ignored her, and she did the rounds meeting old friends and introducing people to each other.

There was another contingent of councillors, who wore an indefinable air of self-conscious inferiority, in contrast to the national-level Power People, retired or otherwise. There was, for example, a female councillor from Ealing who complained about a newspaper story castigating a fellow Tory on Hammersmith Council for sending an email saying that Indian people on a council estate were throwing rubbish out of the window; that they did not know any better because that was what they did in India, but now they were in England they had to learn different ways. She thought the newspaper article was 'all spin'. The reality, she complained, was that the councillor had a right to bring to public attention the fact that people were throwing rubbish out of their windows. The big mistake was to mention 'India' because then the 'the press and left-wing liberals will always twist that into something'. She continued: 'All she said was that the practice of throwing rubbish out of windows was normal in some countries, such as India, but it was not normal in England. She wasn't accusing the Indians directly, just using that as an example.' This struck me as a bit of a fine point, but it suggested the constant, almost knee-jerk mild racism that both David and I had noticed – even in these liberal Tory surroundings.

In stark contrast to the Cheltenham gathering, the food at the party was of the highest quality, multi-ethnic and very expensive. The Cheltenham people, like the punters at the Royal Show, were patriotic in their choice of sausages on sticks, British crisps and flavourless yellow cheese on spongy white bread. Here you had a choice of Vietnamese nibbles, spicy and exciting looking Brazilian-type stuff and specialist treats from every corner of the earth – probably from Azerbaijan to Zimbabwe. There was also a massive quantity of excellent wine and bottles of rare vodka in well-designed, modern bottles, possibly Icelandic. The £15 entrance fee to this public event was terrific value, and to some extent made up for the blatant rip-off of

£75 for the Cecil Parkinson meat and two veg event provided by Conservative Way Forward. Here was the liberal elite of darkest UKIP and Parkinsonian imagination at play, flaunting their couscous and Martin Luther King posters and laughing at the Cheltenham matrons, the Chris Hudsons and the Ian Oakleys of this world with their fried egg sandwiches, packets of Cheesy Wotsits, Harvey's Bristol Cream and saloon bar views.

And everyone was in a good mood after the defeat of Ken Livingstone in the London mayoral election a few days earlier. The (possible) former head of MI6 said that it was good to feel wanted again after 'a decade of being absolutely reviled and ashamed of describing oneself as a Conservative'. Pretty soon everyone had had plenty to drink – the sheer quality of the booze seemed to keep things on track – the booziness was more Dorothy Parker than Shane McGowan. There was about an hour of drinks and chat, during which another and more senior black Tory politician – Ray Lewis – arrived and began working the crowd, with Shaun Bailey and his glamorous female side-kick in tow. Lewis had been appointed as deputy to Boris Johnson, the new Tory Mayor of London. His arrival caused real excitement – like the arrival of a rock star – and seemed to confirm that the Hammersmith party was the hot Tory ticket in London on that particular evening.

Lewis was a short, squat man who looked physically powerful. He had a shaven head with small rolls of fat at the back of his neck. He was wearing a dark suit, with a white formal shirt, open wide at the collar around his thick neck. He glistened with sweat and had a faraway, regal look – nod, nod – and looked very bored meeting all these Tories. One of them said: 'Congratulations on winning' and he replied by rolling his neck, with expansive hand gestures, and using football manager-like clichés: 'Well, at the end of the day we dun well wiv it, because it wuz a team effort'; either that or cheeky chappie self-deprecation. Someone said: 'I've admired all the tremendous work you've been doing' and he sort of shuffled from foot to foot, eyes down, saying, 'Fankyou fankyou like I say it wuz a team effort, y'don't get anywhere wivout yer team.' Then someone else said: '. . . And now you've got some power to take your work forward.' Lewis looked up and said: 'Power? It don't feel like that, I can tell you . . .' and he chuckled and moved on.

When Lewis and Bailey had finished their tour the room was called to order by the constituency chairman. He was a young man with friendly, open features and had a sort of stumbling, bumbling manner of speaking which might have been copied from Boris Johnson, and was a distinctive Tory style. He said that the Conservatives had come back from the brink of disaster to reach the brink of power in the past year. But there was a need to keep working 'on the streets'. He was now 'absolutely sure' that the Conservatives would win the next general election. The London mayoral election, he said, had 'already shown that Conservatives can win, and that they can win in areas that even a few months ago it would have been inconceivable'. Then he introduced Ray Lewis as 'Boris's very capable deputy'. Lewis had to stand on a chair at one end of the kitchen to be seen by the crowd. He was very much more animated now he was doing his performance, rather than the post-match analysis stuff he was offering when he was being shown around.

'Yes, here I am, Ray Lewis, and not Shaun Bailey,' he said. 'I've just been speaking to a lady and she asked: "Which one is Shaun and which one is Ray, it is hard to tell you apart" – there was a surge of delighted laughter at the apparent racism of this remark – 'well, it is easy really – Shaun is the tall guy with the six pack and I am the short guy with the rucksack . . . or, put another way, Shaun is a big black man with a six pack and a lot of testicular fortitude.' There was more laughter and some shock at this. A woman from the audience shouted: 'Shaun's wife can tell you all about that.' So there it was in seconds,

Martin Luther King poster or not – the connection between black men and the size of their genitals, established as item number one on the agenda.

After that Lewis's style was a bit like the best man at a wedding. It wasn't really about politics, just a series of wind-ups and outrages for the audience, to entertain the people at the party. Lewis had a slight cockney accent with not much West Indian influence in there at all. Unlike Bailey, who would slip in the odd 'massif' and 'wicked', Lewis didn't use street language. 'And another thing different is I've got a big booming voice,' Lewis said. 'So you are going to have to put up with that . . . not like Shaun . . . Shaun, he's got this little squeaky voice like this . . .' and then he did a sort of impersonation of Bailey using street slang, 'Oooo oooo ooooo . . . We got to get down with the kids in the street' – and, 'Oooo oooo oooo . . . I don't do crime no more now I have discovered the Conservative Party', and basically making him out to be very effeminate (which he wasn't, though he did have a higher pitched voice than Lewis) and also making him look lightweight and, frankly, something of a joke. Bailey beamed at this, showing he was a good sport. Lewis was presented as the heavy character and Bailey as one of his boys, a protégé. It was very much like the way the best man would try to humiliate the bridegroom at a wedding. The crowd was in tears, practically rolling about laughing.

'I've got a very good idea of what I am supposed to be doing,' Lewis continued. 'I know I've got that idea, but the problem is I don't know what it is yet . . . which is more than you can say about Boris.' (There was sniggering all round at this, as though he had just mentioned a complete and utter imbecile.) Then Lewis did an impression of Boris Johnson's upper-class twit accent and mannerism: 'Crikey, Ray! What are we going to do? Gosh! Crumbs! Have you got any ideas? Golly! Have they told you how it all works? I haven't got a bloody clue!' The room was practically screaming with laughter at this.

'I can tell you this – there's advisers all over the place,' Lewis continued. 'The other day I even saw Boris coming out of the toilet with two advisers.

'No, but seriously, we won that election because, behind the media image, Boris Johnson is really an extremely intelligent man . . . extremely intelligent . . . he needs a complete extreme image makeover, though, because there is a fantastic – fantastic – brain in there and more important than that he has the one thing that this country needs right now more than anything else and that thing is leadership.' The crowd became more serious with plenty of 'hear, hears' and 'well saids'.

'I was at a conference at 10 Downing Street about youth crime with New Labour,' Lewis continued, suddenly serious. 'I can tell you there was no leadership there at all. Whatever the answer was we were supposed to be coming up with, it must have been a stupid question.

'Because that's what's wrong with this country. People are so scared of doing something wrong that they end up doing nothing at all. It is like what Martin Luther King said: "Paralysis through analysis." (From the floor: 'Hear, hear.')

'Boris says to me . . . we're gonna do this . . . And we are not gonna spend a lot of time talking to people and talking to this expert and that expert. Because they are just there to say no. I say you've got to make your decision, do it and take the consequences. You don't wanna lorra of "consultation".

'"Consultation" – that's what the government does and – face it – everything the government touches turns to shit . . .'

There was a shudder of distaste around the room when Lewis used the word 'shit'. He picked up on the bad vibes and seemed to decide to terminate his performance immediately.

'. . . Well . . . anyway you've had y'lot, because I'm paid to be here, but I've been informed that I don't get the cheque until I answer some questions. So, questions then. Fire away.'

This seemed to cheer everyone up again.

The first question came from the back of the room, from an agonized looking, thin, elegant middle-aged woman with a perfect RP accent, like the Queen from thirty years ago: 'Ray, how can you show us how to reach out to the disenfranchised voters in Hammersmith, because we don't know and you do know and we need to know.'

At first Lewis seemed to misunderstand the question. Was she was asking if the Greater London Authority could give the Hammersmith Conservatives some money now they were in charge? There was a bit of toing and froing about this until he got to the point along the lines of 'we are white people, we have no idea of how to talk to black people, can you tell us how to do that please?'

Lewis replied: 'Sister, you have to show 'em leadership. All they need is leadership and they're all waitin' for that.' Then he went off in a completely different direction. 'Y'know, the biggest problem we face today is this idea of the "teenager",' he claimed energetically. 'You allow these youths a period of tolerance when they are allowed to act like adults, and have the rights of adults, but they have no responsibilities.'

He then told a shaggy-dog story about meeting 'three hundred kids' in a school and asking them to put up their hands if they had a TV set in their bedrooms. All of them had. Then he had asked: 'How many of you have got black and white TV sets?' He acted out the sort of gormless, slack-jawed response he had got from the kids, meaning they had never heard of a black and white TV set. 'Next question.' There were gasps around the room about the ignorance about black and white TV, but the woman who asked the question was clearly none the wiser about how she could communicate with black people, and she looked a little disappointed.

Another question – really a long-winded statement – was about the deliberate destruction of family morale by 'the liberal establishment that has plagued this country since the 1960s and 70s' – and it was answered in a similarly evasive way, which led to more ranting against television and television advertising and about shopping. Lewis said: 'Shopping – you hear young women saying they are going into town to go "window shopping"! – they even call it "retail therapy"! . . . We used to go to the shops, to put something in the cupboard that we needed. Now they go out and buy things, just to make themselves feel better.'

There was mild and good-natured heckling from the expensively attired women in the room as if to say, 'You don't understand it, because you are a man . . . we like shopping.'

Then Lewis went into a big routine, asking the chairman if he could have two minutes to explain something important. 'I have to tell you I had a dream before I came here today.' In this 'strange dream' he was walking across a park and he saw a lantern in the grass, and he picked it up and a genie appeared and granted him any wish he liked. Lewis said in the dream that he asked for the biggest sports car there was – 'I'm not very green I'm afraid' – and for a motorway to be built all the way to Los Angeles. But the genie said, 'That's impossible, that ain't even in the genie handbook, you will have to ask for something else.' So in the dream Lewis asked to be able to understand the mind of a woman. The genie paused and said: 'How many lanes do you want on that motorway, four or six?'

Everyone was a bit nonplussed and deflated by this. It was a classic breach of liberal elite etiquette. Here was a black guy being openly sexist in front of a room full of white people, many of whom were women. If they picked him up on that, would that be racist? If they didn't, would it be sexist? If you didn't object to sexism on the part of a black man just because he was black, wasn't that in itself a form of racism? Could you use a form of positive discrimination to allow black men to be sexist, whereas white men would get a hard time? If so, did this mean that white women had an implied right to be a bit racist?

This sort of agonizing had been derailing liberal and left-wing dinner parties for decades. After an awkward silence Ray's sexist outburst was allowed to fall flat on its face. Somebody in the crowd instead quoted Ray's observation that anything the Labour Party touched turned to 'shit'. Lewis seemed annoyed and intensely irritated by this. His act had basically fallen apart with the sexist 'dream' anecdote. He wrapped up with a weak joke: 'You've had your money's worth now. You don't pay enough. That's your lot.' He stepped down from the chair and disappeared into the hall. There was embarrassed laughter and clapping. But the rock star glitter had evaporated.

The chairman took over again and introduced Shaun Bailey as a man who had attracted a lot of local and national media attention and who was 'excellent at appearing on television'. Bailey's speech was mainly about how grateful he was that he had been selected to stand as a Tory candidate, with the hope that he would not let them down. It was genuinely pathetic, in the sense of inspiring sympathy for somebody entirely out of his depth. He said that what he had realized was that politics was teamwork, and that – yeah – he was going to win that constituency, but he was only the tip of an iceberg of helpers and workers who had rallied around him. Then Bailey singled out the guy he had beaten in the selection process and praised him for all the help and support he had given. And that was pretty much it – a very short speech. The high point was when Bailey said that there was an 'African proverb' that went: 'If you don't initiate a child into the village, then he will burn down that village.' This got some sage nods of approval for its apparent profundity, but actually it was the sort of sentiment you might find in a fortune cookie.

Promoting people like Shaun Bailey and Ray Lewis made sense in terms of electoral politics. The Conservatives had left it late in even trying to make themselves appealing to black people. They had missed out on at least two generations of black voters who – if they voted at all – remained loyal to the Labour Party to an overwhelming extent. Black people were largely working class and generally concentrated in inner-city areas represented by Labour or Lib Dem MPs with huge majorities. Even if all the black people – every last one of them – in, say, Liverpool or Manchester voted Conservative that would not necessarily win them the seat. So making any special effort to appeal to black people made little sense, in hard-nosed terms, for the Tory Party. When it came to race they were always better off courting the racist element in the white working class. Those voters were concentrated in seats where there was a chance of overturning a Labour majority. That had been part of the electoral success story of the Tory Party in the 1980s and early 1990s. Lord Tebbit himself had referred to the 'the race issue' as a 'hot button' which could be pressed to cause millions of white Labour voters to switch sides and deliver dozens of marginal seats to the Tories.

In 2005 a version of the Tebbit strategy had been tried, out of desperation. We had seen that go down like a lead balloon in the target seat of Richmond. The 'dog whistle' racism of the Hard Working Families vs Inner-City Criminals had brought out the elderly Tory loyalist vote. But those people were dying out.

There was now a new and significant target audience who could be swayed by the race issue in key seats in the south – liberal-minded, white middle-class and wealthy people who in economic terms were natural Tory voters (who stood to gain a fortune, for example, from Tory promises to abolish or greatly reduce inheritance tax), but who regarded the Conservatives as unfashionable. Racism was universally seen in status terms as the mark of stupid, poor and, probably, old people – the mark of Ian Oakley's White Van Man, the uneducated and the unsophisticated, the knuckle-scrapers of the BNP, bullies in sink-school playgrounds, glue-sniffing skinheads and white redneck trailer trash generally. Racism was a sign of low social status, like having stone cladding and a jumbo-sized satellite dish on the front of your house.

Sensitivities were such that when one of Boris Johnson's advisers made an apparently derogatory racial remark soon after the mayoral election he was immediately sacked. The adviser, one James McGrath, had replied to an email suggesting that the election of Boris Johnson would trigger an exodus of Caribbean immigrations from the country. McGrath had apparently replied by saying: 'Well, let them go if they don't like it here.'

After the talks were over I asked one of the retired big-cheese lawyers what he had made of Lewis's speech. 'Hmmmm . . .' the lawyer replied. 'He was holding back a bit because it is one of the politically correct things you can't say,' he muttered cryptically. 'Leadership, charisma . . . You are just not allowed to discuss it.' He said he had come to know 'Ray' because of his involvement in the Centre for Policy Studies, a Tory think-tank which he supported. 'He says all these things about male role models and fathers, but you just can't discuss that either.' The big question for 'black families', the lawyer said, was just what exactly was the role of the man as head of the family? Men had to be placed back in charge of the family and women had to obey them. Otherwise they had no real role. A lot of the problems flowed from that, he said. Everybody knew that was true, but you just could not say that because of political correctness. 'If the father is not the head of the family, just what is his role? He has no role at all. They won't face that – or even discuss it – so, there you are . . .' He shrugged.

The lawyer then cornered Simon Walker, the host, and began to discuss the PR business, reeling off the names of movers, shakers and mutual acquaintances in various Mayfair PR and law firms. The lawyer just seemed to get bored with the whole race and black fathers issue, and was slightly resentful, I felt, that the annual summer party had been organized around it. It was all just electoral stuff, re-imaging and re-theming for television. All just PR. He was more interested in networking, and in politics at the level of money and power. How was the political consultancy business going, he wanted to know. Walker said that now he was away from the Royal Family he had some contacts who would pay a lot of money – 'and I mean a really lot of money' – to have their image improved. For instance, the Afghan President Hamid Karzai had the money for an image makeover. 'But the pay might be partly in poppies.' This got a good laugh.

Walker then segued into his day at the GMB conference, where he had to deal with a PFI PR fallout. The union had hired a camel and paraded it up and down outside a church for a photo opportunity. It was all 'through an eye of the needle'. 'They were very good,' said Walker, giving the GMB their dues. 'They are just a trade union, though. They don't have any proper PR or any professional PR company, but they do pretty well. They did the stunts and the press things, but they also had strong policy arguments as well. I had to have my wits about me.' His lawyer friend nodded.

Ray Lewis's career in politics turned out to be short-lived. A few days after his speech to the sophisticates and money people in Hammersmith, and just months after being described by David Cameron as 'the most inspirational person I have met since becoming party leader', Ray Lewis was forced to retire from public life after it was revealed that he had faked substantial chunks of his political biography. Specifically, Lewis had falsely claimed that he had served as a magistrate. He had made this claim in order to indirectly deny an earlier record of criminal convictions, since magistrates are subjected to advanced and detailed vetting to ensure they are not ex-criminals before appointment. The deception was therefore both devious and extremely serious.

Lewis had repeatedly used his supposed status as a magistrate to beat down a series of allegations of financial irregularities and sexual harassment involving the youth charities with which he was associated. 'I have never knowingly done anything that would be inconsistent with my position as a justice of the peace,' he told journalists. At the same time it was revealed that Lewis had been subject to the claim that he had been stripped of his ministry in the Church of England in the 1990s amid allegations of sexual harassment of one parishioner, and failure to repay a loan to another.

SIXTEEN

# Majorettes and Export Strength – Dagenham, Essex

The county of Essex occupies a special place in the English imagination. The populations of towns like Dagenham, Basildon, Romford and Southend, running in a line along the A12, have made a big contribution to the popular culture of the country. Linguists have given the white working-class accent and dialect of the area its own title – estuary English – named after the Thames Estuary which is the southern boundary of the area. The accent, with its famously dropped aitches and its glottal stops, has spread right through the country, transmitted via *EastEnders* and hundreds of pop singers and DJs. The people of Essex also have a reputation for being flashy and, to a degree, criminalized – with memories of spivs, the docks and black market of the Second World War. At that time many of the families who now make up the white population of Essex were stuck in the slums of the old East End, riddled with crime, poverty and political extremism.

The Essex Conservative organization was active in the more prosperous parts of the county, such as Chelmsford or Epping Forest, and, generally, the rural and agricultural north of the county. Conservative activity in the former working-class bastions of Basildon and Dagenham was, however, harder to locate. And this was the 'Essex' we were interested in – the badlands of closed car and cement factories, used-car dealerships, derelict 1950s tenpin bowling alleys, rock and roll, *Sun* readers,

Norman Tebbit, Essex Man and Essex Girls, greasers, Terry Venables and Clever Trevor. With nothing in the way of formal politics on offer we decided to attend a civic event, indeed the pride of Dagenham and all of Essex – the mid-summer Dagenham Town Show.

The parade had a unique tradition and, in addition, it was the national focus for the curious activity of competitive drum majorette dancing or promenading, a fad imported into the area in the 1950s as part of Dagenham's and Essex's love of all things American. The whole thing, though, was led off by the mayor, walking on foot behind an army veteran in uniform carrying a flag emblazoned with the borough's coat of arms. He was followed by a group of young girls in long dresses, wearing tiaras and sashes with the word 'Romford' displayed. The first flatbed truck in the parade carried the Black Laws dance troupe. This consisted of four or five black people in African-type costume playing hand drums. Next came the BlueJay Twirlers, a dozen or so girls wearing what looked like matching swimming costumes with sashes. They followed behind a van which crept along blasting Ibiza dance music from its rear doors. They were followed by a man, on his own, dressed in England football kit, wearing an England furry top hat and carrying an England flag; a van towing a mobile hoarding advertising a concert by Status Quo, David Essex and the Bay City Rollers; another flatbed with a variety of people of all ages dressed as ancient Greek gods and athletes – reflecting the official theme of the parade, which was the 2012 London Olympics.

The rest of the parade was pretty shambolic. Majorette groups short on dancers, flatbeds with dismal displays, bass boosters jammed in the open boots of Mondeos followed by bedraggled groups of irregularly uniformed children. A few of the majorette troupes played hip-hop, and there were floats from Age Concern, the St John Ambulance Brigade, the West Ham women's football team, and an Afro dance outfit called the

Bantu Foundation – who were wearing elaborate Brazilian or Notting Hill Carnival-type costumes and danced along to soca music. The Havering Majorettes appeared to be a bit better at the formation marching thing. Their music was Tina Turner, played from the boot of a car belonging to a company offering Caravan Cleaning Services ('full exterior valeting service'). The rear of the parade featured an empty London bus followed by a lot of lollipop ladies who were giving out lollipop lady badges. They were in turn followed by two Community Support police officers on bikes who specialized in doing wheelies in form-ation; a solo Elvis impersonator; a van pulling a mobile hoarding for a Sugababes concert (Central Park, Dagenham); an ambu-lance; a convoy of street-cleaning vehicles and – last of all – a police riot van.

Along the route of the march, which was to end up at the main park and playing field in the centre of Dagenham, near the town hall, people had assembled little rows of deckchairs either along the pavement or in their small front gardens. The weather was reasonably good (warm and dry but threatening rain) and some had set up barbecues in their front gardens. Crummy front gardens are a feature of this part of the world, often littered with spare tyres, old batteries and assorted rusting car parts. The houses consisted of uniform rows of 1930s interwar cottage-style semi-detached or short-terrace council houses – good quality housing stock which had been sold off in the 1980s. One effect of the sell-off was the amazing array of exterior decoration – all the houses got new mahogany-style front doors, many with lots of brass fittings. There was plenty of stone cladding and pebble dashing as well. One cladding job involved what looked like crazy paving on the exterior walls, pointed with luminous lime-green mortar. Another house had been done up to look like a half-timbered mock Tudor job. The owner had named it The White House and attached fake oak beams to the exterior. He was repainting it white as the parade was passing, the noise and distraction causing him to swear and scowl.

There were Croydon facelifts in abundance among the onlookers, and lots of cheap supermarket discount lager being guzzled out of cans on the street. The dress and appearance of onlookers was almost uniform – sports leisurewear, white T-shirts, replica football shirts, beer bellies, baggy pastel tracksuits and sweatpants, combat pants, hoodies, shorts (in various styles), kids on bikes, pushchairs, bald heads and fat thighs.

There were lots of fresh tattoos as well – red-raw on pasty pink skin – the usual stuff: hearts with 'Mum' in the centre, names of soon-to-be-departed lovers, ugly and uneven versions of Maori patterns. There was chunky gold jewellery, crumpled Ralph Lauren polo shirts and many, many dogs on choke chains, mostly Staffs.

Elsewhere there were girls lining the streets – they may have been the older sisters of the majorettes – knocking back Bacardi Breezers, making lewd comments and violently snogging their boyfriends. At one point there was a gang of hoodie-wearing boys, about a dozen of them, sitting on a wall and pointing and laughing at the fat girls (many of the majorettes seemed to be overweight and a few of them were obese) and, even though they only looked about twelve or thirteen, these boys were drinking from long cans of Stella. When the Elvis impersonator came along they shouted 'WANKER!' at him and cackled. He ignored them. A little further on a perfect Samantha Fox-type Essex Girl came out of her done-up council house to have a look at what was going on. She had teased-out blonde hair, bright pink lipstick and was wearing very high heels and a miniskirt. A fat, older woman standing next to her (possibly a relative, maybe the next-door neighbour) nodded towards the parade and said: 'It's the worst one it's bin – usually a lot longer, innit?' The Essex Girl said: 'Yeah . . . it's really shit.' A little further along still what appeared to be a large extended family group had taken over a bus stop, and had installed several fold-up chairs, turning it into a sort of viewing stand. They watched the Bantu Foundation, who stopped in front of them for a while and did a bit of furious and vaguely indecent Brazilian-type wiggling and jumping up and down dancing. The bus stop squatters consisted of a white family, but there was no real racial reaction. One of the females in the group said: 'I couldn't do that! I haven't got the bum for it.' The rest of them were more or less ignoring the parade entirely, conversing instead about some unfathomable but highly fraught family business of one sort or another.

There were three men, probably in their twenties, sitting on a bench on a scruffy bit of grass near a road junction. They were skinheads and were wearing baseball caps. They had a great pile of tins of lager in transparent plastic bags. They, too, were ignoring the parade, but were arguing and spatting with each other, swearing continuously, using not only the f-word, which seemed to function as an all-purpose verb, but the c-word as well. They weren't angry all the time: sometimes they seemed to be enjoying themselves, or expressing admiration for each other, especially for their mobile phones: 'Wow, this is smooth, innit? Man, that's safe. Safe-safe-safe! Smooth. Well safe. Mint!' The other key words were 'geezer' and 'geeze'.

Their women were about twenty feet away, leaning on the railings talking to each other and glancing at the parade in a bored way from time to time. They had their kids with them, and they were running about on the pavement, eating crisps and chasing and thumping each other. They were tiny but they were pretty violent. At one point one of the skinheads noticed that his daughter had spilled some type of junk food on her clothes. He barked in the direction of the women with real venom: ''ere look it's all over her farkin' cardigan . . . clean it off 'er!' The woman, who was overweight, swathed in entirely formless black clothing and was heavily pregnant to boot,

shouted back: 'Narrrrh! Why should I do it? Yoo clean it off
'er.' The man complained that he didn't have any cleaning
materials: 'Whaddama gonna clean it off wiv? Are you farking
stooopid or what?' . . . 'Fark off.' 'Naw . . . you fark off.' The
child had to put up with being streaked with vomit. She had
been crying, but eventually stopped when she became involved
in the thumping, kicking and eye-poking game with the other
kids.

On the other side of the road the gang of boys who'd called
Elvis a wanker had caught up with the parade. They now seemed
to be under the leadership of a fat kid with cropped hair, who
wore a hoodie and looked exactly like the fat dimwit boy in
the *King of the Hill* cartoon. He was about eleven or twelve. He
was drinking from a can of lager, and leading the activity of
teasing the majorettes, many of whom were probably primary
school age – pointing and laughing at them and shouting,
'Carm orn, gewls! Get yer tits out!'

The police were nowhere to be seen. They had gone off to
sort out a traffic problem. At one point the march had got
spaced out and traffic started crossing the route in the normal
anti-social way of drivers – we had noticed – in Essex, getting
trapped between the floats and causing the parade to seize up.

The woeful procession finally arrived at the central muni-
cipal park, a vast tract of featureless fenced-in grass overlooked
by a series of gigantic brutalist tower blocks which gave the
place the look of a more grim and pessimistic version of East
Berlin. There was a judging area where the majorette troupes
did their thing, but not many people were watching.

The rest of the show was divided into two parts, the first a
commercial fun fair which was combined with row upon row
of tents selling junk food of every imaginable variety and, in
addition, a gigantic beer tent. This was the most crowded part
of the show. There was a second, less busy area which featured
displays put on by the multitudinous branches of the local

authority, various charities and some local businesses. One of the largest tents was occupied by the police, where, just outside, the TSG (Territorial Support Group) were giving a continuous display of riot-control techniques. The cops were organizing kids into two groups – one group was encouraged to throw eggs and meaty looking black rubber bricks at the other group, who had to defend themselves with riot shields. 'Go on, let 'im have it,' one ten-year-old yelled, encouraging members of his team to pelt the shield-holders with eggs. Meanwhile, a disabled man in a motorized wheelchair joined in, whacking the shields with something like a baseball bat for all he was worth. The police looked on benevolently, laughing and praising the kids alternately for both their rioting and riot-control skills.

There was an educational tent with the credentials of all the local further education colleges on display, with lots of glossy brochures offering all sorts of weird and unlikely life-changing career opportunities – such as deep-sea diving and psychiatric counselling. They were doing very little business, despite expensive looking video display equipment and more glossy brochures than you would find in the average high street travel agent. A wide variety of council-promoted cultural activity was also being advertised – and widely ignored – including African drumming and poetry.

One of the more popular attractions in the civic area was a tent belonging to West & Coe, the local funeral directors. The attraction here was a newly painted, shiny black Victorian glass-sided hearse manned by a bloke in elaborate Victorian funeral director's costume – a stove-pipe hat covered with black netting – and pulled by two gleaming black horses with black plumes on their heads. The thing was really nightmarish, like something out of a bad 1970s British horror film, but it attracted a big crowd, and people were lifting their kids up so they could pat and stroke the horses while the funeral directors observed them with meaningful looks and thin, chilling smiles. It was hard to explain the prominence of the funeral tent and the lack of effect it had on people. Maybe it was part of the same generalized 'whatever' approach to everything, which extended from the plainly obscene sexual feeling up and French kissing in public, to non-stop drinking and eating. Maybe it was a case of tattoos replacing taboos.

The central row of local authority and voluntary organization tents was like a tunnel of misery. Cheerful things like the Boy Scouts, and similar paramilitary youth organizations such as the Boys' Brigade, had a vestigial presence, but mostly the charities were of the heartbreakingly miserable kind – MS, mental health, diabetes, drug rehab, abused children – all trying and evidently failing to raise cash and sympathy. The British Legion, the organization which cares for ex-servicemen and women, had probably the biggest presence in this part of the show, reflecting the county of Essex's role in supplying the army regularly with squaddies, something at which it excelled and even rivalled Hampshire.

The chairman of the British Legion in Dagenham was a bluff man in his sixties with small eyes set in a pink and fleshy face. He wore a blazer and a British Legion tie. The lapels of his jacket were decorated with numerous enamel poppy badges, and he had another large enamel badge of a Union Jack and a yellow ribbon. We met him in the community action tent which formed part of the show. He got our attention by challenging us to a game of fund-raising tombola. The Legion, the chairman reckoned, was needed more than ever because of the wars in Iraq and, especially, in Afghanistan. 'People call it a "conflict",' the chairman volunteered, angrily, 'but it is not a conflict – it is a war, a full-on war.'

The chairman said people didn't realize how bad the situation was. 'I've been up to Birmingham to see our boys, it is absolutely terrible.' He was referring to the Midlands hospital in which casualties from Iraq and Afghanistan were being treated. 'People know about the fatalities, but what they don't talk about is the injuries – and they are horrific.' At this point a second member of the Dagenham Legion's committee piped up: 'This is a war that can't be won. The Russians couldn't beat them. Nobody can beat them . . . Anyway, we shouldn't be there in the first place.'

The chairman screwed up his face and said: 'The only way you can fight them is from the air. You've got to bomb the bastards. But the do-gooders won't let you.' The other bloke chipped in: 'All you can do is unite all the countries and march through Afghanistan and clear them out . . .' The chairman interrupted: '. . . well, I don't know why we are in Afghanistan. I can't see the sense of it. There's nothing there, nothing worth fighting about. At least in Iraq we're there to get the petrol – we need that – but Afghanistan?', and he shook his head, 'nah!

'Do you know most of the soldiers out there in Afghanistan and Iraq are eighteen or nineteen? That's all. And if you go to the First World War graves, they were all that age as well . . . even the captains and the officers.' He had a theory that the British Army was only being used in Afghanistan because the British government was somehow being paid to be there by 'the Yanks'. But by this stage he was getting a bit irritated with us. He wanted to get on with the main job which was selling tombola tickets. 'This war in Afghanistan . . . we'll never win that. Remember . . . they've got Allah on their side.'

He was also getting a bit shirty with David, but this was a problem for somebody who sympathized with the British Army – a disproportionate number of soldiers in the British Army, including a good many decorated men, were black.

Dagenham was overwhelmingly white. At one point David had been walking along the pavement and a rough looking white bloke had barged into him as he passed, almost knocking him into the road. His normal 'don't react' reflex kicked in and, David reckoned, it was in such circumstances that it was really needed in order to avoid coming to serious harm. In this way the white working class, David thought, were much more of a problem than, say, the Richmond Tories. When they were aggrieved, and when they felt that the target of their ire had only a limited ability to defend itself or strike back, the WWC was much more likely to do something about it – such as follow you for thirty miles down a duel carriageway and then jump out of their white vans at traffic lights, snarling like rabid pit bulls. White Van Man is existentially dangerous not only because of the way he drives but because in the back of that van he has lots of hammers, knives, pickaxe handles, drills, lengths of metal pipe, hacksaws and the like – whereas in the back of his Rover, Richmond Tory Man simply has a box of After Eights and, as we had seen with the likes of Marco Forgione, directions to the nearest model railway club.

Still at the head of the parade as it wound through the town was the mayor of Dagenham; he was a Labour councillor and he was black. David walked with him and they chatted. As they did so they noticed a man among the spectators standing next to a youth in his early teens, almost certainly his son. He had thinning ginger hair and wore regulation sports casual: a cheap blue and white striped polo shirt, stone-washed jeans and a grey blouson casually slung over his shoulder. Every other word he used was 'fuck'. The boy looked bored and unimpressed, as if he'd heard it all before. The man answered his mobile phone and said: 'Yeah, I'm at that stooopid farkin' parade fing . . . Y' know what? The farking mayor – right? – aind the farking mayoress are farking coons! Yeh! FARKIN' COONS! Can you farkin' believe it! Yeah! I can't farkin' believe it neeever!'

The mayor heard all of that – as intended – but he just smiled and looked away. The police did nothing, although they were right there. Surely there was some sort of public order issue at stake. The mayor had been born in Nigeria and was tremendously proud of the honour of leading the town parade. He really was sort of bursting with civic pride which was presumably why he could deal with the racist abuse with such impressive sangfroid.

The mayor's characteristic West African enthusiasm and inexplicable cheerfulness waned, though, when David asked him what he thought of the crowd's reaction to the procession. 'They're not 100 per cent excited,' he said, with an air of seriousness. The lady mayoress continued to wave at the crowd. 'It is to do with the demographic nature of the area,' he added, being careful not to say exactly what both David and he were thinking: Dagenham is basically chock-full of racists, to the point of it feeling actually quite dangerous. He said he was concerned about the lack of diversity in the crowd and he put that down to the absence of adequate information ethnic minorities received about the parade. 'I don't think the whole community is represented here,' he said.

All those immigrant bus drivers, nurses and cleaners and collectors of tickets. They were all in the union and they paid their dues every week. Over the years that probably added up to millions by now. They had built the Labour Party, or a big part of it. That gave them a say – by right – on who got on what committee and who was picked as a council candidate. It was not like the Tory Party where some national ad campaign manager was looking at data from focus groups and deciding he needed a bit of diversity to look a bit more modern, urban, young and up to date.

The white working class might be right-wing, but they were not Conservative. They were developing if anything a kind of anarchic dislike and distrust of everyone and everything. As a political force they were falling to bits. Some might vote for the extreme right, others for the extreme left. Most would not bother, or just give in to the forces of inertia.

But there was a Conservative force at work in the grass roots in places like Dagenham. And it was represented by the Labour mayor of the town. He described himself as a 'Very British mayor of a very British town . . . a British mayor of African descent'. When David asked how he felt about representing a town with a reputation for white working-class racism he said: 'I was elected by white people. Your service to the community can't be hidden. The best thing for ethnic minority people moving to this area is to serve their community. I'm a private person. I like to serve from behind the scenes. Let's serve. That's the best we can do.' It struck us that this guy was a classic civic Conservative, the sort of modest pragmatic, family-orientated man who valued privacy and observed a scrupulous air of modest decency and decorum of the sort that Edmund Burke would have recognized as 'the best sort of civilized man'.

When we headed back to London David visibly relaxed. We got lost in a one-way system and went round a good few roundabouts until, with enormous pleasure, we saw a big green sign marked 'London'.

# SEVENTEEN

# Inside the Magic Kingdom – Chartwell, Kent, and Westminster, London

On a wet bank holiday Monday in May, the grounds of Chartwell, the family home of Winston Churchill from 1922 until his death in 1965, presented a damp if pretty sight. The profusion of trees and shrubs and the long grass in the meadows were luminously green in the murkiness. Wisps of cloud and mist hung on to the treetops along the horizon. At ten o'clock in the morning, the car park was deserted, and by lunchtime it was still only half full.

It struck me that one of the key things about Conservatives was the idea that it was their party leader who had won the Second World War single-handed. If it was never stated openly, there seemed to be an underlying and not unreasonable assumption that without Winston Britain would now be an enslaved province of Nation Europa, a German empire somehow allied with the Japanese. 'England, Their England' in these circumstances would have found its women defiled, its Jews and ethnic minorities exterminated and its male population slaving away in coal mines and labour camps.

As the party of the older generation (certainly in the South of England anyway) the Conservatives could claim moral strength from the idea that they, or their generation, had fought in the Second World War to preserve the freedoms and liberties which made Britain a decent place to live in. If the younger generation and post-war immigrant communities now took all these liberties for granted, it was hardly surprising that some older people found that annoying.

Nor was it surprising that many Conservatives thought that after the war, and the decade of austerity which followed it, the country had begun to go to the dogs in the 1960s. The late sixties (marked by the 'summer of love' of 1968) saw the coming to maturity of the first generation of post-war babies, a generation that mocked the attitude of their parents, those of the wartime era, and one that preferred flower power to fire power, making love rather than war.

For the elderly Conservatives we met during our True Blue tour of Britain, among them many of the wartime generation, the political energy generated by Winston Churchill had been spent, the spirit of the Battle of Britain long since evaporated. Not only had they consigned the war to the past but they had accepted the abandonment of the Union Jack as the symbol of the party. Mention of Margaret Thatcher (never mind Winston Churchill) was now virtually taboo. The marketing and campaigning gurus in charge of the Conservative Party had determined that overt admiration for such individuals and all they symbolized made the party look old-fashioned, elderly, cranky, overly formal and certainly not user-friendly.

In 2002 the BBC carried out an intriguing nationwide poll. It broadcast a programme with an interactive element in which it asked viewers to nominate their choice of 'the greatest Briton of all time'. The poll attracted more than a million votes. In the end, Winston Churchill emerged as the victor, with 447,423 votes. This would have come as a relief to the BBC, who must have dreaded viewers voting for Jordan or Bill Oddie. Still, Churchill's electorate amounted to just 1 per cent of the adult population of Britain.

Apart from a statue which stands near the Houses of Parliament, Churchill has no national, public memorial. Chartwell therefore serves as that memorial and as a shrine of sorts.

Where better to go to try to understand what it was that made Churchill in the eyes of so many 'the greatest Briton of all time'? It was all quite low-key, however. Despite the house's historical significance and its impressive grounds, many of the visitors on that bank holiday seemed to have come only for the tea shop next to the car park. Grandly referred to as a 'restaurant', the tea shop had a clientele that was overwhelmingly old and preoccupied with the quality of the coffee and the cakes on offer.

Almost everyone, even including some of the children, was dressed in expensive wet-weather hiking gear, the sort of kit you would need for a walk up Ben Nevis or a trek in the foothills of the Himalayas. Gore-Tex jackets in either nettle-green or dung-brown, heavily laced hiking boots, matching waterproof gaiters and complicated headgear were de rigueur. Most had rucksacks and some carried lightweight, collapsible walking sticks, which looked a bit like ski poles or perhaps sniper rifles.

The tea shop was decorated in a spartan green and beige, with green emulsion lightly applied over exposed brickwork. Everything felt very puritanical, with rows of tables decked out like a school canteen. Despite the wholesome, eco-friendly look, everything was plastic – plastic tables, plastic wooden panels on the wall, plastic chairs, plastic knives and plastic forks – and there was a rather incongruous old-fashioned hat stand which, from a distance, looked like it was made of polished mahogany but on closer inspection also turned out to be . . . plastic. There was a very definite style to it all, one which might be termed Plastic Puritanism.

There were special children's meals available in cardboard party box affairs. They were colourfully graphic and cheerful but, rather than featuring the usual superheroes and cartoon characters that kids actually like, they were illustrated with drawings of cows and chickens. Outside the main café, an ice-cream kiosk stood closed and padlocked due to the bad weather. Even this had a didactic element to it. It was called The Dispatch

Box, named after the part of the House of Common from where Churchill delivered his speeches. Because this would probably baffle any normal ten-year-old, it would provide a brilliant opportunity for a mind-improving lecture on parliamentary procedure. Yes, politics is fun!

The gift shop next door was the size of a small supermarket and housed in what appeared to be a converted Kentish oast-house; in reality, however, it was a modern building made out of cinder blocks. The shop's interior was tricked out like a barn with plastic-looking wooden beams and a very high roof. Whitewashed breezeblocks maintained the Puritan theme, while powerful halogen spotlights illuminated the shelves of goodies on display, making them gleam. In a further clash of styles, the shop was playing 'In the Mood' by Glenn Miller over the PA, quietly.

Winston Churchill appeared on the shelves but mainly in relation to alcohol. The booze section centred on bottles of overpriced champagne and claimed in a useful information panel that Churchill used to drink a pint of champagne for breakfast every day. Other patriotic booze included English mead, 'England's Oldest Drink', and English Bulldog Bitter. While booze may well have got the great man through the war in private, as with Groucho Marx and Fidel Castro the cigar was very much his public trademark. But when I asked a shop assistant if they had any cigars for sale, it was explained to me, aggressively and with a look of complete horror, that it was against National Trust policy to sell 'anything to do with tobacco in any form whatsoever at all'.

A life-size bronze of Winston Churchill for sale at £4000 watched over all the tat in the gift shop. Smaller, and, at £140, more affordable zinc Churchill busts were also for sale, but they really did not look anything like the great man. There was a boxed set of Churchill's complete speeches, in mono, but that didn't seem like the ideal stocking filler. There was also a fair amount of stuff about fighting on the home front and what have you, but no real indication of who Churchill was fighting, or why.

For no apparent reason there was a scale model of Concorde (£200) on sale, nestling between First and Second World War aircraft, including a Lancaster bomber and some jolly Red Baron-style German biplanes with old-fashioned non-Nazi Iron Cross markings. Flogging Stukas and Messerschmitts, however, would have presented a problem, since this would have involved a public display of swastikas, which in these politically correct times was not a great sales strategy and was possibly even illegal. In fact, there was no mention of Hitler or Germany, the Bosch, Huns, fiendish Japs, Nips, cowardly Eyeties or our great friend Uncle Joe Stalin or anything like that at all. But there were Churchill fridge magnets with various non-political sayings, like: 'History will be kind to me, as I intend to write it'. There was not much patriotism in evidence, no Union flags and no 'V for Victory' signs. Churchill had been repackaged into the history category of 'beyond living memory' and as a bit-part support player in the long-running black and white Hitler show apparently continuously looped on the cable TV history channels. Churchill was well on his way to becoming just another Dead White European Male – like Alfred the Great or the Duke of Marlborough – who had won a war against somebody over something or other at some barely defined point in the past.

As I was leaving the gift shop, I noticed a large Audi with foreign plates sweep into the car park. Germans! I decided to watch what they did. They were forty-something and dressed, in that typically casual German way, like successful architects or furniture designers. They headed straight for the gift shop as though they knew what they were doing and had been there before. As they entered the shop, they bumped into some oldsters leaving. The Germans apologized in heavily accented

English. 'It's OK, my friend,' said one old Englishmen, with genuine amity. The German man went straight to the display of model warplanes where he began examining the Red Baron biplane with Teutonic seriousness and intensity. Then he started sorting through the CDs of Winston Churchill speeches. His German woman friend, rigged out in a bright red skiing jacket, efficiently cleared off and came back with the illustrated guide to Chartwell in German. The German man then spent a while looking at the Churchill books. I could not resist asking him, 'Are you interested in Winston Churchill?' He seemed a bit surprised and defensive and said that he was learning English and hoping to improve it. He had read that Winston Churchill spoke perfect English and he wanted to 'listen and to practise'. Then he was off, moving quickly and scanning all the tat in the shop with a look of disdain.

I wandered out of the shop into Churchill's house itself, which had supposedly been preserved in exactly the way he had had it in the 1930s. All the guides were volunteers, very elderly, mostly female and in uniform, in the sense that they all wore brass-buttoned navy blue blazers, apart from the odd one or two in shades of mustard or salmon. The guide in the salmon jacket had perfectly yellow teeth, twinkling eyes and a habitual smile, which had given her face masses of creases. She also sported an elaborate swept-back hairstyle. 'We are down to the hard core,' she said, flashing her pearly yellows. When I asked if the visitors came, as seemed likely, mainly for the gardens and the architecture, she became strangely vehement. 'No, no . . . it is Churchill!' Was the attraction popular with foreign tourists, I asked, given the distinct absence of European visitors, apart from the odd German couple in search of language lessons? 'Oh, yes. He was a world statesman, a giant figure on the world stage . . .' She then became confidential and lowered her voice. 'Just recently there was a man here from Brazil, and he said it had been his life's dream to visit Chartwell.'

She was then called away to deal with an emergency involving transgression of the velvet rope by a baby buggy.

There was a dignified hush as I shuffled through the rest of the house, which included Lady Churchill's bedroom, a kitchen, library, dining room and a 'trophy room' which Winston Churchill himself had laid out. The room featured, in pride of place, a certificate from John F. Kennedy conferring honorary citizenship of the United States on Churchill, along with some tacky glass fruit bowls given by Stalin and a gold, bejewelled dagger scabbard presented by the Saudi royal family. It looked like something out of a Christmas cracker, only bigger and much more expensive. A visitor asked one of the guides innocently if Churchill had lived at Chartwell during the war. The guide reacted in mock horror, and she explained that it would have been much too dangerous; the Germans would have attacked the house without hesitation. No: in the main he stayed in London, she said, but he may have put up in the gardener's cottage once or twice. The place had been pretty much boarded up during the war and had suffered from terrible rising damp because it was on a hill and had not been maintained for a good few years. 'I know the state these places can get into because my father's house was boarded up as well,' an elderly woman guard revealed. I suggested that with all the cigars he smoked and the brandy and other booze he consumed, the damp must have had a terrible effect on his chest. The guard looked offended. 'Oh no, he lived into his nineties, he was a very healthy man.' It was a conditioned response, semi-totalitarian, that no bad thing must be said of the Great Leader, even about his health.

Outside, in the back garden near a separate building housing Churchill's art studio and collection of astoundingly bad amateur paintings (his hobby), a teenage girl was conducting a school project survey of the visitors. She was kitted out grunge-style, with scuffed Converse basketball shoes, drainpipe jeans that made her legs look like pipe cleaners, a T-shirt, long, scruffy hair and a fur-lined parka. She was happy to share some of her results with me and allowed me to hover nearby watching her grill the punters. Most were retired locals, and some said they came to the house often. Others were from the north and on their way to the Continent for a break and had made a stopover in Kent. They were mostly interested in just coming out for a cup of tea at their nearest major countryside tea room, and the association with Churchill was an added bonus. They all approved of Churchill but were vague about the reason. 'He never gave up' was a standard reply, as was 'He was very determined', but nobody said anything about him saving the country from invasion and German occupation. A slightly younger man, who was pushing a buggy with his long-suffering wife and kids, answered the grunge girl's questionnaire. He said that he'd voted Labour last time but that he was 'probably New Conservative now'. He explained that he was not really interested in Churchill as such (and definitely not in the gardens) but he was interested in the war and the 'equipment' used in wars generally. He was disappointed that there was not more 'equipment' at Chartwell.

Everyone I saw tried conscientiously to help the grunge girl with her school project and seemed delighted that she should be taking an interest in the Olden Days in this way and not just hanging around the local bus stop drinking alcopops and swearing at people. It struck me as a very nice, moderate, decent conservative response. The visitors might have looked a bit boring at first glance, but they were also modest and self-effacing. They listened carefully and very respectfully to the girl even though they did not need to do so, and had to stand in the gentle drizzle to do this to boot. They announced themselves as gently as they could, and tried to put her at her ease. 'I'm not very political, dear . . . probably Conservative, dear,' they would say or, 'I used to be Conservative, my love, but I'm Liberal now . . . for my sins.'

The Chartwell visitors were old; in their younger days, I judged from the look of them, they had kept themselves in work, kept their noses clean and avoided the various disasters of life. Now they were retired and comfortably enough off to be members of the National Trust, eat tea and cake in country house gardens at £7.50 a pop, just about keep a nice motor on the road and enjoy occasional creature comforts. They stayed in the slow lane, had savings and pensions and were decent people. They were interested in the old days, vaguely proud of the history of their country and the look of the countryside, though they would have liked a bit more sunshine for their gardens. They were happy to help other people out, so long as it was not too much trouble. They were nostalgic. They liked preserving things from the past and, in a vague way, thought that the modern world was an unpleasant and frightening place compared to the way things had been when they were in their prime – even though some of them had lived through the war and all of them went through the Cuban Missile Crisis and the Cold War.

The grunge girl asked her questions in the conventional listless and pushy-yet-self-effacing style of teenagers everywhere. Once she had listened to about ten people, presumably deciding this was enough to produce an A* grade collection of plausible looking yet statistically meaningless pie charts, she gave up and slouched off, hood up to protect her head from the drizzle. I left at that point as well, winding through Kent's narrow country lanes back to the motorway and the horrors of the twenty-first century.

And there they were again, the People of Chartwell: obediently driving at exactly one mile an hour less than the legal speed limit, in the heavy bank holiday traffic, maybe discussing ways in which Winston Churchill's take on gardening and watercolour painting could be applied to their own more modest plots and households. They were on their way home to a well-cooked meal of meat and two veg. They would worry a little about the welfare of their grandchildren while comfortably wrapped up in their own very private world of air bags, cruise control, anti-shatter windscreen glass, steel radials, up-to-date third party insurance, AA roadside assistance and Classic FM.

Yes, there they were sitting in the middle lane of life's motorway, sticking to the rules and keeping a sharp eye on the petrol gauge. Yes, they were bland, they were mainstream, they were unadventurous and utterly middle-of-the-road. However they cast their vote at election time, they were Conservatives.

At another point during our True Blue journey, David and I found ourselves standing next to the real dispatch box in the Chamber of the House of Commons. We were in the company of the Tatton Conservatives, on their annual day trip to the Houses of Parliament, and later in the day – as I've discussed earlier in the book – we would go on to the Carlton Club for tea.

One of the Tatton Tory matrons looked around the debating Chamber, taking in the coats of arms and general Victoriana: 'It looks a lot bigger on't telly,' she said, 'dun'tit?' Everyone agreed that it looked bigger on telly. Their guide pointed out the part of the wall of the Chamber which had been replaced by smoked glass. That was where the TV cameras were located, but you wouldn't really notice that unless you were looking carefully: 'Ohhh . . . that's clever int'it?' The guide rattled through the rest of his spiel, pointing to the dispatch box and instructing his charges to note the wear caused by Winston Churchill who had a habit of banging his fist on its leatherwork. It remained more or less as it was in his day, unrestored, a sort of memorial to him: 'Ooohhh that's intrestin', int'it?'

In the Members' Lobby, located between the Central Lobby and the Commons Chamber in the middle of the House, there were a number of bronze statues and busts of legendary prime ministers. Two figures in particular stood out. One was a larger than life Margaret Thatcher on a plinth, the index finger of her right hand pointing in accusatory fashion. The other dominating statue was that of Winston Churchill, hands on hips and gut slightly jutting forward but tastefully slimmed down as a mark of respect. The guide pointed out the wear on Winston's shiny left foot, the result of years of superstitious MPs rubbing it for luck before entering the Chamber, but few of the Tatton Tories were especially interested in him: they seemed keener on Margaret Thatcher. Several started stroking her foot in the hope, we supposed, of starting a new tradition. They were lost in reverent admiration for this statue of their idol. In the cathedral-like Gothic surroundings the moment acquired an almost religious intensity. They all seemed vaguely proud of Winston Churchill, but they actually appeared to be in love with Margaret Thatcher.

Later we sat with the Tatton Conservatives in the House of Commons tourist café, where they complained – not unreasonably – about being ripped off not only in the form of taxes levied by parliamentarians, but by the price of the Cornish pasties in their canteen. They moaned about the Labour Party in a general 'country going to the dogs' way. When one bloke started going on about that day's big news – that David Davies had resigned his seat to fight a by-election on the issue of civil liberties – his wife chided him: 'He's off again . . . wi' 'im it's all politics, politics, politics.' Apart from the moment of ecstasy when they spotted Margaret Thatcher in bronze, the Tatton Tories didn't seem to be enjoying themselves very much. It had already been a long day, an early start followed by the rigours of the coach trip, traffic jams and the crowds of tourists around Westminster.

And yet you could see how the trip to the Houses of Parliament was a treat, which must have given them a powerful psychological lift. If the physical fabric of the Palace of

Westminster was a Victorian imperial theme park, it was also a monument to something even older and more specific – the English revolution and counter-revolution of the seventeenth century. The place was a shrine not to democracy, but to limited monarchy. In the four centuries since the monarchy had accepted, on pain of execution, that its representatives had to rule in conjunction with Parliament, kings and queens had mostly worked with the Tory (or Whig) prime ministers, men who were the precursors of the Conservatives of today.

Since then the Palace of Westminster had been further sanctified by the fact of its survival during the Blitz of 1941 (bomb damage in the Central Lobby had been left untouched on the orders of Winston Churchill himself). As one of the Tatton Tories told us, the place was 'magic . . . proper magic'. It seemed that this might literally be true. There were signs of tribal magic, ritual incantations and ancestor worship everywhere – from the superstitious habit of touching Winston Thatcher or Margaret Churchill's foot, through symbolic paintings and mosaics of national saints and miracle workers on the walls, to the reverence shown towards the vacant throne of Queen Victoria – spooky and empty as if she were still a spectral presence.

All this seemed to explain the attraction of the visit to the Tories of Tatton. They came down every so often, to remind themselves that England was their country, that Blair might come and Brown might go, but they were going to hang on to it. The visit to their Parliament was their pilgrimage. Parliament belonged to them. It was their birthright.

My Tory journey had come to an end and it was time to take stock. I felt a lot better than when I started, but that was largely because I had recovered from a potentially fatal disease that coincided with researching the early part of this book. I had survived but I don't think that the Conservative Party – at least the grass roots of it – is doing the same. At the time of writing, David Cameron is riding high in the polls but he had very little in common with most of the Tories I met. I reckon that if David Cameron and his aides were actually to spend any time with the overwhelmingly elderly and sometimes down at heel Conservative activists we met then there would be embarrassed glances all round. Cameron and his people would probably see many of the activists we met as, if anything, a liability rather than an asset.

This yawning gap between a party leadership's brightly optimistic message and the less telegenic reality of the party's local membership was all pretty familiar to me. I had seen, from a slightly closer vantage point, the way that the Labour Party had been re-themed for television a decade or more earlier – a transformation which had yielded staggering success in the polls. You couldn't re-launch the Tories as the New Conservative Party because, apart from anything else, that would be a contradiction in terms. But at the top of the party nearly everything else had, at least superficially, changed. The union flag has been relegated to the faintest hint of a red cross on pastel blue, grey and green websites; the robust philandering and boozing of the likes of Alan Clark has been replaced by the nappy-changing, bike-riding new man image of David Cameron.

The question David and I had set ourselves when we started out on our journey was 'what sort of person might, these days, become a Conservative activist and what makes them tick'. We had come up with an answer of sorts. Once you got beyond the national marketing campaign and one or two places where party membership offered access to money and moderately glamorous social events, most Conservatives seemed to be very old, not particularly interested in politics or ideology, and slightly hurt – in some cases – to be thought of as the 'nasty party'. Most of the Tories we met didn't seem to be rolling in cash – rather they displayed a type of distressed gentility, the style of people who had once been wealthy but had been living off their savings and capital for longer than they had expected. These grey, wrinkled Tories had waged a lifelong campaign to protect their family wealth and capital from the ravages of taxation and inflation. But socialism was wreaking its revenge, in a way they couldn't have expected. The NHS, publicly funded and staffed by an army of foreign employees, was keeping them – and often their parents – alive for far longer than they had budgeted for. This was steadily reducing them to a condition of dependency upon the welfare state far more comprehensive than anything Arthur Scargill or Harold Wilson might have engineered.

One of the most appealing characteristics of the Tories we met was the care and concern they tended to show for each other. Some of them had clearly been serving on the same committees with each other – and carrying out the same canvassing and other political chores – for decades. They didn't seem to have much passion for it any more, but they seemed to enjoy the sense of community and security these old routines gave them. Like old married couples, they continued to care for each other and show a lot of affection for each other long after the original spark of passion had died.

Almost everywhere we were greeted with courtesy and one or two people seemed, genuinely, to want to befriend us. Many of the older Conservatives had impeccable manners and were very courteous – both increasingly rare in modern Britain, where rudeness and incessant complaining about everything now seems to be viewed as some kind of virtue. One of the strangest moments I experienced among the Tories in the home of an elderly and very proper female Conservative supporter in Richmond, whose small town house was a monument to every imaginable type of chintz. She seemed to be horrified at my presence, but still treated me with the greatest courtesy, as if we were in a play by Noël Coward. At the other end of the spectrum was Ian Oakley, the disgraced Conservative candidate from Watford, who was charged with harassment of rival candidates and seemed, to us, little more than a self-obsessed yob. To be fair the Watford Tories did seem to shun him. The fact that they had chosen him as a candidate, though, seemed to confirm just how desperate the Tories were to involve people who were under retirement age. Even creepy people like Ian Oakley.

Most Conservatives, like the lady in Richmond, were very wary and simply did not seem to believe that anyone such as ourselves (which in David's case meant under fifty and – in addition – black) would want to have anything to do with them. I was confronted only once – by Big Frank during our canvassing escapade in the 'Thatcherite' Tudor ward in Richmond. He narrowed his eyes and looked a bit threatening, in a harmless way. But then he just shrugged his shoulders and got on with the canvassing.

Thus the most glaring empirical finding thrown up by our journey was that Conservatives are old – and the conclusion I draw from that is that the party, at least as it stands, will not be around for much longer. We had glimpses of the Liberals, Labour and Greens during the general election and by-election campaigns and indeed the candidates of fringe, crank parties. They were pretty wrinkly as well. Miss Great Britain – who stood in the Henley by-election – was fairly young. But she was very much the exception to the rule and, anyway, her appearance treated the entire edifice of democracy as a huge joke, strictly for losers and useful only as a cheap publicity gimmick. Who can doubt that this is the general standpoint of young folks generally?

Many of the people we had met – and this included 'small c' conservatives – seemed to be bewildered by the social and economic changes going on around them. Some of them were very fearful. Some of the most disturbing hours of our journey were spent at the protest meeting in Weston Otmoor. Fear permeated the village hall meeting room – caused by the knowledge that those attending would shortly be required to share their small and insular part of the planet with a lot of strangers who were much poorer than themselves. The looks on the faces of those in the meeting room will haunt me for a long time.

Essentially the way of life of those attending the Weston Otmoor protest meeting – at least as they saw it – was being abolished and there was nothing they could do about it. It was like seeing a large group of people simultaneously being told they had been diagnosed with a terrible illness which they would also pass on to their children. Many of the protestors had, it seemed clear, secured their livelihoods on the value of their thatched cottages which – judging by the endless whitewashing and primping – played a vast role in their emotional lives, as well as their economic lives. I imagined many of them had been looking forward to dying with the comfort that they had at least left a large dollop of house price money to their offspring. Now that was all being thrown into doubt. At other, non-Tory political meetings I had seen people affected emotionally by the plight of a persecuted group. But I had never seen a group of people audibly groan with pain and shock because something so crucial to their happiness was to be taken away from them.

Many of the Conservatives we met seemed to have, as the saying goes, arrived direct from central casting. The tendency of people to live up to their stereotypes – much noted by social psychologists – seemed to be strongly in evidence. But some Tories we met defied the stereotypes. At one point we joined the audience of the BBC Radio Four discussion show *Any Questions*, which was being recorded in a church in Rugby. I found myself sitting next to an engineer who worked at the local Jaguar car factory. He was probably about fifty, dressed in jeans and a T-shirt and was with his wife. One of the subjects for discussion was knife crime and, as we waited for the show to start, he shared his very liberal views on the subject. The problem was that kids had no jobs and were bored, as youths had been, he supposed, from the start of time. They were drifting into crime because they had poor prospects and did not see any point in staying on the straight and narrow. Harsher punishments would not deter them. Most of all he thought that young people generally had a hard time, especially if they couldn't get into college. He had been a manual worker most of his life but he had skills, and so he had enjoyed a great career and had just finished doing a degree at the Open University. He said: 'Somebody like me now would have no chance.' Given the views he expressed, I asked if he was a Liberal Democrat or a Labour supporter? The engineer screwed up his face and said: 'No way! I'm True Blue. . . . Conservative, always. Of course.'

In 2005 I reckoned that the Conservative Party was dead and buried – it seemed to have been bereft of strong new ideas, and talent, for so long that a few valedictory words (and possibly a headstone and a floral tribute) were needed. The idea of this book had been that David and I would mingle with the mourners, writing the first draft of The History of the Conservative Party (Now Deceased). Of course, with the apparent demise of Gordon Brown and the arrival of David Cameron, it's now clear the Conservative Party's electoral fortunes are relatively rosy once more. But I still maintain that the Conservative Party as a living, breathing part of our communities – a key part of the complex web of allegiances that Edmund Burke praised as the essence of freedom and the guarantee of decency in public life – is close to extinction, and has disappeared altogether in some of the places we visited. 'Conservative' is now just another brand name, a once meaningful word around which opportunistic marketing men cluster, trying to fill it with whatever off-the-shelf values they think will keep them in a job. Today's Conservative Party has provided a new set of characters for the national reality TV show which politics now consists of, but they are characters who are all sound and fury and don't signify very much.

We live atomized lives now, with very little allegiance to anything. This creates a kind of personal and individual freedom, and this new kind of freedom has almost completely replaced the older idea of being free through belonging. For better or for worse, it now seems that freedom means isolation and detachment.